Care-full
Preaching

Care-full Preaching

FROM SERMON TO

CARING COMMUNITY

G. LEE RAMSEY, JR.

Chalice Press®
St. Louis, Missouri

Cover design: Lynne Condellone
Interior design: Elizabeth Wright
Art direction: Elizabeth Wright

This book is printed on acid-free, recycled paper.

Visit Chalice Press on the World Wide Web at
www.chalicepress.com

10 9 8 7 6 5 4 3 2 1   00 01 02 03

Library of Congress Cataloging–in–Publication Data

Ramsey, G. Lee, 1956-
    Care-full preaching : from sermon to caring community / G. Lee Ramsey.
        p.   cm.
    Includes bibliographical references.
    ISBN 0-8272-0480-9
    1. Preaching. 2. Pastoral theology   3. Sermons, America.   I. Title.
    BV4211.2 .R28   2000
    251–dc21
                                               00-009173

Printed in the United States of America

*To Mary Leslie,
Shelley, and Luke*

Contents

Preface

To readers, acknowledgments can seem routine, part of the standard beginning of any book. Yet for the writer, the names within the acknowledgment represent the people upon whom the creative effort of writing depends. Gratitude seems too small a word for the feelings that arise. But gratitude is a good word, the best one available to acknowledge the people who have sustained and challenged me during the writing of this book.

The whole project began at Vanderbilt University in the Graduate Department of Religion, where I had the good fortune to work with Professors David Buttrick, Liston Mills, Susan Bond, and Bonnie Miller-McLemore. I am indebted to each of them for wise guidance, extraordinary patience, and genuine compassion.

Jon Berquist, my editor at Chalice Press, was able to see the promise of a book buried within a doctoral dissertation, and with keen insight and patience has helped bring the work to fruition. I am grateful.

Colleagues here at Memphis Theological Seminary have provided as much community support as anyone writing a book could hope to receive. I am thankful for various faculty members' comments on portions of the manuscript. I am particularly thankful for the encouragement and suggestions of Paul Brown and Mary Lin Hudson, friends and two of the best preachers and teachers of preaching around. Jane Williamson, Nancy McSpadden, Melissa Hamblin, and Michael Strickland have simplified my research with their efficiency, resourcefulness, and generosity of time and spirit in the library. Eric Corbin, Mary Earheart-Brown, and Randy Leslie have been unfailing in their moral and technological support. If all computer "geeks" are like these three, send us more. Evelyn McDonald has offered a steady hand and enthusiastic support that, while I was writing, helped me keep on track all the other responsibilities of teaching.

I inflicted portions of this manuscript on a number of students during a preaching and pastoral care course here at Memphis Theological Seminary in the fall of 1999: Corrine Adams, Julie Davis, Keith Dodson, Richard Hackleman, Amy Howe, Lori Kleinjan, Russell Little, Mark McNair, Kevin Medlin, Mark Mitchum, Cheryl Penson, Dennis Renshaw, Willa Ross, Richard Smith, and Keith Wright. Their comments on pastoral preaching in general, and on the manuscript in particular, have shaped my own thinking and writing. From them, I have learned more about preaching and pastoral care than I fear is evident in this book.

Several sermons appear in the final chapter because of the generosity of those who preached them. Gina Stewart, James Forbes, Barbara Brown Taylor, and Fred Craddock were all kind enough to allow me to include their sermons as a part of the book. I am indebted to them. My friend and colleague in ministry Don Park provided helpful review of one of the sermons.

Four specific congregations have been on my mind as I have written about pastoral preaching: Iglesia Metodista Unida de San Marcos and St. Paul United Methodist Church, both in Atlanta, Georgia; Bethlehem United Methodist Church in Clarksville, Tennessee; and Trinity United Methodist Church in Memphis, Tennessee. Each of these churches has taught me more about Christian ministry, pastoral care, and preaching than I will ever be able to fully explain. They are pastoral communities who care deeply for the world.

Gilbert and Frances Ramsey, my parents, surely had a hand in all of this. From my Dad, I first heard the sound of pastoral preaching. From the United Methodist congregations that they served, I first caught glimpses of the pastoral community. Who can say for sure where faith in God begins? Who knows how a love for learning is kindled? Many of my answers to these questions lead to their door.

Finally, in Mary Leslie, Shelley, and Luke, my immediate family, God did something fine. Mary Leslie has provided patience and insightful comments about the work from start to finish. Shelley and Luke, who are a whole lot more fun to be around than their bookish Dad, have kept my feet on the ground with joy. In my book, they are simply the best. For them all, I am full of love and gratitude.

Lee Ramsey
Memphis Theological Seminary
January 2000

Introduction

The grace that is the health of creatures can only be held in common.
In healing, the scattered members come together. In health the flesh is
graced, the holy enters the world.[1]

— WENDELL BERRY

As Christian preachers, despite the torrent of words that flow from our mouths, we wrestle with a recurring problem: We are tongue-tied. Thoughtful preachers often stammer when attempting to form words into meaning-full representations of God; we falter when speaking the words of the people before God. The audacity of such a human undertaking often silences those whom God and the church call to speak. Many sermons never find a voice because we accurately perceive the gravity of the task. Like Isaiah, we stand mute before the Holy One. Who would dare speak? On the other hand, Sunday after Sunday countless banal sermons stream from the mouths of many preachers who either by habit or fear do not venture into the presence of the mysterious God, thereby rendering themselves unable to truly speak. Preachers know silence, whether it is born of awe or the deafening remainder when jangling sermons cease.

But there is something else that vexes our words: *care.* Preachers hesitate to speak because we care. Preachers speak among people who call us to proclaim God's word *and* who need God's care. In short, preachers are also pastors. We who preach know in some detail the personal needs of those within the congregation for pastoral guidance, healing, sustaining, and reconciling.[2] We share the grief of the congregation over the death of

---

[1]Wendell Berry, *What Are People For* (San Francisco: North Point Press, 1990), 9.

[2]The first three pastoral categories are identified by Seward Hiltner, *Preface to Pastoral Theology* (New York: Abingdon Press, 1958), and the fourth pastoral category, "reconciling," by William A. Clebsch and Charles R. Jaekle, *Pastoral Care in Historical Perspective* (Englewood Cliffs, N.J.: Prentice Hall, 1964).

1

Reilly Blanton, a sixty-five-year-old salty-spirited saint who seemed to embody the soul of the community. We hear the sound of fifteen-year-old Terri Davis' frightful plea for direction when her friend ends up in jail.[3] Preacher pastors struggle alongside the mission group that seeks congregational commitment to support a safe house for battered women. The desperation of these women haunts us; the violence of their abusers angers us. The loneliness evoked by a family's impending move floats before us as we stand to preach. The congregation's resistance to accepting newcomers bothers the pastor. The sermon surely has some bearing on these pastoral needs. But how? What words can we as preachers speak from the pulpit that will make any difference at all in the lives of the persons among whom we preach? We seek an apt response in the face of complex personal, familial, and communal needs that we know cannot be fully addressed except by announcing a larger word, a word from beyond the context of the existing problem that encompasses the hurting persons with Christ's healing, redemptive presence.

These two dimensions of ministry, preaching and pastoral care, are inseparably linked. I claim in the pages that follow that ministers cannot cleanly separate preaching and pastoral care, nor should we.[4] Yet it is just this interrelation of preacher and pastor in the person and calling of the minister that draws preaching and pastoral care up short. How do we understand the intermingling of preaching and pastoral care in the Christian ministry? Is all preaching a spoken act of pastoral care, a word-deed of compassionate concern? Does every act of pastoral care entail proclamation? If the two, preaching and pastoral care, are so indissoluble, then are we wasting our time trying to define them in churches, seminaries, and the numerous volumes written about both fields?

Maybe we should be content to say that preaching and pastoral care are more or less the same thing. They are distinguished by whether we are speaking from behind a raised pulpit to an amazingly human group of people sitting on hard wooden pews in a stainlit sanctuary, or praying with one or two people holding on to each other for dear life while a ventilator pumps the last dying breaths into the lungs of their beloved. It's all ministry when you get right down to it. The person who preaches is the same one who shows up to pray over a shattered marriage. And when the chips are on the table, with people betting their last dollar that the preacher pastor will say or do something that will make sense out of the bad hand that life has dealt them, who really cares about whether you call it preaching the gospel or offering pastoral care? When you're hungry enough, you don't

---

[3]All names are fictitious.

[4]I assume that pastoral preaching is only understood within the larger unity of Christian worship, but I will not try to point out the pastoral dimensions of worship as a whole. Two such studies are Elaine Ramshaw, *Ritual and Pastoral Care* (Philadelphia: Fortress Press, 1987) and William Willimon, *Worship as Pastoral Care* (Nashville: Abingdon Press, 1979).

worry about the label. Maybe the attempt to define how preaching is pastoral care, or vice versa, is a swell concern for academic types, people who seem to have lots of time to ponder the distinctions. But in the parish, where folks crave a saving word and ache for a healing touch, such discussions can taste like stones rather than bread or feel like cold shoulders rather than open arms. Maybe we shouldn't bother ourselves with knowing whether we are preaching, offering pastoral care, or both. Maybe we should just do it, since the needs of congregations and communities cry out—witness Littleton, Colorado; witness elderly "care" homes stuffed with society's rejects; witness first-grade children in our inner-city schools whose eyes are already dimly burning wicks. The time is so short. Ministers should preach and care as best they know how to set loose the healing and liberating power of the gospel before the lights of our culture go out altogether. Maybe so.

Then again, maybe not. Given half a chance to voice concern, most busy preacher pastors will admit questions about the blurry boundaries between preaching and pastoral care. We know that preaching and pastoral care are like two branches emerging from the central trunk of ministry, entwining, reinforcing each other yet distinct. As Phillips Brooks said years ago, "The preacher who is not a pastor grows remote. The pastor who is not a preacher grows petty."[5] Rigid separation of ministry into distinct domains of prophetic (preaching) and pastoral (caring) leaves the practicing minister in the awkward position of the specialist who dashes back and forth between pulpit and counseling room endlessly changing hats.

The problem is, we're not quite sure where pastoral care stops and preaching begins. Let's ask the question, Does pastoral intent stop when preaching begins? If not, as I assume most everyone reading here answers, how does the sermon convey pastoral freight without sidetracking the gospel? In other words, how does pastoral care inform preaching without shoving gospel proclamation right out of the pulpit? This is not an imagined problem.

Pastoral care has tended to hog the pulpit over the past thirty to forty years in mainstream Protestantism. Preachers have noticed that the sounds coming from many pulpits have often been the psychological tones of therapeutic preaching. In the name of pastoral concern for the hearer, the preacher has often shrunk the grand and awesome mystery of God-with-us down to the miniature size of the individual psyche. Seeking to connect with the real life of the hearers, a good move in preaching, we have defined real life concerns individually and subjectively. Then we have applied a therapeutic solution to the perceived problems—more optimism, less stress, reduced anxiety, coping skills for the harried, better time management, more insight into one's own psychological processes. Even when our preaching hasn't taken such a shallow psychological turn, we have still

---

[5]Phillips Brooks, *Lectures on Preaching* (New York: E. P. Dutton, 1877), 77.

tended to define the needs of the hearers subjectively. The role of preaching then is to therapeutically address the inward struggle of the believer, never mind the location of the believer within a faithful community set within a specific time and place in human history.

Protestant preaching and pastoral care did not concoct this strategy all alone. We have been full-fledged ticket holders on the bus of much broader social trends, documented by sociologists such as Christopher Lasch, Robert Bellah, and a whole host of others.[6] Just where and when Christian pastoral care and preaching took the wrong fork in the road is probably impossible to pinpoint. But somewhere along the line, much of our preaching as well as our pastoral care began to turn, as Brooks Holifield has stated, from the theological concern for salvation to that of self-realization.[7] There is more than enough blame to go around. Without even realizing it, the pulpit, like pastoral care, succumbed to the triumph of the therapeutic in Western culture.[8] The fragile yet essential distinctions between preaching and pastoral care caved in. Without some line of separation, however porous, pastoral preaching took on the character of personal counseling in the pulpit, surely a truncation of the good news that God, in Jesus Christ and by the power of the Holy Spirit, redeems the whole world.

Fortunately, rehabilitation is under way. Pastoral preaching does not have to be erected on the piers of psychological wisdom with borrowed material. Although there have been some gains in this approach to pastoral preaching, it's time to ground pastoral preaching once again in solid theological footings. Pastoral theologians and homileticians are constructing a firm yet flexible approach to pastoral preaching with the bricks and mortar of theology and scripture. In these pages, I hope to demonstrate that in the long run the theological and scriptural basis of preaching determines the pastoral nature of the sermon.

Sermons are not pastoral simply because the pastor preaches them. Nor are they pastoral because the preacher has a particular pastoral need in mind when she bends over the word processor to pour sweat and tears into this Sunday's sermon. Sermons are pastoral, I hope to show, by the way they understand human beings, the sermon's theological anthropology. Just what is wrong and right with us anyway? And how does the living God heal and sustain us? Further, sermons communicate care by their construing of the church, the people of God in the world, as a pastoral community. When we preach with these theological emphases in mind, we are preaching pastorally because we are addressing the fundamental needs of the human

---

[6] Christopher Lasch, *The Culture of Narcissism: American Life in An Age of Diminishing Expectations* (New York: W. W. Norton, 1978). Robert Bellah et. al., *Habits of the Heart: Individualism and Commitment in American Life* (Berkeley, Calif.: University of California Press, 1985).

[7] E. Brooks Holifield, *A History of Pastoral Care in America: From Salvation to Self-Realization* (Nashville: Abingdon Press, 1983).

[8] Phillip Rieff, *The Triumph of the Therapeutic: Uses of Faith after Freud* (Chicago: University of Chicago Press, 1966).

being. We are seeking to identify and bring to life the primary community of the Christian believer, the church, which has always been one of God's main avenues for caring in the world. So we turn not to psychological and interpersonal dynamics between preacher and congregation but to anthropology and ecclesiology to gauge the pastoral nature of the sermon. I'll have a great deal to say about this as the book progresses.

Preaching is indeed pastoral, through and through. The question I address in the following chapters is, How? What is pastoral preaching anyway? If we set aside the modern pulpit's penchant for therapeutic preaching, must we throw away pastoral preaching as well? Preachers of the gospel have always been preoccupied with pastoral concerns, from Paul's heartaches over the divisive Corinthians right on down to a contemporary pastor's compassion for a young father who has leukemia gnawing away at the living cells of his body. *The question is: How does pastoral care occur through the sermon?* Just how does *the sermon* convey pastoral care when the preacher stands before the people, opens the scripture, and beckons, "Listen for the Word of the Lord"?

Relatedly, *who* cares in the sermon? We know the preacher cares about the people. If not, he or she should consider hanging up the stole and stepping aside for another. But who actually cares in the *sermons* that the preacher offers week to week? Who should care? Is it solely the preacher's business to express care for the people week in and week out through the frail vessel of the weekly homily? Or is someone besides the preacher delivering care packages through and because of the preached word? If we look carefully at our sermons, over time we might discover who cares or who doesn't.

This leads us to one final purpose of this book. Just what does a pastoral sermon sound like anyway? Would you know a pastoral sermon if you heard one? Could you name the reasons why you believe the sermon gracefully delivers the healing and sustaining care of God to those who receive it? In the final chapter of the book, we will look together at a few examples of pastoral sermons and explore their pastoral theological underpinnings. They are diverse in approach and content. The preachers may not have preached them with deliberate pastoral intent, which is all the better, because I hope that by the end of this walk through the landscape of pastoral preaching, you will become convinced that all preaching is pastoral to some degree or another. The sermons selected here, and the theological analysis of them, show how this is so. Such examples may lead you to turn toward your own sermons to inquire: Are these sermons pastoral? How do they communicate care?

The questions that I invite you to explore with me here are those that stir me as I preach and offer pastoral care through ongoing ministry within the church. They first occur as questions swirling around the sermon–before, during, and after the preaching of it. Why does this particular sermon based on Luke 15 cause a single mother with two children to say to the preacher,

"We need to hear that sermon every week"? Or how might these sermons be developed to generate congregational commitment to support a community land trust for low-income housing? What theological grounds, scriptural sources, and preaching strategies can we, as preacher pastors, draw on to achieve this pastoral aim? Or how is it that in regular weekly preaching and worship a pastoral environment can be engendered that will sustain the congregation as it is buffeted by the shock waves of global horrors such as Serbia and Kosovo, the bombing of the Murrah Federal Building in Oklahoma City, the slaughter of schoolkids in Denver, Colorado, or the ravages of an earthquake in Turkey, without encouraging wholesale ecclesiastical retreat from the good world of God's creation and redemption?

None of these pastoral dimensions of preaching, nor any other dimension for that matter, is within our full control as preachers. Like all human creatures, preachers are stewards of the gifts of God. God in grace creates and redeems the world by Word (Jesus Christ) and Spirit (Genesis 1, John 1). God gives to preachers the gift of words and spirit to share responsibly in God's ongoing acts of creation and redemption. We do not control nor redeem creation through preaching, pastoral care, or anything else. God does. Our part is to act responsibly and in gratitude for God's gift of God's self and world. That we think we can control our lives, and usually attempt to secure our own existence, is the well-known story of humanity in relation with God that we keep telling to one another but that *we* cannot change or even believe. All of which is to confess from the outset the theological commitments that underlie my own approach to preaching and pastoral care. That we should work hard at anything, in this case to trace out the links between preaching and pastoral care, only makes theological sense in response to God's initiative.

A related assumption is that sustained study of preaching, like pastoral care, becomes suspect if severed from its home within the worshiping community of the church. Serious challenge of this trend in pastoral care specialization is now well under way. Certain distance from the worshiping congregation does indeed offer vantage that can render insight. But God through the church calls preachers to serve God and the church in the world. I want to hold preaching and pastoral care close to the congregation through whom God calls forth the gifts in the first place. Although I am in agreement with Rebecca Chopp, who points out that congregations hold no special *gnosis* for theological education, I do not see how we can take seriously our theological task without the ongoing life of the congregation before us.[9] This does not mean that a narrow parochialism drives our understanding of preaching and pastoral care. Nor does it mean that the

[9]Rebecca S. Chopp, "Practical Theology and Liberation," in *Formation and Reflection*, ed. Lewis S. Mudge and James Poling (Philadelphia: Trinity Press, 1987), 124.

congregation is the only place where preaching and pastoral care occur. It does mean that Christian preaching that is theologically grounded occurs among the people who in the broadest sense of the word are the church and whose practices, rituals, and values cohere around the central symbol of our faith, the crucified and resurrected Christ.

Finally, I write from the dual location of church and theological academy. As an ordained minister and a teacher in a seminary, the questions that I tackle in this book, and for which I seek deepening theological clarity in the academy, are questions that emerge out of congregational ministry, where preaching and worship, pastoral care, education, mission, and organization incessantly swirl together. The sheer variety of responsibilities within local church ministry, while often touted as a vocational blessing of sorts, also frustrates. Ministers learn pretty quickly, though some too late, that we cannot do everything. The temptation arises to grasp at one dimension of ministry, conceive it as a function of one's role, hone it to perfection, and forget about the rest. This functional approach to Christian ministry may save the harried clergyperson from diffusion and forestall burnout. But the choice compromises the theological integrity of ministry. Persons called by God through the church to preach the gospel, serve the sacraments, offer God's pardon, and liberate the prisoner, become instead "speakers," "counselors," "church administrators," and "social workers." Admittedly, it's difficult, but preachers can intentionally resist this solution. At the heart of the people gathered whom we know as church, *ekklesia,* resides God through Christ and the Holy Spirit. Somehow the parish minister in all her many tasks must point to this central truth, no less in preaching than in pastoral care, no less in organizing than in teaching. From where I stand, the church needs the academy to keep this straight, and the academy needs the church, which is the basis for its mission. I am writing from and for both.

No doubt my views on preaching and pastoral care are limited by the very skin and social world that I inhabit. Postmodernism, despite its philosophical vagueness, has surely driven home the point that none of us is value neutral or context free. We each see the world from our own plot of ground; we each tend our own soil based upon how we read the larger landscape. I happen to be a native of the Southeastern United States, male, white, middle-class, formally educated, married, a parent of two children, a United Methodist by birth and choice, and a whole lot of other things. God knows why. All this profoundly shapes my approach to preaching and pastoral care; how could it not? Yet in theological reflection and the practice of ministry, I actively seek to hear and see the matters before me from the perspective of others, recognizing that at best each of us has only a small purchase upon much larger and changing realities. It is no small contribution of postmodern theology to name the demise of Constantinian

Christianity and thereby open the church universal to the various manifestations of the gospel within particular cultures and communities.[10] In the Western church of our era, despite reactionary trends to hang on to the good old days of Christian triumphalism, we may be learning just how much we need one another, not regardless of culture, skin color, and gender, but because of culture, skin color, and gender. Authority is hard to pin down these days in any arena. Theological authority clearly is no exception. I do not write under the illusion that my view of pastoral preaching is *authoritative*, whatever that might mean. Herein, I pull my chair up to the table of theology and Christian ministry, specifically that portion of the table around which are sitting the preachers and pastors, homileticians and pastoral theologians. I listen the best that I know how to those who are reflecting upon pastoral preaching. Then I offer my own two cents' worth in response. Many who see differently than I will correct me. So much the better. I would expect no less from a pastoral community formed by word and sacrament for care in God's world.

Preacher pastors often hesitate before they speak. The stakes are high.[11] For words "name worlds," worlds that can bind or set free, worlds that can build up or tear down.[12] Little wonder that preacher pastors pause before preaching. But then the time comes for preachers to speak. Called and equipped by God and the church, preachers focus on care-full preaching to form a people full of God's care.

---

[10]For the challenges this presents to homiletics on the issue of authority, see Ronald J. Allen, Barbara S. Blaisdell, and Scott B. Johnston, *Theology for Preaching: Authority, Truth, and Knowledge of God in a Postmodern Ethos* (Nashville: Abingdon Press, 1997).

[11]Preaching "is a crisis, a moment of truth, a decision of immense consequence." Fred Craddock, *As One Without Authority* (Nashville: Abingdon Press, 1979), 17.

[12]David Buttrick, *Homiletic: Moves and Structures* (Philadelphia: Fortress Press, 1987), 9.

1

Theology and Pastoral Preaching

*Preaching is...not only done in a pastoral context but is itself a
pastoral act...Preaching not only has a theological context but is itself
a theological act.*[1]

—Fred Craddock

Most preachers are surprised from time to time by comments that
congregational members make about sermons, if they say anything at all.
Sometimes these are painfully humorous. "Well preacher, I thought I knew
where you were going with that one, but I was just confused." Sometimes
they are polite disagreements. "I'll have to say this for you. You made me
think." But occasionally people indicate by their remarks that the sermon
has touched a pastoral nerve, even if their comments are general. "Thank
you for that sermon, Reverend. We needed to hear that today." Or the
more oblique comment that may signal that the pastoral perspective of the
sermon and worship service has registered within the congregation, possibly
evoking pastoral concerns. "Listen, Brother Tom, why don't you stop by
the store sometime for a cup of coffee. I'd like to show you around." The
astute preacher will hear the undertones of pastoral concern within these
comments even if they do not call for direct response.

The pastoral element of the preached word always seeks a hearing. It
moves among the congregation searching for opportunities to provide the
care of God for the broken in spirit, the perplexed, the bored, the desperate,
the haunted, and the harassed, who are all a part of Christ's body. Preachers
who are also good pastors sometimes discover that the caring word has

---

[1]Fred Craddock, *Preaching* (Nashville: Abingdon Press, 1985), 47.

found its answer among the people. This pastoral perspective of preaching has been around since the beginning of the church.

The Christian Tradition and Pastoral Preaching

The Christian church has always set preaching and pastoral care on the same pew. Preaching is evangelical, announcing the good news that God is right at hand. And preaching is pastoral, speaking the palpable nearness of God into the shattered lives of those who are far away, namely, the whole human race. Scripture bears this out. Paul is a preacher (1 Cor. 1:17) and a pastor who lovingly cares for the congregation (2 Cor. 2:1–5). The writer of Timothy calls upon the church leaders to preach and to take care of the flock (1 Tim. 2:1–6:1). You get one, you get the other–preachers who are pastors and pastors who are preachers. The confused lives of the people cry out for the preached word that rings true. The preached word that rings true clarifies the lives of the people. From the disciples on, no preacher worth his or her salt has assumed the burdensome joy of preaching without wearing pastoral concern like a prayer shawl when stepping into the pulpit.[2]

Church history is chock full of examples. We could wander throughout the winding course of church history, and just about any place along the way that we stopped to rest our feet, we'd find a preacher talking like a pastor. Origen's (185–254 C.E.) sermons are not only kerygmatic but pastorally instructive. Like a concerned parent, Origen fusses over the believer's steadfastness in the faith. One slip, and the brothers and sisters in his care are goners, bowing down to imperious idols who in the short run don't hurt the believers nearly as much as the lions, but in the long run drain the blood right out of the heart of discipleship.[3] St. Augustine unites a pastor's compassion with a scholarly preacher's learning and rhetoric. In preaching and teaching, love is Augustine's primary pastoral intent. Indeed, love is his ruling principle for all scriptural interpretation.[4] Gregory the Great sees the pastor as the "ruler of the soul," and the cure of souls as the "art of arts."[5] In *Pastoral Care,* Gregory glides unobtrusively between preaching and personal guidance with deep insight into the human person. Preaching, Gregory asserts, "is far more laborious when on one and the same occasion one has to deal with a numerous audience subject to different

---

[2]The phrase, "burdensome joy of preaching," is from James Earl Massey, *The Burdensome Joy of Preaching* (Nashville: Abingdon Press, 1998).

[3]Joseph Wilson Trigg, *Origen* (Atlanta: John Knox, 1983), 176–88, cited in Paul Scott Wilson, *A Concise History of Preaching* (Nashville: Abingdon Press, 1992), 185.

[4]Augustine, *Writings of Saint Augustine, on Christian Doctrine,* The Fathers of the Church Series, trans. John J. Gavigan (New York: CIMA, 1947), 3–238.

[5]Gregory the Great, *Pastoral Care,* trans. Henry Davis, Ancient Christian Writers series (Westminster, Md.: Newman, 1950). See Thomas Oden's interpretation of Gregory in *Care of Souls in the Classic Tradition,* Theology and Pastoral Care Series, ed. Don S. Browning (Philadelphia: Fortress Press, 1984).

passions. In this case the address must be formulated with such skill that, notwithstanding the diversity of failings in the audiences, it carries a proper message to each individual, without involving itself in self contradictions."[6] Like a gospel doctor, Gregory applies a nuanced, healing word directly on the wounds of the sin-sick soul. He is a preacher pastor who is equally concerned about caring for the souls of the parishioners from the pulpit and in the privacy of the confessional.

Jump ahead in church history and listen to the pastoral intent of the Puritan preacher Richard Baxter in *The Reformed Pastor*. Exhaustive in his instructions for how pastors should care for the individual parishioner, Baxter assumes that pastoral care and preaching are concerned with the whole church.

> The object of our pastoral care is all the flock: that is, the Church and every member of it…[But] one part of our work, and that the most excellent, because it tendeth to work on many, is the public preaching of the Word—a work that requireth greater skill…It is no easy matter to speak so plain, that the ignorant may understand us; and so seriously, that the deadest hearts may feel us; and so convincingly, that contradicting cavilers may be silenced.[7]

Baxter, like Gregory before him, focuses on pastoral care, all right, and he clearly sees that it shares the same aims of preaching: to build up a "sanctified, peculiar people" by tending the household of God.[8]

Finally, consider the preaching of Catherine Mumford Booth (1829–1890), a Methodist and cofounder of the Salvation Army. As a preacher, Booth extends aggressive care to those members of English society who are beyond the direct influence of institutional Christianity. The Salvation Army story is well known, but Booth's preaching for change of heart and life *and* reform of society is not frequently recounted. As Paul Scott Wilson interprets her, "She preached the need for an antagonistic force of good…[Because] the Church, instead of aggressing on the territory of the enemy, is allowing that enemy to aggress upon her!"[9] Wilson points out that in Booth's preaching we go right into the homes of women and children for whom she cares. Her sermons avoid abstraction and are clearly pastoral.[10]

Perhaps this quick glance at several key figures in church tradition is sufficient to outline the historical ties between preaching and pastoral care. A more thorough historical treatment would surely pause at the preaching of Chrysostom, Jerome, Catherine of Siena, Saint Vincent Ferrer, Luther,

---

[6]Gregory the Great, *Pastoral Care,* 226.
[7]Richard Baxter, *The Reformed Pastor* (London: Nisbet & Co., 1860), 11, 128.
[8]Ibid., 297.
[9]Paul Scott Wilson, *A Concise History of Preaching,* 149. See Catherine Mumford Booth, *The Salvation Army in Relation to the Church and State* (London: Salvation Army, 1883), 41.
[10]Wilson, 153.

Calvin, Jonathan Edwards, the Wesleys, Horace Bushnell, Phoebe Palmer, Phillips Brooks, and others.

What we see in the history of the church is that preaching and pastoral care have always been companions. Pastoral preachers' core theological concerns have been for the life of the church, its members, and the wider world. Without concrete awareness of the actual needs of the congregation and world, preaching becomes a monologue with the self. Outside of the corporate gathering of the people formed by the word of God and sustained by the sacraments, pastoral care is a pleasant conversation devoid of transcendent power. Pleasantries are all right, but pastoral preaching promises more. Pastoral preaching promises that through the words of the sermon, God heals. Through the gathering of God's people around word and table, the Holy Spirit sustains the believers, come what may. Pastoral preaching promises that in silence, even the deafening silence that descends upon a freshly dug grave, God speaks and makes all things new.

Where does preaching leave off and pastoral care begin? Apparently, many in the history of the church didn't see the problem in quite the same way that we do today. Sermons were all bound up with the ministry of care. But their binding ligaments were theological–God, Christ, Spirit, creation, the human soul, the church. Pastoral sermons offered theological responses to theological problems. Sermons were laden with care, to be sure. But it never occurred to these earlier preacher pastors, as it does to many preachers today, that they preached to offer mini-doses of psychological healing to isolated individuals. Yes, pastors counseled with troubled individuals and families. In the name of God, they extended sacramental, scriptural, or doctrinal guidance to those in need of care. But when Sunday morning arrived, and the pastor stood in the pulpit, pastoral concern reached out toward the whole people, the church. The *therapeia* (healing) of preaching was not pastoral adjustment of the psyche of the listener. *Therapeia* meant the corporate healing of the broken body of Christ, whose members, when gathered in like prodigals by the care-full preached word, found reconciliation to God, neighbor, and self around a table spread with bread and wine.

Pastoral Preaching and the Therapeutic

What happened? Pastoral preaching takes an odd turn in the twentieth century. Preaching and pastoral care, heretofore more or less integrated at the theological level, begins to fragment and realign under the rising influence of the social sciences throughout Western culture, especially that of psychotherapeutic psychology and its spawns. The wisdom of Freud and followers was irresistible, as much for its processes as for its content. It is doubtful that Freud himself could have imagined the extent to which Western society, deeply pietistic and hungry for individual expressiveness without religious and social constraint, would embrace the therapeutic.[11] The shift is undeniable, however. Christian ministry would not and could not remain the same.[12]

Naturally, the preaching and pastoral care of the church becomes more overtly psychological with the rise of the therapeutic. Modern psychology offers concrete help to those concerned with the cure of souls. It gives to preachers and pastors new concepts and language with which to understand the perennial vexations of the human being. Even more, psychology is not simply a tool with which to diagnose and heal the inner wounds of others. It becomes a valuable avenue for self-awareness of the preacher pastor. Self-understanding, personal authenticity, and integration become leading values in the twentieth-century Christian ministry. Out of the depths of one's own struggle for personhood comes the ability to offer aid and consolation to others.[13] Upon the anvil of these convictions, ministers begin to forge a new version of pastoral care and preaching.

Preaching as Personal Counseling

In the 1950s and 1960s, specialized pastoral counseling emerges whose practices and theories mirror much of secular psychotherapy. For many pastors, pastoral counseling becomes synonymous with pastoral care. Preachers hoist into the pulpit counseling goals, theories, and techniques as a way to increase the effectiveness of Christian proclamation, especially with a concern to address the pain of the individual in the pew. Anxiety, depression, transference, and projection sometimes take center stage in the actual sermonic content as well as the minister's own self-understanding of the dynamics of the sermon as a therapeutic (healing) encounter. By the mid-1960s, humanistic psychology's ethic of self-realization finds fertile ground in Christian pastoral care and preaching, and in many pulpits today it still masquerades as gospel.[14]

Broadly speaking, this kind of psychologically based preaching, though still attentive to biblical and theological sources, becomes known as "pastoral" preaching. It achieves an almost normative status in mainline

---

[11]This is Phillip Rieff's contention in *The Triumph of the Therapeutic: Uses of Faith After Freud.* Freud could not have foreseen the optimistic spin-offs from his own psychological insights that gave birth to today's self-help psychologies.

[12]See Allison Stokes, *Ministry After Freud* (New York: Pilgrim Press, 1985). E. Brooks Holifield accurately documents the impact of this shift on pastoral care in *A History of Pastoral Care in America: From Salvation to Self-Realization* (Nashville: Abingdon Press, 1983).

[13]This notion attained broad acceptance in contemporary ministry with Henri Nouwen's popular *Wounded Healer: Ministry in Contemporary Society* (Garden City, N. Y.: Doubleday, 1972). It appears now throughout pastoral care and preaching literature. For example, as applied to pastoral preaching, see David K. Switzer, *Pastor, Preacher, Person: Developing a Pastoral Ministry in Depth* (Nashville: Abingdon Press, 1979).

[14]See Holifield, *A History of Pastoral Care in America*, 307–48.

denominations. But pastoral preaching in this sense is a preaching that aims to address the personal psychological problems of the individual listener or the family. Pastoral preaching now means pulpit pastoral counseling. The pulpit becomes an extension of the counseling session or, as some pastoral theologians such as Howard Clinebell argue, "pre-counseling."[15] Numerous twentieth-century preachers adopt this easy alliance between preaching and pastoral care, especially through their use of psychological concepts and therapeutic techniques to enhance what they understand as the pastoral or personal dimension of preaching

Harry Emerson Fosdick's oft-quoted dictum that "preaching is counseling on a group scale" may be the most notable example of this approach.[16] In his "project method" or "life situation" model for preaching, Fosdick unapologetically employed insights from the various psychological movements of the first half of this century.[17] This was not, however, because Fosdick wished to propagate a psychological gospel. He simply believed that preaching's primary concern is people's real problems. If psychological wisdom could help the preacher to understand and meet the needs of the hearers through the sermon, so much the better. In contrast to topical and expository sermons, whose starting points begin in scripture or a general subject, Fosdick's life situational or counseling sermons began with the actual needs of the individual, often understood psychologically, though not exclusively so. "We need more sermons that try to face people's real problems with them, meet their difficulties, answer their questions, confirm their noblest faiths and interpret their experiences in sympathetic, wise and understanding cooperation."[18] For Fosdick, the true test that a sermon had found its mark was how many individuals requested personal counseling from the preacher after the sermon.[19] Fosdick saw little difference between the task of preaching and pastoral counseling. One is public; the other, private; but both are addressing the consoling word of the gospel to individuals in various forms of distress from fear to anxiety, loneliness to grief. The titles of Fosdick's sermons are indicative: "The High Uses of Trouble," "When Life Goes All to Pieces," "How to Stand Up and Take It," "The Conquest of Fear."

In fairness, it should be stated that Fosdick's sentiments in the pulpit were not restricted to private concerns. Maturing during the social gospel movement and the fundamentalist-modernist controversy, Fosdick spoke

[15]Howard J. Clinebell, Jr., *The Mental Health Ministry of the Local Church* (Nashville: Abingdon Press, 1965), 86–88.
[16]Harry Emerson Fosdick, "Personal Counseling and Preaching," *Pastoral Psychology* 3, no. 22 (March 1952): 11–15.
[17]Fosdick, "What Is the Matter With Preaching?" *Harpers Monthly Magazine* 157 (July 1928): 133–42. He restates this formulation in several places throughout his work. See *The Living of These Days* (New York: Harper, 1956), 94.
[18]Fosdick, *The Living of These Days,* 97–98.
[19]Fosdick, "What Is the Matter With Preaching?" 141.

forcefully in his early years on issues of race, poverty, hunger, and war, remaining a pacifist even after Pearl Harbor. His 1922 sermon "Shall the Fundamentalists Win?" launched Fosdick to national attention and earned him a symbolically central place in the ongoing debate between fundamentalists and modernists. In the liberal theological tradition, Fosdick sought to make Christian faith understandable (defensible) to the modern mind, beginning with the questions posed by Western culture and moving toward the answers offered by Christian tradition, theology, and scripture. That psychological interpretations of both the problems and answers to modern existence should slowly attain greater influence in Fosdick's preaching seems natural, given his confidence in Western culture as a whole.

The crucial point that Fosdick wishes to make is that preaching is in fact counseling, "personal counseling on a group scale." The characteristics of the counseling sermon, according to Edmund Linn, are that it (1) expresses clear convictions based on personal experience, (2) involves speaking as to a single person, (3) relates to people where they are, (4) deals fairly with objections, (5) applies the gospel to persons, (6) retains the values of the older methods of preaching (expository and topical) and (7) makes a directed effort to learn people's strengths and weaknesses in order to know the questions for which people seek answers.[20] This person-centered approach to preaching gave Fosdick's sermons broad appeal for hearers and other preachers. Listeners felt that Fosdick addressed them personally right where life was most difficult. Tired of arid trips through biblical exposition or rebuffed by preachers' futile attempts to speak authoritatively on every subject of the day in topical preaching, Fosdick's sermons cascaded over the beleaguered hearers like spring showers sent personally by God. Indeed, Fosdick's counseling approach to preaching may still be the most influential one on North American pulpits today.

But there are problems with this therapeutic approach to preaching, influential as it was and remains even today. Maybe the problems are obvious, but the fact that many preachers today continue to preach out of these well-worn grooves (take a look at the Saturday paper announcements of Sunday's sermon) suggests that a lot of preachers do not spot the problems. To begin with, the most obvious flaw in Fosdick's approach is that he subordinates proclamation of the gospel to counseling. Proclamation, teaching, exhortation, and prophecy all take a backseat in Fosdick's model. The individual needs of the person in the pew come to the fore. What drives this model are the private aches and pains of the hearer, not that God has done something startlingly new in Jesus Christ.

> Every sermon should have for its main business the solving of some problem—a vital, important problem, puzzling minds,

---

[20]Edmund Holt Linn, *Preaching As Counseling: The Unique Method of Harry Emerson Fosdick* (Valley Forge, Pa.: Judson Press, 1966), 16–20.

burdening consciences, distracting lives–and any sermon which thus does tackle a real problem, throw even a little light on it, and help some individuals practically to find their way through it cannot be altogether uninteresting.[21]

This keen interest in personal, psychological struggle is what makes this type of sermon seem relevant to the hearer. Yet Karl Barth raises fundamental objections to this trajectory of preaching in Christian liberalism. Consistently beginning a sermon with the need of the listener, a need discerned through counseling and answered by counseling's wisdom, leaves little room for the preacher to announce the gospel in its fullness.[22] The dialectical theologians remind us that precisely because proclamation begins in God's grace, humanity can hope in redemption. Constant attention in preaching to the particular needs of the hearers, while admittedly retaining listener appeal, obscures the truth that God's answer to human suffering is already and ever again given in Christ. Even more, the prophetic element of preaching calls the hearer beyond her own personal need for healing into the wider pain and redemption of the world.

Fosdick's turn to pulpit counseling pivoted on heightened individualism in North American culture. But if preaching counsels individual persons in their existential need, what shall we say about the people-making dimension of gospel proclamation? What about God's word spoken in community and celebrated at the eucharistic table, which creates a body of believers who do not exist alone but with and for one another? While Fosdick may never have intended it, sermons that consistently counsel individuals over the hardships of life fragment Christian community and may lead to religious consumerism. If the sermon does not speak to "my" needs, what's the use of listening? When we take the individual counseling session into the pulpit, the whole gospel may not actually reach anyone at all, given that such an approach funds private religious expression rather than corporate belonging and responsibility. Robert Bellah dubs this approach to Western religion "Sheilaism," for its extreme privatism.[23] Granted, such a state of affairs cannot all be laid upon Fosdick's doorstep, but pulpit counseling greased the skids of an already slippery slope within North American Protestant Christianity.[24]

---

[21]Fosdick, "What is the Matter With Preaching?" 134.

[22]See Karl Barth, *The Word of God and the Word of Man,* trans. Douglas Horton (New York: Harper, 1928), 56.

[23]This term is coined by Robert Bellah after a series of interviews with a woman whom he fictitiously names "Sheila," who understands religious life as extremely private, individualistic, and idiosyncratic. See Bellah et al., *Habits of the Heart: Individualism and Commitment in American Life* (Berkeley, Calif.: University of California Press, 1985), 221, and chap. 6.

[24]See Christopher Lasch, *The Culture of Narcissism: American Life in an Age of Diminishing Expectations* (New York: W. W. Norton, 1978), chaps. 1–2. Lasch comments, "Therapy has established itself as the successor both to rugged individualism and to religion" (13).

I stress Fosdick's influence upon pastoral preaching because of his vast impact on the Protestant pulpit, not because he was the only advocate of this approach. Fosdick generated a largely unexamined equivalence between preaching and pastoral counseling. Yet preaching, a liturgical act of naming the grace of God within the church and world, is not really counseling any more than counseling, an interpersonal act of responding to the felt needs of hurting individuals and groups, is really preaching. Many preachers, however, in the wake of Fosdick, have been unable to note this distinction. Brooks Holifield assesses Fosdick's impact on preaching and pastoral care:

> Possibly more than any other person, it was Fosdick who persuaded a large segment of the liberal Protestant clergy to refashion the sermon in the image of the counseling session...[F]osdick was a living illustration of the burgeoning therapeutic sensibility. Under his tutelage a generation of ministers constructed topical sermons on the mastery of depression, the conquest of fear, the overcoming of anxiety, and the joys of self-realization. Unfortunately, few of them shared Fosdick's other talents and sensitivities. Most sermons that masqueraded as personal counseling probably collapsed as banality.[25]

Holifield is correct. And even as preacher pastors uncritically clambered aboard Fosdick's therapeutic homiletic, others attempted to expand its theoretical construction.

Preaching as Group Counseling

One such attempt was made by Edgar Jackson. Jackson is representative of many pastoral preachers during the 1950s and 1960s who embraced and extended Fosdick's outlook. It is no coincidence that Fosdick comments in the preface to Jackson's *A Psychology for Preaching,*

> The insights of the new psychology involved in personal counseling can add immeasurably to the preacher's power; and his [or her] preaching, using the matrix of a worshipping congregation, can gain a penetrating quality so closely akin to personal counseling that its effect is much the same. This is what Mr. Jackson is driving at.[26]

In other words, Jackson ties pastoral preaching to counseling and psychology, just as Fosdick does, but he adds another layer of psychological knowledge to the model.

The unique element in Jackson's work, at least unique in 1961, is an application of group dynamics to the sermon process itself. Jackson rightly

---

[25]Holifield, *A History of Pastoral Care in America,* 34.

[26]Harry Emerson Fosdick, preface to *A Psychology for Preaching,* by Edgar N. Jackson (Great Neck, N.Y.: Channel Press, 1961), 10.

perceives that the sermon is not simply directed toward a collection of individuals. Occurring within the context of communal worship, the sermon has a larger and differing effect upon the hearer than does an individual conversation. He claims that preaching and worship are the "oldest form of group therapy," and that by analyzing group dynamics in worship and the impact of preaching upon the group, he will "throw an experimental bridge across the gap between preaching and counseling." Noting the growing distance between preaching and pastoral care resulting from the contemporary counseling movement, he wants to help preaching become "an instrument for serving the needs of persons in groups at the same time that it prepares the way for meeting the special needs of those who seek counsel."[27]

Jackson gives priority to psychological and sociological perspectives in pastoral preaching. He wants to harness psychological insight, experimentation, and method for preaching by going underneath the preaching event and establishing its therapeutic value in psychological terms, whether he speaks of the individual or the congregation as a whole. With more psychological training and sophistication than Fosdick, he begins to label the moments, moods, and persons engaged in Christian worship with psychological terminology, lending, he seems to think, scientific authority to the work of Christian preaching and pastoral care.

Jackson builds on the same shaky foundations as Fosdick, although he adds some new timber to the construction. He hammers a psychological brace between pastoral care and preaching that ties them both to psychological dependency. While Fosdick calls for preaching to be personal counseling on a group scale, Jackson makes the dubious equation between preaching and group psychotherapy.[28] Meanwhile, he tosses the theological substructure of both preaching and pastoral care into the scrap pile. This is a mistake. People's anxieties come and go. Our personalities remain constant, or evolve slowly, or undergo radical transformations through insight and life experiences. But how we understand ourselves in relation to God and one another, and how God is active within creation is the bedrock of preaching and pastoral care. Jackson buries these beneath his psychology for preaching.[29]

Jackson and Fosdick alike see the preacher as a dispenser of therapeutic wisdom. With enough psychological sophistication, the preacher might even know in advance how certain types of sermons will impact the neurotic or obsessive-compulsive personality and adjust accordingly. The preacher as

---

[27]Jackson, *A Psychology for Preaching,* 14–15.

[28]Ibid., 123.

[29]This critique does not mean, however, that such approaches are without merit. Clearly, group dynamics and personality structures impact the speaking and hearing of the gospel. Such studies deserve attention. But to make psychological dynamics the primary link between preaching and pastoral care misses the mark.

counselor administers care from the pulpit like a skilled pharmacist doling out medication for each person's illness. There is no argument here that such a view of pastoral preaching lacks pastoral sympathy and compassion. I would agree with Jackson that the preacher pastor must see with "no unreal blind-eye view of life and people." She must see persons "whole" in all their struggle and satisfaction.[30] But the pulpit is not the place where such personal needs come into focus, at least not in the way that these preachers advocate. This hierarchical, individualistic model of pastoral preaching crowds out the central role of the Christian community in pastoral preaching. It sets up the preacher as the community psychologist. And it puts God and the preacher pastor (as God's agent) behind the drugstore counter. As David Switzer cautions, "Preaching in such a way as to meet persons' needs does not imply that the pulpit is to be the regular weekly source of psychological self-help." Or again: "We must certainly always beware the trap of developing as our image that of the sanctuary as a large couch and the preacher as a stand-up shrink."[31] Surely we are now at a time when pastoral preaching cannot simply help people cope with anxiety, stress, fear, or loss on a personal level, as important as these matters are. But pastoral preaching, as I shall develop later, must begin to take seriously how preaching contributes to a community and world that God has inaugurated that sees us in interdependence, God's people on the way of loving and just relations.

Pastoral Preaching as Relationship

There is one more tricky, therapeutic knot that ties up pastoral preaching. Untangling it can cause some temporary confusion because many preacher pastors do not experience it as a bind. What I am talking about is the personal relationship between the preacher and the members of the congregation. Most clergy and laity would agree that the pastoral relationship between the preacher and the person in the pew weighs heavily on the scales when determining the pastoral effectiveness of the sermon. The hearer tends to listen more carefully when the one who is preaching is the same one who showed up last week at Billy's ball game or last month when Mama had her heart attack. Theologically speaking, the character of the preacher does not determine the ultimate efficacy of the gospel, but it clearly impacts the extent to which a congregational member finds the words of the preacher to be true. We are talking about the pastoral authority of the preacher pastor, an authority that the hearers can give and take away. Please don't misunderstand me. The authority of the one called to preach and offer pastoral care is based on more than the collective approval of the particular congregation in which he or she happens to serve. The

---

[30]Jackson, *A Psychology for Preaching,* 78.
[31]Switzer, *Pastor, Preacher, Person,* 51–52.

congregation should not be confused with God, although God does call ordained representatives through the people. But preachers and congregational members establish relationships built on trust, authenticity, and truthfulness that naturally augment or diminish congregational receptivity to the sermon.[32] If the pastor demonstrates loving-kindness on Thursday, the congregation may hear more clearly the voice of the God of love that the preacher proclaims on Sunday. Without solid pastoral relationships, the reasoning goes, the sermon arrives either as suspect or as a less-than-convincing witness to the truth. Preachers and hearers view such interpersonal rapport as the "pastoral" element in preaching. This is clearly a convincing way to integrate pastoral care and preaching. It is largely what Phillips Brooks intended when he called preaching "bringing the truth through personality."[33] The person of the preacher and his or her human relationships determines the pastoral impact of the sermon. Who can argue?

Well, here's the problem. Kept in the background on Sunday morning, this pastoral relationship does give specificity to the weekly proclamation of the gospel. We will see this dynamic in some of the sermons at the end of the book. A solid pastoral relationship with the people strengthens the message. But here's the bind. Let loose out of the sacristy, and invited to sit front and center in the sanctuary, the pastoral relationship can overwhelm the congregation. Preachers who build their sermons by relying too heavily upon their pastoral relationships wind up with lopsided sermons. Such sermons display a lot of pastoral planks, but they are skimpy on theology, biblical understanding, and insight born of sweat and reason.

The real problem is that such a pastoral approach sometimes devolves into a "personal" approach, meaning the personal life of the pastor as text for the sermon. This is a serious misunderstanding of a pastoral approach to preaching. Preachers like Fred Craddock, who skillfully bends his own personal experience toward deeper identification with the hearers, may not have foreseen how contemporary preachers would misuse this approach. Rather than allowing a biblical text, theological theme, or cultural concern to govern the sermon, the personal voice of the preacher begs for all the attention in the sermon. Stories from the preacher's life, his or her family, or their most recent vacation, come rushing onto the podium and drown out the mysterious sounds of God and the genuine cries of the people. For what reason? Maybe because in the remarkably patient congregation, the preacher has found someone who will actually listen to him. But this is hardly proclamation of the good news. As William Willimon asserts, "Thank God, we preachers have something to preach other than ourselves."[34]

[32]See Willard F. Jabusch, *The Person in the Pulpit: Preaching as Caring,* in Abingdon Preacher's Library, ed. William D. Thompson (Nashville: Abingdon Press, 1980); Charles F. Kemp, *The Preaching Pastor* (St. Louis: Bethany Press, 1966).

[33]Phillips Brooks, *Lectures on Preaching* (New York: E. P. Dutton, 1877), 5.

[34]William H. Willimon, *Integrative Preaching* (Nashville: Abingdon Press, 1981), 61.

You can see the problem with this personal, mistakenly called "pastoral," approach to preaching. It shrinks the otherness of God's Word to the pint-sized shape of the pastor's personality. It commandeers the sermon and the worship event to prop up the pastor's fragile ego (or serve a gargantuan one). Personal preaching often casts the preacher as either the hero of his or her own stories or the buffoon who never seems to get the point. Either way, what happens is that the focus of the congregation shifts from the gospel to the life of the preacher, or at least the sermon courts this risk. For this reason, David Buttrick claims that such use of the personal should rarely enter the sermon.[35] While I would not categorically rule out the use of personal experience in the sermon, we should heed Buttrick's cautions. We should carefully screen the presentation of personal experience in the sermon.[36] Because of the danger of subverting the gospel, we should hold use of the personal to high standards of discipline, asking ourselves who is being served when we begin or conclude a sermon by saying, "The other day, I was…" As Buttrick points out, "All in all, we are a poor substitute for the Gospel."[37] Just because the material is personal doesn't make the sermon pastoral. Just because the story is interesting, or funny, or tragic doesn't mean that God among us will be illuminated. Personal anecdotes seem to have become favored stock among contemporary preachers. But we have to ask, does the personal tale in the sermon, however skillfully handled, reveal or obscure sin and grace, judgment and forgiveness, the present and absent God?

Perhaps the affinity for the "personal touch" in today's preaching and worship is a reaction to the impersonal nature of our social existence, a desperate bid for communion in a seemingly inhumane world. But this is really the tortured religious fruit of a bureaucratic, materialistic, and individualistic culture that consigns religion to the private sphere, where lonely individuals seek relief from a therapeutic God. We fashion this God in our own private image. Then we preach "personal" sermons that serve up a God who can be counted on every week to bless our mistakes, share our confusion, unpack our troubles. But what about the God who says to the people, "My thoughts are not your thoughts, nor are your ways my ways" (Isa. 55:8)? What about the Jesus of the gospels who calls the church into, not out of, big trouble and whose sign of blessing is a crown of thorns?

Furthermore, therapeutic preaching blots sin out of the homiletic vocabulary, as Marsha Witten has documented in her study of protestant preaching *All is Forgiven.* "The application of therapeutic tolerance to the idea of sin quashes even the possibility of authoritative religious speech, rendering the speaker silent on any matter except for the musings of his

---

[35]David Buttrick, *Homiletic: Moves and Structures* (Philadelphia: Fortress Press, 1987), 94, 141–43.

[36]See Tom Long's suggestions about the use of personal examples in *The Witness of Preaching* (Louisville: Westminster/John Knox Press, 1989), 177–78.

[37]Buttrick, *Homiletic,* 106.

own subjectivity."[38] This is problematic for pastoral preaching because without a firm notion of sin we cannot announce the healing words of grace. Therapeutic preaching leaves us desperate yet not quite sinful individuals to solve our own dilemmas by the dim light of our own wits. "What, for example, of the immensely potent Protestant doctrine of grace, which appears eviscerated in much of the speech as speakers [preachers] fail to acknowledge notions of human depravity and separation from a transcendent God?"[39] In this therapeutic approach to preaching, notions of human sin and righteousness give way to the language of "unhealthy" and "healthy."[40] As Robert Bellah comments, "No autonomous standard of good and evil survives outside the needs of individual psyches for growth."[41] The preacher expresses care to the people, in this case, by doling out helpful hints to achieve healthy lifestyles or personal well-being, not really much different than the secular brands of self-help that are readily available to us eager consumers of self-fulfillment culture. With enough pointers, we seem to think, we'll straighten the whole mess out. This trajectory in preaching threatens the church as a whole. Gerhard Forde correctly points out that, severed from preaching's commitment to the language of theology and the distinctive values of the church, therapeutic language in the pulpit drives "us more deeply than ever into the black hole of the self, turns the pastor into a shrink or guru and worship into mass therapy."[42]

If this is what we mean today by pastoral preaching, we have clearly tied the pastoral pulpit in some bizarre knots. I may be overstating the severity of the case. Obviously, not all preachers and congregations have capitulated to the therapeutic. Many creative preachers and churches have remained close to scripture, theology, and liturgical tradition. For example, narrative theology has impacted preaching with its call to incorporate the church into the world of the gospel (the story revealed in Christ and scripture) that confronts us with its peculiar Christ-shaped belief and action.[43] Others insist that preachers dare not turn inward away from the brokenness of the world and the reign of God.[44] Still, the Protestant pulpit,

---

[38]Marsha G. Witten, *All is Forgiven: The Secular Message in American Protestantism* (Princeton: Princeton University Press, 1993), 101.

[39]Ibid., 140.

[40]Erskine Clarke, ed., *Exilic Preaching: Testimony for Christian Exiles in an Increasingly Hostile Culture* (Harrisburg, Pa.: Trinity Press International, 1998), 3.

[41]Bellah, *Habits of the Heart,* 232.

[42]Gerhard O. Forde, *Theology is for Proclamation* (Minneapolis: Fortress Press, 1990), 150.

[43]See Walter Brueggemann, *Cadences of Home: Preaching Among Exiles* (Louisville: Westminster John Knox Press, 1997); Charles L. Campbell, *Preaching Jesus: New Directions for Homiletics in Hans Frei's Postliberal Theology* (Grand Rapids, Mich.: Eerdmans, 1997); James William McClendon, Jr., *Making Gospel Sense to a Troubled Church* (Cleveland: Pilgrim Press, 1995).

[44]See David Buttrick, *Preaching the New and the Now* (Louisville:Westminster John Knox Press, 1998), esp. chaps. 2 and 7; Walter J. Burghardt, *Preaching the Just Word* (New Haven: Yale University Press, 1996); Christine Marie Smith, *Preaching Justice: Ethnic and Cultural Perspectives* (Cleveland: United Church Press, 1998).

when it turns to care, speaks often and easily in the therapeutic language of self-fulfillment, personal growth, self-help, and individual salvation. Those who preach alternatively, and those who decry so loudly the state of the therapeutic pulpit, do so because the knots are so tightly cinched. Theology will help us loosen the narrow and private constraints of pastoral preaching.

Pastoral Preaching Is Theological

Thinking Christians, when all is said and done, do not show up at worship to hear about the pastor's personal life or to receive seven effective habits for overcoming life's difficulties. Pastoral sermons are not for the primary purpose of conveying the preacher's personal care for the congregation, though the preacher pastor certainly communicates this in and out of the pulpit. People attune their ears to the preached word to hear of *God's* care for them and the world. God through Christ is the one who redeems our humanity. Jesus Christ–God's care for the world–is the central character in Christian pastoral preaching. God is the one who "so loves the world," not the preacher pastor, even though the preacher pastor seeks to love the world with the love of God. Pastoral preachers want to link the hands of the hearers with the outstretched hands of God.

This means that pastoral preaching is theological, above all else. The pastoral theology of the sermon makes it possible to bring reconciliation home to the hearers. The theological commitments of the preacher, which inevitably crop up in the sermon, determine whether the Word will sustain the congregation like an ark when the creeks begin to rise. Like a compass, the pastoral theology of the sermon may guide the faithful when they stumble in chains through the Babylons of contemporary existence. Like fresh bread, the pastoral theology of the sermon can satsify the hungry hearts and unite strangers around a common table. Why must we insist that for a sermon to be pastoral it should be either personal or psychologically derived? When it comes down to care, the theology of the sermon will do just fine.[45]

So how does the pastoral theology of the sermon express care? We are accustomed to thinking that persons, such as the pastor, offer care to the congregation. Theology, on the other hand, conveys concepts, beliefs, interpretation of doctrine, scripture, and life. Theology drives toward clarity of religious thought. Theology serves the church by defining its commitments to God and neighbor. Practically speaking, how can the pastoral theology of the sermon really convey care?

---

[45]For contemporary homiletic theology, in addition to works already cited of David Buttrick and Gerhard Forde, see Ronald J. Allen, Barbara S. Blaisdell, and Scott B. Johnston, *Theology for Preaching: Authority, Truth, and Knowledge of God in a Postmodern Ethos* (Nashville: Abingdon Press, 1997); Rebecca S. Chopp, *The Power to Speak: Feminism, Language, God* (New York: Crossroad, 1992); Richard Lischer, *A Theology of Preaching: The Dynamics of the Gospel*, Abingdon Preacher's Library, ed. William D. Thompson (Nashville: Abingdon Press, 1981).

Such a view of pastoral theology is actually a misunderstanding. When we assume that the theology of the sermon is divorced from the sermon's pastoral intent, all kinds of problems occur in preaching. In the worst case, theology becomes irrelevant to the sermon, at least in the mind of the preacher. Theology must stay seated on the dusty shelves of the pastor's study while the sermon takes flight. Presumably, the sermon has some freight to deliver, in this case marked "care," that theology cannot assist. Better to leave theology in the backroom whenever the person in the pulpit stands among the congregation.

Another sticking point occurs when we discount the pastoral importance of theology in preaching. Most preachers readily admit that theology matters to preaching; we're just not sure how. But because we believe that theology is secondary to either scriptural interpretation or personal experience in preaching, we abandon theology to find its own way through the hedgerows of the sermon. Here and there theology raises its head above the shrubbery, pokes an arm through, or awkwardly tries to vault over the fences of the sermon to make a glancing point. This yields more than a few tiresome sermons, where preachers take long excursuses to chase down theology before returning to "my main point." Or the sermon simply careens around between experience, scriptural interpretation, and theology without ever going any place in particular. John McClure notes, after studying the use of theology in contemporary preaching, that often such use of theology is highly inconsistent and even contradictory within the same sermon.[46] Here, theology is like the embarrassing cousin of preaching, whom the preacher, for love and duty, will not ignore but can't figure out how to introduce to the neighbors. This is a step in the right direction, but preachers aren't quite sure what to do with this thing called theology in the sermon.

One further misuse of pastoral theology occurs in preaching. Many preachers are convinced that theology belongs in preaching, as it always has. Yet our clearest models of theological reflection come from the classroom, usually of the seminary or divinity school. Academic theology, or at least the study of theology in academic settings, comes to mind. Systematic reasoning often holds the upper hand in the classroom, whether you agree with this approach to teaching or not. With this as our example, we despair of ever making a bridge between theology proper and the sermon, leading us to set aside theology as discussed above. Or we make a valiant effort to teach theology from the pulpit, to instruct persons how to think theologically about Christian faith and life. There is clearly a place for teaching the faith from the pulpit. C. H. Dodd's strict separation between

---

[46]John McClure, "Changes in the Authority, Method, and Message of Presbyterian (UPCUSA) Preaching in the Twentieth Century," in *The Confessional Mosaic,* ed. Milton J. Coalter, John M. Mulder, Louis B. Weeks (Louisville: Westminster/John Knox Press, 1990), 108.

kerygma and *didache* no longer convinces us.[47] But a steady diet of "teaching" sermons, whether the content is biblical interpretation, doctrine, culture, or social principles, will not satisfy the congregation's appetite for pastoral theological depth in the pulpit. And preaching that incorrectly seeks to imitate the academic study of theology may considerably dampen the congregation's hunger for gospel food. Here, the congregation has the uneasy feeling that the preacher has been off taking exotic culinary classes for academic credit when a well prepared, basic meal would suffice.

Pastoral theology in the sermon leads in another direction. The pastoral theology of the sermon is not an add-on to the finished product. It is not an afterthought tossed into the sermonic mix. Rather, pastoral theology is part and parcel of the entire sermon. Pastoral theology is present in the sermon whether we recognize it or not. Theology is there because the preacher pastor, as all Christians, is a theologian, albeit a practical one. As Christians, we think about God's ways with humanity. We puzzle over the godly meaning of birth and death, of trust and betrayal. We see God stitched into the fabric of domestic life. We stare with wide-eyed wonder when a knee-high youngster sits down at a piano to play. We wonder about God's silence when bombs fall upon Serbia and soldiers brutalize civilians. We vow to God, when hearing the anguish of abused wives and children, not to remain silent ourselves. All Christians are really theologians, though some are more systematic than others. Preacher pastors just happen to have the opportunity and the calling to put their theology to work on a daily basis in the hospitals, in the aisle of the grocery store, or standing on someone's front lawn. Where the theology often comes to bear upon the life of the people is in the sermon, as the preacher pastor speaks of God before humanity and humanity before God. When you get right down to it, all preaching is pastoral, and all preaching is theological.[48]

This means that the true pastoral intent of our sermons lodges in the theology of the sermon itself. Pastoral care in preaching does not rely primarily upon the caring attitude of the preacher or psychotherapeutic categories that shed light upon troublesome situations. Theology is the bedrock from which pastoral sermons emerge, or don't.

Pastoral Perspective of the Sermon

But how do we uncover the pastoral theological foundations of preaching? A generation ago, Seward Hiltner, in his now classic treatment of pastoral theology, *A Preface to Pastoral Theology*, offered a helpful way to

---

[47]C. H. Dodd, *The Apostolic Preaching and Its Developments* (New York: Harper, 1936). On teaching sermons see Ronald J. Allen, *The Teaching Sermon* (Nashville: Abingdon Press, 1996).

[48]Ronald Allen makes the observation that prophetic and pastoral preaching cannot be separated. The prophetic occurs within pastoral preaching as a corrective to false understandings of God, the community, and its mission in the world. "The Relationship Between the Pastoral and the Prophetic in Preaching," *Encounter* 49 (Summer 1988): 173–89.

sort out the relationship between pastoral care and preaching. Hiltner links preaching and pastoral care through the concept of *perspectives*.[49] While Hiltner's primary interest was the pastoral, or shepherding, perspective of ministry, he outlines two other perspectives that interact with the former—communicating and organizing. The perspectives model suggests that in each act of ministry one perspective is dominant while others remain secondary. Preaching brings one perspective forward; pastoral care events bring another. But regardless of which perspective is dominant, the subdominant perspectives remain operative in the background of the ongoing act of ministry. For example, if the pastor is engaged in individual conversation to offer guidance to a questioning parishioner, say concerning unemployment, she will also be aware that the concern at hand could be addressed through a sermon. Similarly, while proclaiming the resurrection in worship, the preacher remains tacitly aware of those who are bereaved. Proclamation of the gospel receives the main focus, but the pastoral perspective concerning grief hovers on the edge of the spotlight. Ministers may even shift perspectives from preaching to pastoral, or pastoral to preaching, within any event, depending upon changing circumstances.[50] Or both perspectives may be at work without the preacher pastor's awareness. Indeed, most preachers have had the occasional experience of a parishioner who says that a particular sermon spoke "directly to me" about a pastoral concern when the preacher was unaware of the need.

Pastoral Theology of the Sermon

Specifically, we see most clearly the pastoral perspective of the sermon in two theological locations: theological anthropology and ecclesiology. All sermons rest on certain notions of the human being in relationship to other humans and God (theological anthropology) and certain notions of the purpose and identity of the church (ecclesiology). These theological foundations may be explicit or implicit in the sermon. The preacher may be conscious of them, or they may simply stand outside of the preacher's awareness, subtly though powerfully shaping the orientation of the preacher and the sermon. This seems obvious, although many preachers may not have stopped to consider the implications.

These theological foundations telegraph the pastoral perspective of the sermon. The theological anthropology and ecclesiology of the sermon signal how the preacher understands care. Over time, because of the power of sacred speech, they begin to orient the congregation's approach to care. In chapter 3 we will explore how language shapes congregational identity, and we will look specifically at theological anthropology in chapter 4 and ecclesiology in chapter 5. But for now, I simply wish to state that the pastoral

---

[49]Seward Hiltner, *Preface to Pastoral Theology* (New York: Abingdon Press, 1958), 18, 55–69.

[50]Ibid., 152–53.

theological commitments of the preacher and the sermon give direction to the pastoral care of the congregation. They are the signposts that tell the congregation who cares, who should care, and how care is offered. For example, one preacher's sermons may suggest that pastoral care is an act of individual healing, while another's sermons may indicate that care is the sustaining action of an entire congregation for each and every member. The pastoral theology of one sermon may be simply translated, "I (preacher pastor) care about you (parishioner) in this manner–empathically, reservedly, with control, carelessly, faithfully." Or the pastoral theology of the sermon may communicate an entirely different message. "We (all of us in this sanctuary) care about one another (all other members of the congregation) in these ways–with tenderness, respect, caution, avoidance of conflicts–for these reasons because God loves and cares for us just as God always has," or "because we are afraid of those people out there." Varied as they are, each of these approaches to care comes across in the pastoral theology of the sermon, specifically through the theological anthropology and ecclesiology of the preacher. While we can see this in any particular sermon, the pastoral perspective in preaching is especially evident through numerous sermons preached in congregations over time.

Anthropology

Why theological anthropology and ecclesiology? In the first instance, pastoral care's widest sphere of interest is clearly the human being. Certainly, we cannot cleanly separate anthropology from other theological beliefs. Christian anthropology implies theology, soteriology, christology, and so on. But our concept of humanity, however vague or clear, sets the direction for our pastoral care. It is the ground floor for pastoral care. Pastors are preoccupied with the needs and motivations of human beings in relationship with others and God. For instance, when pastors enter conversation with parishioners who are searching for vocational direction, the primary focus is on human goals and motivations. Theologically speaking, the issue concerns telos, the goal of human beings in the world. To take another example, a pastoral visit to a bereaved family whose members have suffered a tragic death focuses upon the ubiquitous experience of human loss. Simultaneously, the pastor enters into the particular experience of this family's grief, a grief that is not quite like any other. The theological issues at hand are finitude and response. Praying with a couple who have just given birth to a child, the pastor faces any number of human realities: the embodiment of maternal/paternal love and suffering (the excruciating pangs of childbirth); joy and fulfillment of the human desire to nurture; fear of failure and the weight of responsibility; identity and role confusion; or in the case of complications at birth, perhaps shock, guilt, and confusion. In this case, theological meaning clusters around the image of God, co-creation, and even corruptibility or the fall. In such pastoral situations, pastoral care spotlights human nature in its fullness.

As pastors, we carry along these notions of the human being when we show up to preach. How we see the human being unavoidably shapes our approach to care in the sermon. For instance, the theological anthropology of the sermon may define the human problem as individual sin, understood as disobedience of God's laws. What is needed, therefore, is for the disobedient one to come down to the altar, confess his or her sin either privately or to the preacher, and receive the forgiveness of God. Here, the sermon is communicating that individual reconciliation constitutes pastoral care, given the definition of the problem as sinful disobedience. In a psychological approach, the sermon may typify the human problem as lack of self-esteem. The solution is for the hearer to follow the sermon's instructions about how to learn to love oneself. Presumably, in such a sermon, care boils down to self-care, an odd admonition from a preacher who stands in a tradition that proclaims human beings cannot do much at all without the care of God. Or take another example from an activist orientation in preaching. The sermon may define the human dilemma as our unwillingness to confront the forces of evil in the world—racism, economic injustice, militarism, and so forth—because of either fear or selfishness. The response that the sermon calls for is for the hearer to shake off the fetters that bind and confront evil with moral force. In this case, the sermon expresses care as moral guidance of the faithful who, because of their inaction, have become faithless. Each of these examples shows how a sermon's grounding theological anthropology determines the preferred approach to care. Of course, theological anthropology is not always clear in every sermon. And a preacher may hold inconsistent or highly complex understandings of the human being. Yet over time the anthropology will establish the course of care in the sermons.

Ecclesiology

As for ecclesiology, this theme emerges in part from the previous one. Contemporary theological anthropologies have been creatively focused on human relationship as one answer to the conundrums of human beings. In particular, feminist theologies have shifted our focus from the isolated human being as representative person to human beings together. Mutuality, interconnectedness, and the unity of body spirit thematize feminist anthropologies.[51] Likewise, liberation and African American theologies have changed attention from individual to corporate conceptions of sin and salvation, not necessarily a new emphasis in theology but with new contextual weight. These developments turn us toward communal themes

---

[51]See Catherine Keller, *From a Broken Web: Separation, Sexism, and Self* (Boston: Beacon, 1986); Bonnie Miller-McLemore, *Also a Mother: Work and Family as Theological Dilemma* (Nashville: Abingdon Press, 1994); Christie Cozad Neuger, "Women and Relationality," in *Feminist and Womanist Pastoral Theology,* ed. Bonnie J. Miller-McLemore and Brita Gill-Austern (Nashville: Abingdon Press, 1999), 113.

in theology; hence, ecclesiology, the study of the nature and purpose of the church, becomes central in postmodern Christian thought.

Pastoral care has not missed this most recent theological fork in the road. Indeed, pastoral theologians have turned to Christian community as a logical correction to the individualism that underlies many therapeutic approaches to pastoral care and counseling. Pastoral theologian John Patton has appealed for a "communal-contextual" care that seeks to refocus pastoral care within the ecclesial community while honoring the need for contextual specificity in pastoral care.[52] Charles Gerkin sounds a similar theme in *Prophetic Pastoral Practice*, claiming that the time is overdue for pastoral care to return to its home base of the church.[53] Various pastoral theologians have held this position throughout the contemporary pastoral care and counseling movement. Now, however, their wisdom seems to be taking root. So ecclesiology offers a natural and renewed link between preaching and care that might open up fresh discovery for pastoral preaching.

A caution: The tendency to romanticize the church and "community" plays around the edges of this return to ecclesiology. One wonders just how much actual community commitment emerges out of all the discussion today on the need for community. Discipleship always dogs community. But by and large, pastoral care comes closer to the heart of its discipline when it moves back inside the sanctuary and fellowship hall. The church, with all its promise and problems, moves into the foreground of pastoral care and theology. As Kathleen Billman summarizes, "The first conviction, widely shared in contemporary pastoral care literature, is that pastoral care is a communal art, bringing together laity and clergy to offer ministries of care to one another and to those outside the boundaries of their congregations."[54] This is not to say that pastoral care is becoming parochial. Rather, pastoral care is recognizing the church as the natural base from which to offer care to the wider community and world.

It follows that we will glimpse the pastoral perspective within sermons through attending the images of the church therein, because it is in and through the church that care occurs. As we saw with theological anthropology, the preacher pastor's views of the church may be spelled out or implied. Often we will find more than one image of the church in a sermon.[55] Yet there will usually be one or two dominant views of the church

---

[52]John Patton, *Pastoral Care in Context: An Introduction to Pastoral Care* (Louisville: Westminster/John Knox Press, 1993).

[53]Charles V. Gerkin, *Prophetic Pastoral Practice: A Christian Vision of Life Together* (Nashville: Abingdon Press, 1991).

[54]Kathleen D. Billman, "Pastoral Care as an Art of Community," in *The Arts of Ministry: Feminist-Womanist Approaches,* ed. Christie Cozad Neuger (Louisville: Westminster John Knox Press, 1996), 10.

[55]Paul S. Minear identifies more than one hundred images of the church within the New Testament in *Images of the Church in the New Testament* (Philadelphia: Westminter, 1960). Avery Dulles explains six basic ecclesiological models in *Models of the Church* (Garden City, N.Y.: Doubleday, 1974).

that indicate the sermon and preacher's understanding of care. For instance, a preacher's sermons may often point toward the church as a loving fellowship of believers, something akin to Avery Dulles' church as mystical communion. Such a theology of the church suggests that pastoral care is the mutual sharing of one another's burdens in the power of the Holy Spirit. Or the images, stories, and scriptural allusions of the sermon may indicate a church that understands itself as a suffering servant in the world. In this case, the theology of the sermon constructs care as binding the wounds of those beyond the boundaries of the faithful community. Either way, the sermon points toward its pastoral perspective through the nature and purpose of the church that it presents. Discover how the sermon and the preacher construe the church, and you will be on your way to discovery of how the sermon and preacher offer pastoral care.

Summary

All this talk of theological anthropology, ecclesiology, and pastoral perspectives in preaching may seem unnecessarily complex. After all, pastors and preachers are busy people with precious little time to read and reflect. I admit that it is no easy task to assess the pastoral theology of our sermons. Sometimes we just want to preach. Let the theology of the sermon take care of itself. But I am convinced that too much is riding on our preaching to leave theology orphaned.

Preaching is care-full. Sermons express the fullness of care theologically, especially through the ways that they understand the human being and the nature and mission of the church. We must handle with care the pastoral theology of our sermons if we wish the sermon to do the work of pastoral care.

This leads us toward the next concern of this book: the pastoral community.

2

The Pastoral Community

It is grace, nothing but grace, that we are allowed to live in Christian community.[1]

—DIETRICH BONHOEFFER

A harried pastor friend once remarked to me, "There's just not enough of me to go around." Most pastors have experienced the frustration. There are too many pastoral needs within the congregation and too little time and energy to respond. We do the best we can with congregations large and small. We seek to establish regular visitation of persons in hospitals, retirement centers, and at home. We review the studies that conclude that what people really want from their minister is good preaching (however defined) and a pastor who knows them by name. So we dig a little deeper in our sermon preparation, and we double our efforts to keep in touch with the persons in the congregation. We know that we live in a society where technological advances, for all their contributions, propel us toward lack of human contact ("We're glad that you called. Touch 1 for a directory of personnel. Touch 2 if you wish to correspond with our automated teller. Touch 3, and hold if you wish to speak with an attendant."). So we work even harder to make our congregations into face-to-face communities. When God calls us through the church into the ministry of the gospel, we take pastoral care of the people with utmost seriousness. But there is never enough of us, at least as the ordained representative, to go around.

Pretty soon, we begin to reflect on the ministry of care of the entire congregation. Pastoral care, properly understood, does not belong to or

---

[1]Dietrich Bonhoeffer, *Life Together* (New York: Harper & Row, 1954), 20.

depend solely upon the ordained clergy. Care is the action and attitude of the *laos*, the people of God, as much as it is the work of the pastor. If we wish to retain the biblical imagery of shepherd, or pastor, as the guiding imagery for Christian care, we need to broaden its conception to include the shepherding ministry of the community as a whole. As Kathleen Billman says, "An important task of the pastor as caregiver is to…communicate a vision of pastoral care that has at its heart the creation of communities of care."[2] For the pastoral work of the church does not flow downward from God, through the ordained pastor, to the people. Rather, by the power of the Holy Spirit, care flows among the people of God and out into the wider world. Yes, the ordained pastor plays a key role in gently directing the care of the congregation, maybe stirring it up, sending it off in new directions, and thanking God for blessing the people with compassion, but the ordained minister cannot presume to be "in charge" of all the pastoral care that goes on within the community.

The theological basis for this claim is the doctrine of the priesthood of all believers, which in turn rests upon the biblical foundation that all believers in Christ are partners in the gospel (Heb. 3:1) and priests for one another (1 Pet. 2:1–10). The church gives the ordained clergy certain responsibilities of pastoral oversight. In specific situations the ordained representative symbolizes the church as a whole when he or she offers pastoral care, for example by offering prayers at a funeral or sharing the sacrament with the homebound. But pastoral care goes on within the congregation all the time among the members and between the members and those whom they encounter outside the congregation.

We are all familiar with the routine though nonetheless important ways that churches carry on pastoral care: phone calls of concern, sharing meals with grieving families, prayer lists, celebrating births and marriages, quiet gifts of money during tough times, and so on. We are also familiar with extraordinary ministries of pastoral care that occur within churches: supporting immigrant families over several years, caring for persons with AIDS, after-school programs for latchkey children, providing shelters for the homeless or abused. In so many ways congregations are directly involved in pastoral care. Dietrich Bonhoeffer captures the mutuality of care within the Christian community when he writes, "Strong and weak, wise and foolish, gifted or ungifted, pious or impious, the diverse individuals in the community, are…cause for rejoicing in one another and serving one another."[3] The burden of pastoral care need not fall so heavily on the pastor if he or she understands that every person within the congregation

---

[2]Kathleen D. Billman, "Pastoral Care as an Art of Community," in *The Arts of Ministry: Feminist-Womanist Approaches,* ed. Christie Cozad Neuger (Louisville: Westminster John Knox Press, 1996), 10.

[3]Bonhoeffer, *Life Together,* 93.

brings care-full gifts to the altar. The Spirit of God empowers every person within the congregation to freely offer his or her pastoral gifts.

The central claim of this book is that preaching helps create a pastoral community. The true ministry of pastoral care grows out of the caring community that forms through pastoral preaching. As Rudolf Bohren wrote a number of years ago, preaching builds up the congregation so that it can fulfill the communal task of "being a community of pastors."[4] Clergy simply cannot and should not assume the full responsibility of pastoral care of the congregation. Such attempts always fail because the pastor, no matter how gifted, isn't capable of responding to all the pastoral needs of the congregation, large or small. More importantly, the congregation exists for the purpose of extending godly care to one another and the neighbor. For the preacher to attempt to corner the market on care robs the community of its core purpose and limits the mission of the church. Preachers want to preach the gospel in such a fashion that the congregation develops its own ministry of care, complemented by the pastor to be sure, but not dependent on him or her. In other words, pastoral preaching forms pastoral communities.

Most pastors will probably agree with this general endorsement of the pastoral care ministry of all Christians. And most will probably agree that preaching can contribute to the formation of the congregation as a pastoral community. The rub, of course, is how the pastoral nature of the congregation actually plays out. Just what is this pastoral community that our preaching seeks to form? Are there specific characteristics that identify the Christian community as a pastoral community? Before we can talk concretely about how preaching fashions a pastoral community, we need to see a quick portrait of it so that we will know the traits of the community that pastoral preaching hopes to shape.

The Nature of the Pastoral Community

We must acknowledge a danger from the outset. There is always a tendency to describe community in ideal terms. We do this because our sense of loss of community is so great. Whatever else bothers us in postmodernity, the breakdown of community has left much of Western society reeling and rootless. The absence of community is real, at least community in the traditional sense of persons belonging to and understanding themselves as part of a specific people in a specific locale whose commitments and values endure over time. Lamenting the loss of communal identity, Flannery O'Connor once made a comment about certain types of commercial writers: "You know what's the matter with

---

[4]Rudolf Bohren, *Preaching and Community,* trans. David E. Green (Richmond: John Knox Press, 1965), 123.

them? They're not from anywhere."[5] Because of many sociological factors, the cohesive meaning fabric that traditional community provided for us in Western society is irreparably torn.[6] Excessive individualism and unbridled materialism has gnawed at the roots of public life. We see this in politics, where the electorate swings widely in its political allegiances every two years, belying a profound distrust in the ability of any government to provide for the common good. Universities graduate professionals who are highly skilled to compete in the marketplace yet frequently hold no vision of social morality. Without extended kinship and social ties, isolated family "units" assume more and more responsibility for raising the children. Under the weight, marriages implode. To be sure, the effects are not uniformly felt across society. Some pockets of Westerners continue to escape the erosion of community either through bold resistance (The Amish and old order Mennonites), cultural tenacity (various immigrant groups), or sheer geographical isolation. But by and large, our community fabric is severely shredded. This is frightening. So we tend to idealize what we have lost, dressing our notions of community in romantic, nostalgic, and utopian clothing. One prominent cultural indicator of this is the rapid rise in mainstream popularity of country music over the past fifteen years. One of the musical genre's reiterated themes is idealization of the rural, small town community. The fact that country music sings so constantly and nostalgically about this communal ideal belies just how far it has vanished from the social landscape.

The church itself, once a center of community life, has not been immune to this steady erosion of community. In many ways the church, too, has capitulated to the dominant economic and political models that define American public life. It is no coincidence, for example, that the church growth movement of the past thirty years has adopted the shopping mall as its main image for the successful church. In this model, the church is not the Christ-centered community where persons learn the life of discipleship. Rather, it is a place where individuals go to choose what they need from a vast smorgasbord of programs that will help them feel fulfilled. Furthermore, like government, the institutional church is mired in impersonal and debilitating bureaucratization that drains off valuable energy and resources from the ministry of the local congregation. The church does care about the increasing needs of a society that is profoundly broken, yet we are not clear about how to respond.

We do know that community is central to the church's own history and self-understanding. From our beginnings, the church has been communal. Jesus didn't summon persons to follow him one by one. He beckoned to them in groups of two, three, twelve, and five thousand. We

---

[5]Cited in Betsy Fancher, "My Flannery O'Connor," *Brown's Guide to Georgia* 3 (1975): 16–22.
[6]See Peter Berger, *The Sacred Canopy* (Garden City, N. Y.: Anchor Books, 1969).

call ourselves an *ecclesia,* which means in translation from the Greek, "a public," a "people called out." That is, the church is a people (plural) called out by God. Yes, the church scatters throughout the world, just as individual members of a single congregation come and go from the gathering. But every time we leave the white frame building, or the storefront location, or the gray stone gothic structure where the people meet, we carry the community with us insofar as those who are truly in Christian community do not exist alone but as a part of one another. It is Christ, of course, who unites the Christian fellowship. We celebrate this union with Christ and one another every time we break bread together and share the cup of blessing. The eucharist, or holy communion, actually seals the bonds of community that Christians profess. Christians have always found themselves in community—it is part of the definition of the Christian church.

Our communal nature may be the most important seed that the church can sow for public renewal in Western society. We will not rebuild wider community all at once. But the church yet bears within itself God's gift of human communion. The fact is that people still show up in large numbers at our churches looking for caring and committed community life. You can see them every week in congregations large and small, urban, rural, and suburban. Whether they find authentic Christian communities, communities with enough of the imprint of Christ to make a difference in God's community-hungry world, is another question.

The pastoral dimension of Christian community is the one that concerns us right now. What are caring congregations like in today's culture? When people become a part of pastoral communities, how do they act? What are some of the values of the caring congregation and how are these values translated for others? If we can find answers to some of these questions, we can take a hard look at our preaching to see how it contributes to pastoral formation in the congregation.

I will try to avoid painting a rosy, trumped-up picture of the ideal pastoral community, one that is far beyond actual human realization. Krister Stendahl refers sarcastically to this sentimental tendency among clergy as "playing Bibleland."[7] But theologically speaking, the church lives between the reality of who we now are and the promise of who we shall yet become. The Christian community's identity is already rooted in Christ, but the fullness of the church will be realized in the future of God. I may fall off the tightrope that stretches between the "is" and "ought" of the church (it's inevitable), but when I fall, I hope to fall with the church toward God's future.

We will explore three characteristics that I understand to be central to the pastoral community: *mutuality in ministry, hospitality, and compassion.* These categories are not exhaustive, though they suggest much of what I

---

[7]Cited in William Muehl, *Why Preach? Why Listen?* (Philadelphia: Fortress Press, 1986), 14.

understand to be the core features of pastoral community. If space permitted, we could certainly add other pastoral categories to the list. Hopefully, readers will fill in some of these as we proceed.

The Pastoral Community Is Mutually Edifying

In one of his most insightful works, *In the Name of Jesus,* the late Henri Nouwen tells the story of his efforts to discover mutuality in ministry in a *L'Arche* community in Toronto, Canada. *L'Arche* communities are based on Jean Vanier's vision that persons with severe mental, emotional, and physical challenges can live creatively in community with other persons. Nouwen commits himself to the *L'Arche* community, which causes him to practice community mutuality in a way that he has never done before.

As the book unfolds, Nouwen tells about the time that he invites one of the members of the *L'Arche* community to join him for a speaking engagement. Nouwen thinks that while he gives the speech his companion, Bill Van Buren, will simply sit quietly on the platform. This arrangement doesn't satisfy Bill, however. He stands directly behind Nouwen on the platform. When Nouwen begins to speak, Bill interjects, "I have heard that before." Bill's comments irritate Nouwen. But they are refreshing for the listeners as Bill unwittingly chips away the pretense that usually accompanies Nouwen's formal speeches. The speech proceeds, as does the rest of the conference, in this joint approach to Christian leadership. On the flight home, Bill says to Nouwen, "And we did it together, didn't *we?*" Nouwen replies, yes, "What we did, we did together in Jesus' name." In the end, this occurrence beckons Nouwen into deeper community mutuality in the ministry of pastoral care. It is a mutuality that he could not have ever imagined without the actual involvement in *L'Arche.*[8]

Status

There is nothing easy about mutual care within the Christian community. Difficulty riddles our *koinonia* (communion, partnership, fellowship). Status differences based on role, gender, race, age, economic and social class, education, talents, and physical and mental abilities all create roadblocks to mutuality. Wherever human beings gather, including the church, power impinges on care. Pastors learn something about the politics of pastoral care when they land in the hospital bed themselves. Suddenly the roles are reversed. Care doesn't seem quite so desirable or well intended when the pastor is the one using the bedpan. The tendency of many ordained ministers to hold tightly to the reigns of pastoral care shows just how problematic the matter is.

In one sense, distinctions are practically and theologically necessary in Christian community. If you have ever participated in a congregation

---

[8]Henri Nouwen, *In the Name of Jesus: Reflections on Christian Leadership* (New York: Crossroad, 1989), 75–81.

where everyone is falling over one another attempting not to assert leadership, you know what I mean about distinctions being practically necessary. Conversely, you may have seen some churches where a lot of the people want to chart the course but very few want to hoist the sail. Groups, even Christian ones, need some semblance of ordering to fulfill their purposes. Churches need some people who can see the big picture, others who can sketch it out, and still others who can fill in the details. There is one Spirit, but many gifts, as Paul instructs the Corinthians (1 Cor. 12). God intends them all to be used for the common good of the body. Theologically, those with leadership gifts would be negligent stewards not to exercise their abilities in service of the community, just as those with other talents are indispensable to the Christian community. As a friend told me recently about his role in the church: "I'm not the one to chair the committee. But I'm happy to be the 'go-to' guy when they need a job done." Christians have always understood these social and theological realities. The orders of ministry, lay and clerical, are the church's organizational attempts to be faithful as the body of Christ in the world.

When I speak, then, of mutuality within the pastoral community, I am not suggesting the abolition of priestly ordination or the erasing of distinctions between the laity and the clergy. In fact, God extends vocation (a call) upon all Christians through our baptism into Christ. The call to all believers is to love God and our neighbors through Christ, who dwells among us in the power of the Holy Spirit. The church then determines whom God is calling for representative ministries of service, preaching, sacraments, and oversight of the church. In this sense, the clergy are always part of the *laos* (the people). They arise for a time from their place within the congregation to move to the pulpit and lift up the cup. Thomas Long makes this point humorously with respect to preachers. He says that preachers do not drop down into congregations as "visitors from clergy land, strangers from an unknown land, ambassadors from seminary land, or even, as much as we may cherish the thought, prophets from a wilderness land. We are members of the body of Christ, commissioned to preach by the very people to whom we are about to speak."[9] Preachers stand up from the middle of the congregation and walk down the aisle to the pulpit. Orders within the community are a necessary distinction if the church is to fulfill God's calling. In and of themselves, orders should enhance mutuality in ministry. Yet these necessary distinctions within the church often thwart Christian community.

Power

The problem is the use of power within the ordering of the Christian community. Distinctions should not hinder mutuality, but they do. Why?

---

[9]Thomas G. Long, *The Witness of Preaching* (Louisville:Westminster Press, 1989), 11–12.

Because we "live among a people of unclean lips" (Isa. 6:5), because we "do the things we ought not to do, and cannot do the things we ought to do"(Rom. 7:15, rev.). While we are a people who profess that in Christ there is neither Jew or Greek, slave or free, male or female (Gal. 3:28), our body, like Christ, is broken, and unlike Christ, has not yet received the fullness of a new body in the resurrection. Where Christ intends a whole people whose only status and power rest upon the folly of the cross, we set ourselves up as individual lords over one another, clawing and kicking like James and John (Mk. 10:35–45) for the seats of privilege (who gets the big chair, the highest salary, the solo, the name in the newsletter, etc). When our capacity for sin runs its destructive course, we wind up in the Christian community with whole groups of people who are second-class citizens, usually in Western churches the women, persons of color, children, the poor, and the physically and mentally challenged, though not in any particular order. If there is one thing that the feminist, black, and liberationist members of the body have taught the church over the past thirty years, it is to recognize that someone's interests are always being served within every human community. It is usually the interest of those who are controlling the rules and the language of the community under consideration. I'm not saying that anyone intentionally sets out to make the church this way. But given who we are as sinful creatures, once the privilege of power locks into place within the church, it seems that all heaven must break loose before just and loving community comes.

So let's not be too sanguine about mutuality within the pastoral community. There are many forces that work against it, the largest being the power of sin within human society to corrupt even our best intentions. Christians, like all the rest of the human race, tend to act out of self-interest despite our professing that our sinful selves are buried with Christ. Every day in society we see the painful and dehumanizing results of our corruption. We don't have to drive far in any city or small town in North America to see just how unequally the power is distributed across socioeconomic groups. The President of the United States recently took a trip to highlight poverty in the country and to try to focus public policy toward greater concern for the poorest members of our society. But the President didn't have to travel to the delta of Mississippi or the barren hills of South Dakota. The blight of poverty and violence born from inequality is no greater anywhere in the United States than on the streets of Washington, D.C. We are dealing here with more than the lack of good human intentions. We are dealing with sin perpetuated by powers and principalities that only the active forces of God's goodness can counter.[10] This same force of sin distorts our use of power within the pastoral community. So if we wish to build up

---

[10]See Walter Wink, *Naming the Powers: The Language of Power in the New Testament* (Philadelphia: Fortress Press, 1984).

a pastoral community where mutuality defines the relationships, let's at least be aware of what we are up against.

Care of One Another

Yet mutuality does characterize pastoral community, even if only achievable in fragments. First, through our preaching we seek to form communities where members freely extend mutual care to one another. Pastoral communities "encourage one another and build up each other" (1 Thess. 5:11). Members of the pastoral community seek to serve each other in the Spirit of Christ. "We who are strong ought to put up with the failings of the weak, and not to please ourselves. Each of us must please our neighbor for the good purpose of building up the neighbor" (Rom. 15:1–2). As James Cone points out about the importance of Christian community in the African American experience, "Suffering is not too much to bear, if there are brothers and sisters to go down in the valley to pray with you."[11] Pastoral communities carry out their day-to-day work by bearing one another's burdens. We bear one another up in times of suffering, pain, and joy. Feminist theologians, such as Letty Russell, have particularly stressed the importance of mutuality as one of the hallmarks of Christian community. *Koinonia*, she says, "usually stresses a common bond in Jesus Christ that establishes mutual community. The emphasis is on a two-sided relationship of giving or receiving, participation or community."[12] Her metaphor of partnership opens up the pastoral nature of the church, wherein all the members care equally for one another as partners in the gospel.

But what does such mutuality of care look like in the congregation? For one thing, it means that care flows around and across the entire network of the pastoral community. The community is more like a circle, or as Russell imagines it, "a church in the round."[13] Care is not the privileged responsibility of official caregivers, clergy or lay. Christians treat one another care-fully because in Christ they know who they are, a people who care as God cares. While lay care teams may benefit from special training, for example to learn about the emotional dynamics of sickness and death, approaches to pastoral visitation, and listening skills, such is not always necessary. In fact, some such programs work against mutuality by labeling the participants in the programs either "caregivers" or "care-receivers," and then assigning roles to both. When this happens, it is little wonder that there are not enough "care-receivers" to sustain the program. Who wants it? Within the pastoral community, we can see each other simply as those who care in the name of God. Sometimes we receive care and sometimes

---

[11]James Cone, *The Spirituals and the Blues, An Interpretation* (New York: Seabury Press, 1972), 64.

[12]Letty M. Russell, *Growth in Partnership* (Philadelphia: Westminster Press, 1981), 24.

[13]Letty M. Russell, *Church in the Round: Feminist Interpretation of the Church* (Louisville: Westminster/John Knox Press, 1993).

we give it, because the care flows among the community. Communal care is more like music, less like a business transaction. Yes, discrete moments of the composition build as note proceeds upon note. But in the end, the people are more interested in making music than in designating who plays the piano and who plays the saxophone. The music is the thing as each person adds his or her own gifts to the whole. So, too, with care among the community.

Countless opportunities to express care occur within every Christian congregation. We carry one another along when predictable, though nonetheless painful, crises happen—illness, death, leaving home, personal failures. Members of pastoral communities also sustain one another through those unexpected events that create disruption and pain, such as natural tragedies, tornadoes and floods, outbreaks of violence, tragic accidents, divorce, loss of a job, loss of purpose, and emotional disturbances. Mutual care is called for in each of these occasions. We don't have to look around for the experts when someone chokes up before Sunday school class and says, "I need to tell everyone some bad news." We are members of the pastoral community, so it's time to do our job—to listen, hold, console, sustain, and heal one of our wounded members. As Roy SteinhoffSmith has written recently in *The Mutuality of Care*, "Care is constitutive of community; it characterizes the activities of everyone."[14] Each member offers care within the pastoral community, though with different gifts and in distinctive ways.

Once I was the pastor of an in-town congregation in Atlanta, Georgia, St. Paul United Methodist Church, whose education building burned to the ground. The fire consumed sixty years of congregational memorabilia and more than a million dollars worth of property in less than six hours. A firefighter broke his leg during the blaze, but gratefully, no one was killed. In the aftermath of the fire, youth and young adults from the surrounding neighborhood, some who were members of the church and some who were not, began the painful and dirty work of cleanup and salvage. For days we hauled stuff from the shell of the building—old Sunday school class photos, smudged dishes, soggy hymnals, twelve ruined pianos, smoky stuffed animals, and charred cribs from the day care that occupied the ground floor of the building. You've never seen a people work any harder than after this crisis. At one point shortly after the fire, some of the senior adult members were standing around in disbelief that the building was destroyed. So much had gone up in smoke. One of these older "saints," in shock, kept saying, "I just don't know what we're gonna do; I just don't know what we're gonna do." To which another lifetime member of the church said, "Well, I do. These people that are doing all this work are

---

[14]Roy Herndon SteinhoffSmith, *The Mutuality of Care* (St. Louis: Chalice Press, 1999), 16.

going to need some food and something to drink. I'm going home to cook." There are enough needs and enough ways to care to go all the way around the circle of the pastoral community.

Mutuality in care goes further, however, than these examples. Sometimes congregations overlook what persons have to offer to the ministry of pastoral care. This is a failure of the pastoral imagination of the church. It perpetuates condescension in pastoral care.[15] For example, churches are accustomed to expressing their care for church members who are homebound or live in nursing homes. We send them cards, make occasional visits, and every now and then the youth group will go sing. But we do not often think about how these members can provide care for the community. We forget that care is mutual, even in these difficult situations. Care doesn't have to be unidirectional just because someone is confined to the bed or the home. I once heard of a small congregation who decided to act on their conviction that every member of the church has something to offer to the congregation's ministry of pastoral care. They linked up new members of the church with the members who were homebound or in nursing homes. Those who were homebound agreed to pray regularly for the new members by name, and vice versa, a sort of homebound intercessory prayer chain. For example, one member who had had cerebral palsy all her life and was unable to attend worship prayed every day for a family with elementary-age children. Consider how this awareness would affect your faith and action if you were a member of the family. Think about the purpose that the homebound member found in her daily life knowing that someone else was holding her in prayer. Every person who joined the church knew that someone was praying for him or her regularly. Even more, the homebound persons who were praying had lots of time and emotion to invest in the prayers. These were some powerful prayers rising like incense from the lips of the saints. Remarkably caring and mutual relationships emerged from this endeavor. Pastoral communities stay alert to the creative ways that mutual care can be fostered within the diversity of the community as a whole.

Mutuality between Clergy and Laity

But what about the matter of role distinctions within the Christian community between clergy and laity, as touched on earlier? Most clergy and laity experience a certain distance from one another even when we value the mutuality of the Christian community. A space always seems to exist between those who are the ordained representatives of the church's ministry and those who are carrying out their ministry among the *laos*. Is mutuality possible here? Is it desirable?

---

[15]Ibid., chap. 3.

Clergy *and* laity do sustain one another in weakness and strength. Pastors need not hide their moments of real suffering from the congregation any more than they would want the congregational members to bury their problems. A pastor who has undergone loss, for example, can surely confide his grief with certain members of the congregation, knowing that they can share the burden as brothers and sisters in Christ. A certain degree of vulnerability on the part of the pastor does invite openness among the members. A willingness on the part of the pastor to receive the care of the congregation will allow the congregation the opportunity to offer their gifts of care to the pastor in his or her time of struggle. As I have already stated in the previous chapter, rarely is this vulnerability called for in the pulpit, since preaching is not the same thing as pastoral care, but if the preacher is pastorally engaged with the people, the people will make the connections in and out of the pulpit.

Please note, however, that mutual vulnerability between pastor and congregation can be and often is counterproductive. The emotionally needy and unaware pastor can turn such an approach into a constant request for sympathy and support from the congregation. In this case, the shepherd will consume the sheep. Furthermore, pastoral boundaries require that the clergy remain vigilant to the possibility that his or her own vulnerability will confuse the congregation. People do not wish to know every painful detail of their pastor's life anymore than they wish to know such about their neighbors. And never should the pastor use his or her own pain, loneliness, frustration in ministry, or confusion as an excuse for transgressing appropriate emotional and physical boundaries within the community. The result is *always* destructive of Christian community, no matter how much the clergy and parishioner plead otherwise.[16] Vulnerability between clergy and congregation contributes to mutuality only if it edifies the community as the body of Christ. Vulnerability for the sake of vulnerability has no place in pastoral ministry; it should be saved for the therapist. As Letty Russell cautions, vulnerability does not become a strength in our lives "unless the perception of continued need for growth and cooperation with others leads to a willingness to share in responsibility and self-determination as a way of overcoming unnecessary weakness."[17] Good pastors will be careful about how they share their own weaknesses and for what purpose if they wish to engender caring communities.

Accountability

Accountability is another crucial element of mutuality within the pastoral community. Most congregations find it difficult to talk about accountability. In our privatized and individualistic era, most of us shudder

---

[16]See Marie M. Fortune, *Is Nothing Sacred?* (San Francisco: Harper San Franciso, 1992).
[17]Russell, *Growth in Partnership,* 21.

at the thought of calling others into account for their decisions and actions, and most of us don't take kindly to someone else "meddling" in our affairs. The church is a public gathering where, despite some very clear official values, we are often reluctant to hold one another accountable to them. In other words, the underlying value of individual freedom within the congregational culture overrides other Christian communal values such as love of our neighbors, honesty in human relationships, and concern for the poor and oppressed. From time to time, the preacher will challenge the congregation from the pulpit on some public concern. But rarely will preacher or layperson speak directly to individuals about their broken commitments, faithlessness to God, or lukewarm service within the community. The contemporary pulpit grows silent on sin, as Marsha Witten explores in *All is Forgiven*.[18] The members of the pastoral community do not hold one another to account. We're much too polite for such accountability. And we're much too afraid of congregational conflict.

We fear that holding each other accountable will disrupt communal harmony. But often what passes for communal harmony is suppressed conflict within community. Parker Palmer claims that churches, consciously or not, perpetuate the illusion that the Christian community is an ideal family in which people are protected from the impersonal conflicts that typify mass society. "Our image of community forces people to hide their disagreements instead of getting them into the open where we might learn from them, where the problems might be worked through. Though such churches may achieve an apparent unity, it is fragile and unfulfilling, and behind it one often finds anger, frustration, and other taboo emotions."[19] Or as a colleague of mine says, churches and seminaries are where we learn how to "make nice." But making nice within the church glosses over the reality that human beings in community always experience conflict. It is unavoidable whether we acknowledge it or not. "Community is that place where the person you least want to live with always lives!...And when that person moves away, someone else arises to take his or her place," continues Palmer.[20] The truth is, like it or not, community will always confront us with those very people and situations that we wish to avoid. The ability of the members of a pastoral community to offer genuine accountability to one another depends upon our willingness to engage conflict creatively.

To achieve accountability within the pastoral community means that we will sometimes confront one another in love. We do not aim to harm one another but to build up the community of care by showing that we

---

[18]Marsha G. Witten, *All is Forgiven: The Secular Message in American Protestantism* (Princeton: Princeton University Press, 1993).

[19]Parker J. Palmer, *The Company of Strangers: Christians and the Renewal of America's Public Life* (New York: Crossroad, 1988), 120.

[20]Ibid., 126.

care enough about one another to speak up whenever necessary. This is especially true whenever important decisions are to be made on behalf of the community. From the outset, the Christian church has passed through the thickets of conflict on the road of faith. Some want to eat meat; others want to abstain. Some want to worship in ecstasy; others want to speak the plain truth in love. Some want to admit the Gentiles to the sanctuary; others want to keep them behind the rail. Every church has a long list of important decisions that get settled in meetings and around the coffeepot. Some of these decision-making processes turn nasty. They destroy community because the members of the community do not deal creatively with conflict. Members of the community shy away from practicing accountability with one another, so the conflict overwhelms the community. The more we can foster a willingness within the community to actively engage one another, even in disagreement, the more we will be able to see that genuine pastoral care within the community commits us to finding wholeness within our differences.

Confession and Forgiveness

Theologically speaking, what we are talking about is the pastoral community's ability to practice mutual confession, forgiveness, and reconciliation. Within the United Methodist church, some congregations are attempting to recover the tradition of communal confession and forgiveness through covenant discipleship groups. Within these fellowships, members covenant with God and one another to practice certain spiritual disciplines such as worship, daily prayer, reading of the scriptures, and acts of service. Confession and forgiveness comes in when members gather to give an account of their discipleship to one another, accounts which usually make the members painfully aware of their shortcomings with respect to the covenant. By hearing one another's confession, then offering the words of mercy, these communions give flesh to the reality that God through Christ and the church is the basis for our life together. God is the one who through Christ extends the gift of reconciliation. God is the one who sustains the pastoral community and promises faithfulness to us even when we are unfaithful to God and each other.

I am not suggesting that such accountability groups are necessary within every Christian congregation. Wesleyan pietism is obviously not the only route to pastoral community (thank goodness). I am saying, however, that a pastoral community will find ways for confession and forgiveness to take flesh among the people. General prayers of confession and pardon are always appropriate in Christian worship. But members of a pastoral community also need to find ways to hear one another's personal confessions in the spirit of love. This mode of pastoral care has been significant throughout the history of the Christian church, though it has all but dropped out of contemporary church practice.[21] Listen to the counsel that Dietrich Bonhoeffer gave to the pastoral community at Finkenwalde.

> In confession, the break-through to community takes place. Sin demands to have a man by himself. It withdraws him from the community. The more isolated a person is, the more destructive will be the power of sin over him, and the more deeply he becomes involved in it, the more disastrous is his isolation. Sin wants to remain unknown. It shuns the light. In the darkness of the unexpressed it poisons the whole being of a person. This can happen even in the midst of a pious community. In confession the light of the Gospel breaks into the darkness and seclusion of the heart. The sin must be brought into the light. The unexpressed must be openly spoken and acknowledged...[The sinner] finds the forgiveness of all his sin in the fellowship of Jesus Christ and his brother...It can no longer tear the fellowship asunder. Now the fellowship bears the sin of the brother...Now he stands in the fellowship of sinners who live by the grace of God in the Cross of Jesus Christ.[22]

Such words fall strangely on our individualized Christian ears, even though we live in a society that hungers for relentless exposure of the private lives of public figures. Perhaps we ask our public figures (politicians, movie stars, sports players) to endure the torturous public confession of their private lives that we ourselves are unwilling to undergo. But such vicarious confessional drama will not purge the pain and secrecy that accrues within a pastoral community whose members are unwilling to name, confess, and receive forgiveness for their sin. We don't like it. But mutuality within community requires honest confession to one another followed by the offering of God's pardon.

Presence in Community

Many students where I teach, at Memphis Theological Seminary, take a course that we call the clinical practicum in pastoral care. Sooner or later the students grapple with the significance of pastoral presence. They begin to explore what it means as the symbolic bearer of Christ to stand with others who are undergoing suffering and crisis. Some students come to the painful awareness that there are certain situations when they have nothing to say. Such as when they must stand by someone whose body is being eaten away by cancer from the inside out. The pain is too great, the

---

[21]See William A. Clebsch and Charles R. Jaekle, *Pastoral Care in Historical Perspective* (Englewood Cliffs, N. J.: Prentice Hall, 1964).

[22]Bonhoeffer, *Life Together*, 112–13.

theological questions too immense. So words fail, as they should before the abyss of human suffering. Reflecting upon this experience, the students then say something like this: "Just being there, if I can stand it, is important. Because my presence shows that God and all of us have not forgotten them. They are not alone." I agree with my students when they make this theological evaluation of the ministry of presence in pastoral care. It is a theological model of care that is incarnational. It reminds pastors that we are not "answer people" in the face of suffering, and that if nothing else, we can stand quietly by to offer the comfort, if sought, of human companionship.

But I challenge my students to think further about presence in pastoral care. Because as a representative of the people of God, the body of Christ, our presence speaks sacramentally. It speaks of the servanthood of Christ who empties himself of his godliness in order to enter our humanness, even the torment of being strung upon the rack of suffering (Phil. 2:5–8). We do not really stand by bereaved moms and dads with nothing to say. Our standing by says that we, *like* Christ, are truly present, willing, and able to shoulder some of the pain. And though *not* Christ, we bear witness to the one who goes all the way into the depth of death when Mom and Dad would rather die than live without their precious daughter. Charles Gerkin talks about this in *Crisis Experience in Modern Life* when he says that the pastor can go to the edge of the abyss with those who suffer, but Christ will go all the way down.[23] This is the meaning of pastoral presence. It requires that as pastors we learn, insofar as possible, to actually be present when present, and to recognize that our presence intimates the far greater, more redemptive presence of God.

Pastoral communities practice this virtue of presence. The members of the pastoral community are actually present to one another as bearers of Christ in bodily form. We recognize that most interactions within society are instrumental, built upon exchange transactions. Count them up: a stop at the station to buy gas, a call to the library to get a book, a take-out order for pizza, a check for the child care center, a trip to the courthouse to pay a fine. The list is endless of the daily activities that we engage in where our primary purpose is to exchange goods and services, and we have very little opportunity to see deeply into the faces of those with whom we interact. ("That will be $6.95. Please pull forward to the first window.") The church, however, promises something different. The church as a pastoral community offers the members the gift of real, human presence. The church is one community where people can attend lovingly and concretely to one another through interpersonal relations. They are what theologian Edward Farley calls "communities of the face."[24] The pastoral community avoids idealizing

[23]Charles V. Gerkin, *Crisis Experience in Modern Life: Theory and Theology in Pastoral Care* (Nashville: Abingdon Press, 1979), 100–103.

[24]Edward Farley, *Good and Evil: Interpreting a Human Condition* (Minneapolis: Fortress Press, 1990), 289–92.

love and justice; it opts for the real thing. Pastoral communities question whether husbands love their wives if they are never around to act on that love. It doubts that mothers love their children, except in a twisted and pathological sense, when they abuse them. Caring members of congregations don't say, "Your problems aren't really all that bad." They say, "Would you like to talk?" Pastoral communities don't just send money to buy flowers for a grieving member of the fellowship; they show up to honor the dead and sustain the living. (If you want to take a quick pulse of a pastoral congregation, see how many of the faithful show up at the funerals.) I once had a friend tell me after a tragic death in his family, "Your prayers don't mean much to me right now. But your being here does." The pastoral community shows up whenever a member of the community is torn apart. They offer themselves as binding ligaments for the wounded member.

Pastoral communities resist the bureaucratization of mass society by practicing presence. As the social worker in Mary Gordon's novel *Final Payments* says when she struggles to break out of the bureaucracy of her social service work, "You [don't] walk into people's lives carrying a briefcase, carrying forms, and then go back as if you were just another person."[25] Pastoral communities do not live by the briefcase, though of course organization is necessary. They live by the power of Christ, whose presence among the community makes it possible for the community members to be present to one another. This presence within community does not disregard the wider world, as we shall soon discuss. But the community practices presence in order to be fully present to the world that often seems to have lost the ability to care. As Robert Webber and Rodney Clapp explain it, people in community "concentrate on being present to their companions in the community not because they regard the people of the world as less worthy, but because they know that presence is learned only in particularity and that they can be present to the world only to the degree they have learned to be present to one another."[26] God entrusts a rich treasure—the presence of Christ—to the earthen vessel of the pastoral community, who in turn practices Christ's presence for the world.

Some of the most significant moments in the life of the community occur whenever members are awakened to one another's presence and the presence of God among them. To be sure, no community can sustain an ethos of presence all the time. The fact is that we are only partially present to each other most of the time. But if we look carefully at the people who gather at the communion rail—see Mr. Thomas, he always carries his hat with him, even to the Lord's table; see that Langston girl, she's a math whiz, but she's flunking out of school; look at the Renwicks, they'll be married fifty years next month; and there's William, he says AA is making

---

[25]Mary Gordon, *Final Payments* (New York: Random House, 1978), 130–31.
[26]Robert E. Webber and Rodney Clapp, *People of the Truth: The Power of the Worshiping Community in the Modern World* (San Francisco: Harper & Row, 1988), 66.

a difference this time—we'll see the wonders of the God-created human community present before our very eyes. There they are sharing the presence of Christ, reflecting the reconciling love of God. And when we see God present in those around us, then within the pastoral community we stand half a chance of becoming present to one another.

Mutuality for the Common Good

In the pastoral community, members do not simply support one another *individually*. It should be obvious by now that through these various aspects of mutuality within the pastoral community—presence, confession and forgiveness, accountability, shared power, and care of one another—that the members of the pastoral community are concerned about the body as a whole. The pastoral community is not a therapeutic community that each individual person attends in order to find personal healing and then move along. Value for the wider society occurs through such communities, but we should not mistake the pastoral community for the therapeutic one. Robert Hovda lays it out clearly by saying, "There is no point in individual dignity and freedom if the necessary community of reconciliation, common support, and action is lost."[27] Pastoral communities do not exist for the primary purpose of making individuals get over whatever ails them. This would not be a community in the Christian sense of the term.

Members of the Christian pastoral community edify the community as a whole. In other words, we are more than shepherds for one another within the pastoral community, however important this is. We are shepherds of the common good of the community, each one contributing his or her pastoral gifts for the caring nature of the entire fellowship. Community is the ground zero of who we are as the people of God. Out of the Trinitarian community, God creates us in human community and redeems us through the Christian community. This emphasis on our communal nature is important because the individual members are only as strong as the body as a whole. Psycho-social systems theory would tell us this, even though Pauline theology says it much more eloquently and is truer to the identity of the church. So the pastoral community assumes, along with the preacher pastor, responsibility for its ongoing edification as a community.

I claim throughout this book that one of pastoral preaching's primary tasks is to form pastoral communities. This may seem as if I am placing more weight on the work of the preacher for edification than on the community. But since the members of the pastoral community are mutually caring and interconnected, they assume responsibility for their continuing formation as the people of God as well. Lucy Rose, who develops a model

---

[27]Robert W. Hovda, "The Amen Corner," *Worship* 65 (January 1991): 71. Cited in Paul B. Brown, *In and For the World: Bringing the Contemporary Into Christian Worship* (Minneapolis: Fortress Press, 1992), 66.

for "congregational preaching," is on track when she says there "needs to be a shift from the preacher's responsibility for upbuilding the church by providing answers or truths to the community's responsibility for its own formation and reformation."[28] We will see a little later some examples of sermons that point toward mutuality within the pastoral community, in which the preacher honors the congregation's gifts and responsibility for mutual care.

More importantly, members of the pastoral community attend to the common good because the purpose of the pastoral community requires it. That purpose is to receive the stranger and witness to the care of God in the wider world. Without this move, the pastoral community degenerates into a mutual-aid society for "paying members only," at best, or at worst, into the illusion, as Parker Palmer puts it, of a "family at play."[29] In other words, the pastoral community that only ministers to the needs within "the church family" does not understand clearly what it means to be the people of God in the world.

So we turn now to briefly discuss two other characteristics of the pastoral community: *hospitality* and *care for the world*.

Hospitality and Pastoral Communities

Recently my family and I learned some lessons in Christian hospitality. Moving from full-time parish ministry into the teaching ministry of a seminary, we found ourselves for the first time in fifteen years without a church home. This is an unsettling experience for a United Methodist pastor, because from the time of our ordination we are appointed to a local church that, like it or not, at least for a season is our church home. The fact is that Christian community for the ordained pastor in a local church is sort of ready-made. To a certain extent this is true whether you happen to be United Methodist, Presbyterian, Missionary Baptist, or Disciples of Christ. True, at least, until you are no longer the pastor within a local congregation.

That's where our latest lessons in hospitality came in. My move to the seminary cast us in the role of visitors to various congregations in Memphis. We had the awkward sensation, though familiar to many laity, of entering churches and asking ourselves, "Could this be home?" We would visit the Sunday school with our two children, attend worship, and meet the people during fellowship time (if there was a fellowship time); then we'd leave and say, "Now, was that home?"

We felt so eager for hospitality, so vulnerable, even though we (my wife is also an ordained clergyperson) knew and understood many of the dynamics of Christian community. Some churches simply do a better job

---

[28]Lucy Atkinson Rose, *Sharing the Word: Preaching in the Roundtable Church* (Louisville: Westminster John Knox Press, 1997), 98.
[29]Palmer, *The Company of Strangers*, 125.

at making visitors feel welcome than others. Certain congregations are simply more hospitable either by design or by habit. They know how to welcome and receive the guest. We felt relieved when we landed for a visit in such a congregation, and we felt miserable when hospitality was absent or poorly conveyed.

Imagine yourself as a first-time visitor to a church. You are standing in front of a table piled high with brand new pictorial directories. People behind the table are busy passing out the directories to all the members as they pass by in the hallway. They do not seem to notice that you are standing there with your children. Several minutes pass, and no one acknowledges you. You haven't a clue about the location of the Sunday school rooms. So you interrupt and ask someone, "Excuse me, could you tell me where the children's Sunday school is?" And the people behind the table look at you as if you dropped in from another planet. Ouch!

Now imagine yourself in another church as a first-time visitor. You stand after worship. Before you can turn to leave the sanctuary, the person to your right offers a handshake and welcomes you to their congregation. Then two other people come directly up to you, introduce themselves, and invite you to the congregational lunch. You're feeling cautious about accepting the invitation because you don't want to get in over your head, but something about the way they invite you is welcoming. The invitation is genuine, open, and free. They are inviting you, the stranger, to break bread with them. You can say yes, or you can say no. So you say yes. As I said, some churches are better at the ministry of hospitality than others.

Pastoral communities create a hospitable space for the stranger. This is an act of communal care through which the congregation says in word and deed to the stranger, "You are welcome here," period. Church growth types say that such hospitality is the basis for effective evangelism. But we should be cautious here, because genuine Christian hospitality is not the same thing as making people feel comfortable so that they will join our church. The latter is a form of subtle manipulation; the former, an act of care. Hospitality within the pastoral community is not for the purpose of meeting institutional goals—more members, a bigger budget, more people to support our programs. Hospitality is an act of Christian care on behalf of the outsider who seeks prayer, shelter, food, strength, and human companionship. The pastoral community offers hospitality to the stranger because it is the nature of the community to do so. Having received the hospitality of Christ, who is the host of Christian worship and thanksgiving (eucharist), the pastoral community incorporates hospitality into itself and becomes the hospitable community for others.

Years ago I traveled to Costa Rica and was the houseguest of a Costa Rican family for a year. Have you ever thought about entertaining a foreign visitor in your own home for an entire year? Someone who doesn't speak your language and hasn't a clue about how to survive in your culture? This challenges your sense of family, of communal ties, of home. For many of us, it is an exhausting prospect. But the Elizondos, my host family, welcomed me with a gift of hospitality that I still find humbling and instructive. They did not attempt to make me feel special every day. I wasn't. In fact, I was often a nuisance, a bother to their way of life and daily family rhythm. So they did the only thing that genuine hospitality requires. They took me in. They made me welcome, at home, which meant that I was free to enjoy their family as community, and over time, to accept the responsibilities and demands of the family. I learned this about hospitality. Good hosts and hostesses do not fuss and fidget over their guests, never allowing the guests room to be at home. If we always treat our guests with deference, they are unable to move from being a guest to belonging to the community. Those who practice hospitality well have a way of making the guest feel perfectly at ease, so that if they wish, they may settle into home. That's what good hospitality is.

Another theological dimension to Christian hospitality is that the stranger bears the gift of God. We encounter this theme repeatedly in scripture, from Abraham and Sarah's visitation by the angelic strangers at Mamre (Gen. 18:1–15), to Elijah in the home of the widow of Zarephath (1 Kings 17:8–24), to the hidden presence of Christ among the poor, despised, and outcasts of the gospels (Mt. 25:31–46). Those who arrive from beyond the congregation bring the startling newness of God. They help the community to see that God is Other, other than themselves. Many North Americans are surprised the first time that they invite someone from Korea or Japan into their homes. The guests always arrive with gifts for their hosts. They turn hospitality inside out; guest becomes host and host becomes guest. Like the resurrected Jesus on the road to Emmaus, the stranger guest becomes the welcoming host.

God, you see, will not be contained within the mutuality of the pastoral community. God always creates anew, extends the banquet table, widens the circle dance of community.[30] Yes, God is present among the pastoral community, but not wholly so. This side of the eschaton, the pastoral community is always incomplete. The pastoral community always awaits the knock at the door that signals the arrival of God in the guise of a stranger. The care-full community will open the door and welcome the stranger home, knowing that the stranger bears God's wondrous surprises.

After I graduated from seminary, my first pastoral appointment was to a Hispanic congregation in Atlanta. Just before Christmas of my first year, I received a call from a North American woman who was in the process of

---

[30]Leonora Tubbs Tisdale explores the "circle dance" metaphor in *Preaching as Local Theology and Folk Art* (Minneapolis: Fortress Press, 1997), 124ff.

"releasing" a domestic helper, Maria, who was Venezuelan. They wanted to know if our congregation could help Maria get back home since her visa was about to expire and she had recently had a baby boy, whom the employer family was not willing to support. Basically, they had decided to boot the mother and infant out of the house, but they at least were decent enough to call a few of the Hispanic churches and community agencies that might assist.

It's a lengthy story, as you can imagine. But the end result was that Maria and her infant son wound up in the apartment of my fiancee, Mary Leslie. They would remain there for a couple of days until our congregation could pull together funds and secure the necessary papers for Maria to return home. Mary Leslie was not entirely happy with the arrangements, since she was busily involved in a night shelter ministry in another congregation during the coldest month of the year. Having a houseguest who did not speak English, with a newborn child, sleeping on her couch in a small apartment was not her idea of fun. I understood that, but it was the best option that I could come up with at the time.

Mary Leslie relates that on the first night when she got home late from the night shelter, she begrudgingly prepared a meal for herself and Maria. She attempted to communicate with Maria, but the language barrier was pretty tough. After a great deal of sign language, broken English, and Spanish, they began to make some headway. Mary Leslie discovered that she actually liked Maria. Her patience and kind disposition under extreme circumstances was moving. The young mother clearly adored her child, and she was desperate to get him home to Venezuela where they would be among family. Mary Leslie asked Maria the name of the baby. When she replied, Mary Leslie could not understand the name because of the Spanish pronunciation. So Maria dug through her bags and proudly produced the birth certificate. She passed it over to Mary Leslie. And then Mary Leslie saw the baby's name: "*Jesus.*" The baby was named *Jesus*.

You can make the connections for yourself. It is Christmas, a foreign mother is homeless, and in a cramped apartment she cradles an infant child whose name turns out to be Jesus. Every now and then in the caring church we stumble upon (are confronted by?) people and situations that are so analogous to the core elements of the Christian story that the two stories merge into one. We realize that the Christian narrative does indeed interpret our world and us, and it gives us new eyes to see and ears to hear the gospel that Christ is among us. Often this good news comes through the presence of strangers, foreigners in our midst who beckon us to be who we are, communities deeply formed by the hospitality of Jesus Christ. Jesus is the unexpected stranger who turns out to be host of the unending banquet where bread and wine runs clean out into the streets.

One further word needs to be said about hospitality. Within the pastoral community, hospitality should not be confused with intimacy. We live in a culture that constantly promotes the value of intimacy, especially intimacy understood as intense (though not necessarily lasting or deep) emotional and physical bonds between persons that enhances the development of the self. This is what Parker Palmer, following the social analysis of Richard Sennett, calls the "ideology of intimacy."[31] Many factors are responsible for this, including a reaction to the crushing bureaucratization and impersonal nature of mass society, our cultural love affair with psychology, and the ubiquity of marketing and advertisement that promises (but cannot deliver) to sell us what we most crave–human intimacy. I'm not opposed to intimacy in human relationship. In fact, I think emotional and physical intimacy is an important and good thing between spouses, parents and children, and close friends, though in each of these relationships emotional and physical intimacy is distinct. Failure to recognize the distinctions can lead to devastating lunges for intimacy such as sexual abuse, battering, and incest. Intimacy is not value neutral, though the way we talk about it in North American society often sounds so. Intimacy, we seem to say, is good, without stopping to define it, ask why, under what circumstances, and what are the costs and commitments that true intimacy requires. Intimacy is a deepening pattern of emotional and physical attachment between persons within an ongoing relationship of trust and commitment. Without trust and commitment, intimacy isn't really possible, because intimacy is the result of the committed relationship, not the foundation. The fact is that much of what our society projects on the screen as intimacy is usually anything but intimacy. It may be emotional fireworks, steamy sex, or therapeutic encounter, but it hardly qualifies for intimacy. Pseudo-intimacy is what sells, but buying the counterfeit only makes us that much more empty.

This is why pastoral communities do not seek to *create* intimacy among the members. Over time intimacy may arise between certain participants within the community. But as a communal value, intimacy, as we understand it in the proper sense of the term, is too restrictive of the pastoral community. For one thing, no more than a handful of persons can actually sustain intimacy over a long period of time. Pastoral communities grow slowly as members extend and receive the ministry of care throughout the seasons of life. Such a community cannot maintain the emotional demands of real intimacy over the long haul. For another thing, genuine intimacy requires exclusion. For example, marriages are built on covenants between two persons rather than four, ten, or thirty. The choice of a partner is an act of exclusion of all other potential partners so that the relationship has the chance to flourish and yield intimacy. For a pastoral community to adopt an exclusive position in the name of intimacy would be an affront to

---

[31]Palmer, *The Company of Strangers*, 108, citing Richard Sennett, *The Fall of Public Man* (New York: Alfred A. Knopf, 1977), 337.

the gospel, which always opens up the church to others. Too much congregational intimacy actually undercuts the caring ministry of Christian hospitality. "It draws some people in too deep, excludes many others, and cannot serve a public function," points out Parker Palmer.[32] Pastoral communities do not attempt to draw outsiders into an intimate family to make them "like us." Pastoral communities welcome the outsider who can show *us* more how to be *for others.*

Please don't misunderstand. The pastoral community does value mutuality of care that includes trust, honesty, and commitment among the members. Along the way of congregational life, there will be moments of emotional intimacy within the congregation, for example the congregational joy at a wedding or birth, the sadness over the death of a beloved member, or the group fear that sweeps over a congregation in the wake of tragedy. But such genuine moments of intimacy do not rule community relationships; they are not the goal. They simply happen whenever people commit themselves together to follow Christ, love God and neighbor, and put in the worship, time, and sweat to become a pastoral community.

We need to be guarded, then, about family analogies with respect to the church. The church is only like a family to the extent that each member is related to the other in Christ. The church is a "household," as the scriptures suggest, but it is a household of God (Eph. 2:11–22). The family of God knows neither Jew nor Greek, slave nor free. In other words, you don't have to be like the family to belong to the family. The family of God, it turns out, is a whole lot more diverse, more tolerant of difference, more open to wider society, and less "intimate" than many of our churches are. So we need to either broaden the content of church family, rely more upon other metaphors such as "body," "communion," "people," or retrieve the Greek sense of the word "church," *ecclesia,* which means the "public."

Pastoral communities are public communities. Our worship and preaching is a gathering of the public, the people called out. Preaching is not an exercise in creating intimacy among the members, although many understand the task of preaching this way. As Patrick Kiefert analyzes contemporary worship, "The pastor and any other performers on Sunday morning are required to expose their deepest feelings in an attempt to create the intimate community." This approach sets up the preacher as a personality hero who is effective if he or she is "vulnerable" and "winsome." "They need to act as if they and the audience have always been intimates."[33] This pseudo-intimacy, however, defeats the real purpose of the Christian pastoral community. It allows the congregation to remain an isolated

---

[32]Palmer, 121.

[33]Patrick Kiefert, *Welcoming the Stranger: A Public Theology of Worship and Evangelism* (Minneapolis: Fortress Press, 1992), 23, 26.

aggregate of individuals who think they have a warm, open, caring relationship with the preacher pastor, but who do not need to commit themselves to the public community at all. Persons remain isolated within worship and congregational life precisely because we pretend that intimacy exists or should exist within a public gathering. Very little pastoral care will emerge within such a congregation because we are inadvertently looking to the "intimate care" of the ordained leaders as our model. We define care as being so intimate as to be exclusionary of the rest of the caring activities of ordinary folks.

Hospitality within the pastoral community is open, welcoming, and warm. But the openness is toward the friend and stranger. The stranger helps the community to see that godly care is not the same as feeling close to one another, not the same as agreeing on everything, not the same as private security within a closed family. Caring communities will allow the fantasy mask of intimate community to fall away and awaken to the reality of the Christ-led community that turns its face toward the world.

Care and Compassion for the World

Thomas Merton, the Christian monastic, recounts in *Conjectures of a Guilty Bystander* an occasion in which he leaves the monastery at Gethsemane, Kentucky, to go into Louisville on official business. While standing at a corner waiting to cross the street, he sees through the eyes of faith how deeply he is connected to all the strangers who surround him there on a busy city sidewalk. He says,

> In Louisville, at the corner of Fourth and Walnut, in the center of the shopping district, I was suddenly overwhelmed with the realization that I loved all those people, that they were mine and I theirs, that we could not be alien to one another even though we were total strangers. It was like waking from a dream of separateness, of spurious self-isolation in a special world, the world of renunciation and supposed holiness. The whole illusion of a separate holy existence is a dream...We are in the same world as everybody else, the world of the bomb, the world of mass media, big business, revolution, and all the rest. We take a different attitude to all these things, for we belong to God. Yet so does everybody else belong to God. We just happen to be conscious of it, and to make a profession out of this consciousness...This sense of liberation from an illusory difference was such a relief and such a joy to me that I almost laughed out loud.[34]

---

[34]Thomas Merton, *Conjectures of a Guilty Bystander* (New York: Doubleday, 1968, reprint 1989), 156–57.

Merton's insight is helpful. It challenges our tendency to see the church over against the world. If anything it seems that a monastic member and contemplative like Merton would maintain clear distinctions between church and world. But Merton sees that such separation is false. Given a strong theological foundation of creation and incarnation, Merton clearly sees the presence of God active in the world and within the church. Such awareness led Merton to a natural joining of spirituality and justice in the latter years of his life. A strict separation of the world into the disjunctive realms of the sacred and the secular denies the wholeness of God throughout creation. It appoints Christ as Lord over the church but not the world, an odd position for us who claim that "God so loves *the world*" (Jn. 3:16). The pastoral community offers God's care and compassion for the world rather than hoarding the precious gift of God's care. The care that the pastoral community derives from Christ at the center always leads the community outward to find and express care on the margins.

Some would claim that this worldly emphasis shifts the focus from pastoral to prophetic concern. Others would say that this turn carries us beyond the scope of pastoral care into the field of mission. But I am claiming throughout this book that the pastoral and prophetic, the formational (catechetical) and missional dimensions of ministry cannot be separated. As we saw in the previous chapter, each perspective in ministry contains all the others. Charles Gerkin began his pastoral care work with a fairly direct focus on care as interpersonal counseling. By the time Gerkin arrived at his later years of teaching and writing in the field, he was convinced that pastoral care is "*prophetic* pastoral practice." He says,

> It is not a vocation that can be found within the secluded privacy of that community's own life, though that life should seek to become an exemplar of what it means to be a people of the covenant. Rather, the Christian community's vocation will be realized and God's call to God's people will find appropriate response, as ways are found to provide a leavening presence in all the places where human beings are together.[35]

Gerkin is on track. He understands that the pastoral community's vision of care must be guided by God's caring activity through Christ for the whole world. This naturally leads the pastoral community into considerations for persons and events that some would call prophetic or missional.

Writer Kathleen Norris in *Dakota* discusses how the small church, Hope Presbyterian, that she attends on the Great Plains, while seemingly isolated from the wider world, is actually creatively involved with global concerns. "The thing that makes hope so vibrant is that the congregation is so alive

---

[35]Charles V. Gerkin, *Prophetic Pastoral Practice: A Christian Vision of Life Together* (Nashville: Abingdon Press, 1991), 161.

to the world. Hope's members take seriously their responsibility as members of the world's diverse and largely poor human race."[36] Caring for the world is not determined by a congregation's size or location. It is determined by the congregation's theological self-understanding of what it means to be a faithful community of Christians who live in God's world.

I will explore some of these themes more fully in chapter 5, in which we discuss ecclesiology in pastoral preaching, for our theology of the church undergirds communal care. But for now, I want to stress that the pastoral community resists the centrifugal pull that occurs when Christians gather together. This is not easy because the warmth, support, and security that community provides seem far too scarce in the first place. We naturally grow fond of those with whom we worship. Common experiences bond us together. The allure of community inwardness is always present. Yet to care solely for those within our fellowship corrupts Christian care. Sinfulness may pull us toward insularity in community, but Christ pushes us outward toward care for the world.

The pastoral community seeks wholeness, an overall ecology of care. The community of care does not make a sharp distinction between inner and outer needs. We do not minister now to the inward community and later to the world. Elizabeth O'Connor's *Journey Inward, Journey Outward* has had a huge impact on congregations that take seriously the link between spirituality and missional care.[37] Unfortunately, the book is premised on a false distinction between the inward and outward realities of the Christian life. It suggests, though O'Connor may not have intended it, that Christian community has a split focus–inner and outer. In this model of care, the goal is to maintain a delicate balance that focuses on both the inner spiritual needs of the believer and the community and the outer needs of the world that spirituality directs us toward. But the anthropological assumptions of this model of care are problematic, as we shall explore in chapter 4. The Christian understanding of human beings in community suggests that the fabric of life is all one piece, not inner and outer but whole, complete. Admittedly, our fabric is terribly torn. But we care for the whole of humanity–individuals, society, and persons together. When the pastoral community ministers to God's world, we are seeking to mend the entire fabric of life so that external and internal can become integrated. Communal care rests on the theological conviction that world and church, individual and society, are united in God's Kingdom; all express the fullness of creation that God intends. To heal the world is to heal the individual in the world. To express care within the church is to contribute to the wider environment of care that extends to the end of the earth. This is why distinctions between

---

[36]Kathleen Norris, *Dakota: A Spiritual Geography* (Boston: Houghton Mifflin, 1993), 164.

[37]Elizabeth O'Connor, *Journey Inward, Journey Outward* (New York: Harper & Row, 1968).

pastoral (inward) and prophetic (outward) are not only incorrect but counterproductive within the caring community of the church. Since God loves the whole world, redeems the whole world by Christ, and blesses the world with the Holy Spirit ("Parthians, Medes, Elamites" [Acts 2:9]), the pastoral community will eagerly seek the completion of its ministry of care within the world. Ultimately, pastoral care is pulled forward by the vision that energizes the entire church, the vision of wholeness, of *shalom*.

Summary

Preaching helps to create a pastoral community that can be identified by certain characteristics. While it is difficult to name these pastoral traits without hopelessly idealizing the Christian community, we can sometimes see their shape emerging in those congregations where preacher and people take to heart the breadth and depth of the community's ministry of pastoral care. These qualities include, but are not limited to, mutuality, hospitality, and care for the world. Pastoral communities will live out of these virtues, though always partially because of the ongoing disruption of sin within human community.

The question arises now: How does preaching actually help form such real pastoral communities? What about preaching, its language, content, and form, might give birth to the kind of pastoral communities that we have explored in this chapter? Is it possible to link preaching with communal care? This will be the focus of the upcoming pages.

3

Pastoral Preaching Forms
Caring Communities

The real presence of Christ in the Christian community is God's
pastoral care for the world. And this must be preached![1]

—RUDOLF BOHREN

Pastors are usually greatly relieved when they discover that pastoral care is the work of the entire community, that is, if the pastor wants to belong to a church that values the priesthood of all believers. Pastors who are weary of the Lone Ranger approach to Christian ministry welcome mutuality in pastoral care. Like opening a window within a stuffy room, shared pastoral care between preacher and congregation sends fresh breezes through the entire house. On a practical and emotional level, it takes an inhumane pressure (sometimes self-imposed) off pastors and may save them from a foreshortened ministry. But on a more substantive level, it opens up new depths within the congregation's ministry of pastoral care. Now the pastor can join with other members of the congregation to discern the gifts and needs of the congregation for pastoral care. Together they can focus on engendering an environment of care, a web of care that is responsive to many more of the needs within the congregation and community than the pastor could ever hope to reach.[2] The pastor does not abdicate his or her

---

[1]Rudolf Bohren, *Preaching and Community,* trans. David Green (Richmond: John Knox Press, 1965), 131.

[2]For the image of the web as developed in pastoral care, see Archie Smith, Jr., *The Relational Self: Ethics and Therapy from a Black Church Perspective* (Nashville: Abingdon Press, 1982), 53ff.; and Bonnie J. Miller-McLemore, "The Human Web: Reflections on the State of Pastoral Theology, *Christian Century* 110 (April 7, 1993): 366–69.

ordained leadership in this community of care but is delighted to witness other members of the body of Christ extending the church's arms of compassion. The pastor knows and rejoices in the fact that someone else in the congregation may have the right word when words are needed, the right touch to bring consolation to those who are grieving, or guidance to those whose lives are breaking upon the jagged shoals of the twenty-first century.

So how do we go about forming such pastoral communities? Well, we could attempt, church-administration style, to set up a few committees to manage this pastoral care goal by objectives. "Let's all set out to re-form ourselves as a caring congregation. Who wants to be on the committee?" Or we could call in an outside consultant who will train our congregational leaders in the ministry of pastoral care. There are some very effective models available for such lay caregiving.[3] But this organizational approach to care is not what I am after. Don't misunderstand me, organization does matter with respect to congregational care. It is usually needed in a formal way when the congregation, because of size, lack of resources, or better theological awareness, understands that it cannot be pastor dependent.

But the kind of community care that I am pointing toward is of a different order. It does not depend on organization so much as on the nature of the congregation as a whole. Some might call this the organic nature of the Christian community, although I doubt that Christian communities are any more naturally caring than all sorts of other non-Christian communities, given that thickheaded and surprisingly self-centered human beings like us make up these communities. What we are attempting to define is the congregation's *ethos* of care. As Rodhey Hunter writes, "It matters to what and to whom we belong…A major concern of ministry is to help form those communities and to help individuals become a part of them."[4] The people who come together on Sunday mornings, weekday evenings, and around one another's breakfast tables come together as a pastoral community because in their very makeup they exist for care of each other and the world.

This has much less to do with organization, I am contending, than it does with preaching and worship. Preaching, believe it or not, goes a long way toward establishing and maintaining a pastoral community, as does corporate worship. Preaching, because it occurs regularly, and because of the way in which public, sacred speech shapes the body of believers, helps form the congregation as a community of care. To understand this, we

---

[3]See Howard Stone, *The Caring Church: A Guide for Lay Pastoral Care* (Minneapolis: Fortress Press, 1991); and Ron Sunderland, *Getting Through Grief: Caregiving by Congregation* (Nashville: Abingdon Press, 1993).

[4]Rodney J. Hunter, "Participation in the Life of God," in *The Treasure of Earthen Vessels: Explorations in Theological Anthropology,* ed. Brian H. Childs and David W. Waanders (Louisville: Westminster/John Knox Press, 1994).

will want to consider the effect of our preaching language within the congregation.

The Language of the Pastoral Sermon

The language of preaching and the identity of the congregation are all bound up together. Pastoral communities do not emerge *ex nihilo* wherever people gather together in the name of Christ. Maybe they should, given our confession of faith in Christ, God's care for the world. But some professing Christians gather together with little pastoral commitment to one another or the rest of humanity. Pastoral communities take shape over time. They constantly evolve in response to the gospel, the changing context of the congregation and its community, and the influence of all participants within the congregation. One of the most significant factors that shape the pastoral identity or ethos of the congregation is the preaching language itself. As Leonora Tubbs Tisdale summarizes, "Preaching, then, has to do with the formation and transformation of Christian identity—not only of individuals, but also of congregations."[5] The sermons of a particular pastor in a specific congregation help to build up a pastoral community as the congregation forms and re-forms around the preached word of God. Clearly, preaching is not the only factor that determines congregational identity, but it is a contributing factor that only the most indifferent pastor would ignore. This is so because of the sacred nature of Christian proclamation and because of the power of language to meld human community.

Theologically speaking, preaching lays claim to a mystery: The Word of God that forms and transforms believers in faith comes "from what is heard"(Rom. 10:14–17). Maybe it's time for preachers to reconsider the pastoral power of language, of words. Heaven knows we use enough of them on Sundays. But do we stop to measure their height and depth? When was the last time that we preachers considered the power of words to hurt— "chink," "fag," "bum," "old woman,"—or to heal—"I love you," "I have a dream," "I'm sorry"?[6] When was the last time that you crafted a sermon and were fearful that the words and images of that sermon might be pulsating with *the* Word? After all, God speaks and creation springs forth (Genesis 1). God's Word raises valleys and lowers mountains (Isa. 40:3–5). Jesus the Christ is God's Word, God's logos, for the world (John 1). And Martin Luther once called the church the "mouth-house," or speech place.[7] Bonhoeffer states baldly that "the proclaimed word is the incarnate Christ himself."[8] Through Jesus Christ and the Holy Spirit, God speaks in the

---

[5]Leonora Tubbs Tisdale, *Preaching as Local Theology and Folk Art* (Minneapolis: Fortress Press, 1997), 57.

[6]See *Words That Hurt, Words That Heal* (Nashville: Graded Press, 1990).

[7]Martin Luther, *Sermons of Martin Luther: The Church Postils,* vol. 1, trans. John Lenker (Grand Rapids: Baker, 1983, 1995), 44.

[8]Dietrich Bonhoeffer, *Worldly Preaching: Lectures on Homiletics,* ed. Clyde E. Fant (New York: Crossroad, 1991), 126.

words of our frail sermons. It's a frightening thought, God in human words, God in your and my human words. Given their theological freight, we might want to handle words with care. As Annie Dillard queries about the way we handle God-language in *Teaching a Stone to Talk*, "Does anyone have the foggiest idea what sort of power we so blithely invoke?...We should all be wearing crash helmets. Ushers should issue life preservers and signal flares; they should lash us to our pews."[9] In words, and in the silence between them, preachers are the bearers of a potent gift—God-with-us.

If we aim to form pastoral communities through preaching, preachers must take seriously that language matters. Theologians and philosophers, rhetoricians and linguists have all pointed out the critical importance of language. Language is not simply expressive of the ideas, values, intentions, and desires of the speaker, a one-way communication from preacher to congregation. Rather, language constitutes the human being in community. Language is the medium in which we swim. This was the key insight of Heidegger, who philosophically defined language as the "house of being." Preachers are the human architects of this language house in the church, and the sermon is one of the primary ways in which we construct the house. To be sure, the preacher draws sermonic language from a rich treasury of biblical stories, church tradition, cultural expressions, and communal and personal experience. And with all these linguistic elements, the sermon over time builds a congregational world that preacher and community inhabit. "The purpose of the sermon is to provide a world in which the congregation can live," says Walter Brueggemann.[10] Through selection of scriptural texts, use of images and stories, doctrinal assertions, and recounting of daily events, the preacher holds before the congregation a way of seeing themselves in the world and before God. The sermonic language identifies the people—who they are and how they live together. Whether the preacher stops to consider this evocative power of language or not, the weekly sermon steadily defines congregational realities. "How one speaks and what is said are not peripheral matters but at the heart of human existence and social identity," notes Paul Brown.[11] Pastoral communities come to life not simply because the preacher or the people are caring persons. Pastoral communities form around sermonic language that the pastor intends to be theologically and pastorally formative.

Isn't this giving too much weight to the sermon in the life of the congregation, some might ask? After all, many pastors inherit congregations that are already pastoral communities. And a whole lot more goes on in congregations than the weekly sermon (thank goodness). Yes, many Christian communities are deeply pastoral; even some despite the best

---

[9]Annie Dillard, *Teaching A Stone to Talk* (New York: Harper & Row, 1982), 40.

[10]Walter Brueggemann, "The Social Nature of the Biblical Text," in *Preaching as a Social Act,* ed. Arthur Van Seters (Nashville: Abingdon Press, 1988), 143.

[11]Paul B. Brown, *In and For the World: Bringing the Contemporary into Christian Worship* (Minneapolis: Fortress Press, 1992), 13.

efforts of the preacher to undercut their pastoral nature. In this case, the identity of the congregation is in direct tension with the vision of the pastor, and this tension will affect the congregation in numerous ways.[12] Among wise congregations, the people will carry on the work of pastoral care even if the pastor does not. The pastor is a thorn in the flesh, but he or she can be endured for the sake of the gospel. And in other cases, without homiletic undergirding of the pastoral identity of the people, the care of the congregation will deteriorate. Inexperienced pastors, however well meaning, will sometimes snatch the care away from the congregation in a bid to feel important. The sermon subtly conveys that genuine pastoral care is the responsibility of the trained clergy. Without ever meaning to, the preacher, through the sermon, runs roughshod over the pastoral community, leaving ruptured relationships littering the house. Just because congregations do a good job of carrying on the ministry of pastoral care doesn't mean it will always be so. The pulpit can deform as well as transform when it comes to pastoral communities.

Certainly many other things contribute to the pastoral nature of the congregation besides the sermon. The Spirit of God is the most significant agent in the life of the congregation. Without the presence of God through the Spirit, our words and our worship are noisy gongs. Congregations are based in meaning-fraught histories that come to light in present pastoral activity. The complex interactions of every participant in a congregation create a dizzying array of possibilities for how the congregation will carry out its ministry of care. The wider social world of the particular congregation profoundly impacts the pastoral identity of the people inside the Christian community. For example, rural congregational members may communicate care by sharing with each other fruit from their gardens. Suburban congregations may develop e-mail networks to pass on quick words of support to their fast-paced membership. Care goes on in congregations in a variety of ways that is uniquely responsive to the people within the church and the immediate social world that they inhabit. Congregational studies can assist the astute pastor in discerning the diverse levels of pastoral meaning that occur within congregations.[13]

My appeal, therefore, is not that the language of the sermon be the only means to form pastoral community. But the sermon may be one of the most overlooked ways of creating pastoral community. Why? Because, as a whole, preacher pastors do not take seriously enough the pastoral importance of sermonic language. We know a lot about how to form support groups in congregations. We understand the importance of organizing small-group life, especially within large congregations, to sustain and heal the

---

[12]See Carl S. Dudley and Sally A. Johnson, *Energizing the Congregation: Images that Shape Your Church's Ministry* (Louisville: Westminster/John Knox Press, 1993).

[13]See Tisdale, *Preaching as Local Theology and Folk Art,* and James Hopewell, *Congregation: Stories and Structures* (Philadelphia: Fortress Press, 1987).

members of the community in times of distress. Specialists in counseling have convinced us that reparative and growth-producing work through therapy is sometimes necessary whenever our psyches become unglued. But many preachers do not take seriously the power of language, infused by the presence of God, to construct and alter reality.[14] Jewish scholar Abraham Heschel has said, "To the person of our age nothing is as familiar and nothing as trite as words…We all live in them, feel in them, think in them, but failing to uphold their independent dignity, to respect their power and weight, they turn waif, elusive—a mouthful of dust…Words have ceased to be commitments."[15] Preachers' most precious gift is the gift of the Word in words. It is also our most burdensome responsibility to handle words with care.

Any spoken communication between persons is a highly complex undertaking. The worlds embodied in the words of each participant meet, adjust, and sometimes collide. Whether addressing a congregation or one other person, the speaker seeks to bring the hearer a little closer to her or his own worldview by way of language. In response, the hearer may in turn address the speaker and so attempt the same. Between them a world of meaning emerges that is necessarily dependent on the occasion (context) of the exchange.

The language of preaching is one of the deepest, must constant streams feeding into the pool of the pastoral community. Over time, sermonic language slowly, almost imperceptibly, carves out the shape of a people who care. We can ignore the effects if we choose. But like water flowing over rocks, the words of the preacher will alter the substance of the congregation even as the congregation channels the words.

How Language Matters in Pastoral Preaching

So let's look a little more closely at language in pastoral preaching. Some would say that it doesn't matter as much what the preacher says as whether or not she is a caring person. The people will understand, the saying goes, whether or not you care for them, regardless of how you preach. To the contrary, how we preach in form and content is precisely what communicates care at the deepest levels. Congregations hear a lot of sermons from many preachers. They discern readily, even if preachers don't want to admit it, whether the preacher is careful with the content and the form of the sermon. Listeners know whether the preacher has haphazardly slapped together a few lines from biblical commentaries, a couple of anecdotes, and a punch line from Doonesbury, and blessed it

---

[14]For a concise statement on the social function of language in preaching see Ronald J. Allen, "The Social Function of Language in Preaching," in *Preaching as a Social Act: Theology and Practice,* ed. Arthur Van Seters (Nashville: Abingdon Press, 1988).

[15]Abraham Joshua Heschel, *I Asked for Wonder,* ed. Samuel H. Dresner (New York: Crossroad, 1986), 30.

with a rushed cup of coffee, or whether the preacher has put the biblical text, life stories, congregational realities, images, and symbols of the sermon through the refining fire of a whole week of thought, prayer, and Spirit-led sifting that results in a living word—a word that might heal the wounded, sustain the weak, guide the perplexed, and reconcile the lost. The hearers know the difference because the words of the preacher tell them. This is not about eloquence in the pulpit. Astute congregations will hear the hollowness of even the most melodious sermons if the preacher has not forged the words on the anvil of caring faith. As the rhetorician Richard Weaver eloquently stated years ago, language itself "is sermonic."[16] When it comes to care, the language of the sermon tells the whole story. If preachers want to help create caring congregations, they will take care with the words they use in the pulpit. Our preaching language shapes and forms our congregational worlds. Let's look more directly now at some specifics regarding preaching language and pastoral communities.

Presence in Pastoral Preaching

Every preacher, every week, must make the irrevocable decision of what goes in and what stays out of the sermon. Preachers who do their homework by reading widely, staying abreast of biblical and theological scholarship, listening to the voices of those around them, enjoying the world that God creates, and spending time in silence wind up with more sermonic material every week than they can possibly include in one sermon (though many of us try our best to overstuff the homily). Some material simply doesn't work. At first light the seed looks promising, but by full sunlight at midweek, it is clearly a weed; we toss it out. Other material gets a sticker flag—a scholarly insight, a line of poetry, the conversation you heard on the radio, an event that happened downtown. The material is good and meaningful, but it doesn't belong in this week's sermon. Flag it for later. Some material, after you turn it over and over again to see its jagged and smooth edges, seems to fit. It is appropriate. So it finds a home in this week's sermon.

But here another decision arises for the pastoral preacher—the question of *presence*. We are not speaking of pastoral presence as discussed in the previous chapter. We are talking now about how the sermon gives presence to certain emphases. To what material will the preacher render presence, and how? This is more than a question of arrangement of sermonic material, although arrangement does matter. Presence, according to the rhetorician Chaim Perelman, designates the various ways that a speaker brings into the foreground of the hearer's consciousness a certain element

---

[16]Richard Weaver, "Language is Sermonic," in *Language is Sermonic: Richard M. Weaver on the Nature of Rhetoric,* ed. Richard L. Johannnesen et al. (Baton Rouge: Louisiana State University Press, 1970).

on which the speaker wishes to center the discourse, in our case, the sermon. By presence, the speaker can "make present, by verbal magic alone, what is actually absent but what he [or she] considers important to the argument or, by making them more present, to enhance the value of some of the elements of which one has actually been made conscious."[17] In other words, presence in preaching is where and how we focus the sermonic spotlight(s). David Buttrick says that preaching is a "bringing out" or a "bringing into view" our understandings of God and God's ways among humanity.[18] We find ways, if we are intentional in our preaching, to bring into sharp focus for the hearer those beliefs, commitments, values, narratives, and symbols that we deem to be most important. We hope that by giving presence to these elements they will become more snugly nested into the life of the congregation. This requires, as already stated, that the preacher become quite intentional about what he or she deems most important in the sermon. Then we develop homiletic strategies that will plant these commitments into the soil of the congregation or water the commitments that we find already growing there. Insofar as the preacher hopes to build up a pastoral community through preaching, he or she will be aware of how the presenced material of the sermon either does or does not contribute to fulfilling this aim.

Let me stress that the rhetorical element of presence in preaching does not displace the work of the Holy Spirit. God either moves or doesn't move within the community of believers based on God's own initiative. The revealed word of God through biblical text and sermon is never ours to control. Perelman's use of the term "verbal magic" may be misleading in this context. Perelman was not addressing his remarks to the church but to a community of scholars. In preaching, the Spirit of God always goes before the preacher and the congregation and "blows where it wills." But this does not let the preacher off the hook. Since God has given us the gift of language and, through the church, the call to preach, we want to use this gift wisely. Perelman's explanation of presence in public speaking can assist us as we handle the language of the sermon without causing us to believe that our efforts are ultimately responsible for the final outcome of the sermon. Preachers are stewards of the word. Good stewards, like good farmers, learn how to best use their tools to care for the land.

This raises the important question of sermonic intent. Regardless of how long the preacher listens to the congregation, culture, and text, at some point he or she must decide the purpose of the sermon. This may be done through discussions with congregational members in advance, by a disciplined approach to the lectionary, or through a careful exegesis of the

[17]Chaim Perelman and L. Olbrechts-Tyteca, *The New Rhetoric: A Treatise on Argumentation,* trans. John Wilkinson and Purcell Weaver (Notre Dame: University of Notre Dame Press, 1969), 117.

[18]David Buttrick, *Homiletic: Moves and Structures* (Philadelphia: Fortress Press, 1987), 41.

congregation.[19] But like it or not, the preacher is the one whom the congregation has chosen to speak. Eventually the preacher must land on some purpose for which to preach. Despite all the nods toward sharing the pulpit in recent homiletic studies, nods that are pastorally motivated, the preacher designs and delivers the sermon for some intent. The full meaning and action of the sermon occurs during and after the sermon, but the preacher has the burden to set things in motion. Our words, the selection of a scriptural text, the ornamentation and use of the physical space of the pulpit and sanctuary, accompanying music, gestures, silences, all these symbols are the "stuff" by which we seek to involve the cooperation of the congregation. For example, in earlier expository preaching, Richard Baxter intends to explain (teach) the meaning of a scriptural text and apply that meaning to the hearers' lives. He wants the hearers to appropriate the sermon's instruction for the edification of their lives, in short, to prepare them for salvation. Other preachers, like Henry Mitchell, may set out to create an experience through the sermon, for example, celebration of the gospel.[20] Still others may want through preaching to open up an eventful encounter between the hearer, God, and the text of scripture whose outcome is not predetermined.[21] Or the preacher may want, regardless of the sermonic method, to persuade the hearers to get up and do something, such as withdraw one's investments from weapons manufacturers or come forward to the altar and receive forgiveness. Social action or revival fervor, the preacher still aims at a response.[22]

The congregational response that the pastoral preacher has in mind is that the people who gather around the word and table will become a pastoral community. Our aim is to shape pastoral communities through the preached word. This is not the only intent of preaching, far from it. But it is a primary intent when we are talking about pastoral preaching.

The preacher's aims are often clear in the sermon's delivery and content, if not to the preacher, then to the listener. If the preacher is not sufficiently convincing at the explicit level, other messages take over the sermonic communication. For example, "The preacher is confused." "He seems tired." Or "Well, at least the music was pretty." Or "Look at those cute kids." People will find some sense in what is going on in preaching and worship, but unless the sermon achieves a certain level of clarity of rhetorical intent

---

[19]For a collaborative approaches between preacher and congregation see John McClure, *The Roundtable Pulpit* (Nashville: Abingdon Press, 1995), and Lucy Atkinson Rose, *Sharing the Word: Preaching in the Roundtable Church* (Louisville: Westminster John Knox Press, 1997).

[20]See Henry H. Mitchell, *Celebration and Experience in Preaching* (Nashville: Abingdon Press, 1990).

[21]See Fred Craddock, *As One Without Authority* (Nashville: Abingdon Press, 1979).

[22]Since the early 1960s preachers have joined hands with literary critics of the Bible in asserting that biblical language, like sermonic language, is performative in nature. See Amos N. Wilder, *Early Christian Rhetoric: The Language of the Gospel* (New York: Harper, 1964); and George A. Kennedy, *New Testament Interpretation Through Rhetorical Criticism* (Chapel Hill: University of North Carolina Press, 1984).

and persuasion, it may not be the sense that the preacher desires. This means that a certain level of intentionality on the part of the preacher does (or does not) communicate. To say otherwise is to concede that the preacher has no ability to affect a hearing. If this is the case, we might naturally ask, "Why bother?"

So let's admit it. The pastoral sermon proceeds upon intention. By presence in preaching, we are concerned, with Perelman, about "the influence which a speech has on the entire personality of the hearers."[23] When Martin Luther King, Jr., asks a congregation, "Is anyone here on the brink of despair?" and then responds to the assumed reply, "God is able," he seeks to do something. By the use of rhetorical questions and direct speech, King wishes to highlight for the congregation a reality, namely God, in such a way that the congregation experiences God's sustaining power for themselves. King is not simply expressing himself or an opinion. He isn't merely articulating what he has heard the people say. He aims by the use of rhetorical presence to sustain the weary, lift up the downtrodden.[24] To take another example, if the preacher hopes to enable the congregation to know and experience itself as a "community of equals," she will seek to attain presence for this symbol in the full consciousness of the congregation. She will intentionally build the sermon's language through various strategies such as "repetition," "amplification," "synonymy," "interpretation," and "imaginary direct speech," all to give presence to the guiding image of a community of equals.[25] She hopes that each sermon (and other acts of ministry) will further the congregation's self-understanding as such a community. In a large degree, according to Perelman, whether or not the preacher is able to affect the congregation's awareness of themselves as a community of equals, or to agree with the preacher that this is indeed true, depends upon her ability to achieve presence in the sermon.

Sermons always involve selection. By the images, symbols, stories, doctrinal systems, values, and the ways in which the preacher pastor joins these elements in a sermon, he seeks to make certain realities present to the congregation and to obscure others. The preacher "chooses the elements and the method of making them present."[26] The importance of this selectivity by the preacher cannot be overstressed. As Perelman notes, such selection is the means whereby things that seem distant can be brought near, and things that seem close at hand, by excluding them from the sermon, can fade away. When something achieves presence for the hearer,

---

[23]Perelman, *The New Rhetoric*, 54.

[24]Martin Luther King, Jr., *Strength to Love* (Philadelphia: Fortress Press, 1981), 112.

[25]Perelman, *The New Rhetoric*, 171–79.

[26]Ibid., 119. For an in-depth treatment of presence in the overall scheme of Perelman's work, see Louise A. Karon, "Presence in the New Rhetoric," in *The New Rhetoric of Chaim Perelman: Statement and Response,* ed. Ray D. Dearin (New York: University Press of America, 1989), 163–78.

the total impact of that something upon the hearer is much greater; it cannot be ignored. Perelman cites the example of how in war when soldiers actually see the face of their enemies, the individuals become more important than the cause for which they are fighting. The enemy who before was an "evil" abstraction now achieves presence evoking sympathy, while the war fades into abstraction. Some of the material that we handle in sermons is far removed from the day-to-day reality of the congregation. Biblical narratives, quotations from ancient Jewish and Christian tradition, historical allusions, biographical examples, anecdotes about persons whom the hearers do not actually know, situations distant in time and space from the worship service, recounting of films and novels that the listeners have not seen or read–all this material must somehow come alive for the hearers if the preacher desires effect. And it must come alive in a particular way–to effect congregational formation as a pastoral community.

It is easy to see why this concept of presence is significant for homiletics in general and pastoral preaching in particular. Aware or not, preachers use the criteria of presence all the time when selecting sermonic material. Perelman illuminates just how crucial the selections become. To the point of this study, how one "presents" the human being and the church in preaching week after week has direct bearing on the pastoral impact of the sermon. We will see this in more detail in chapters 4 and 5 and in the sermons of chapter 6. Given the formative power of language, what and who achieves presence in the sermon will shape the congregation's self-understanding and activity in the world. As Richard Weaver clarifies, "Rhetoric...is an art of emphasis."[27] The preacher cannot afford to forget that the sermon helps shape a congregation's world. Whatever material she selects, and however she presents it for the understanding of the listeners, helps determine the shape of that world. It may be a hearty pastoral world where mutual care and concern feed the people of God to become bread for the world. Or it may be a meager private world where individuals sip scraps of sustenance from a thin pastoral soup.

Presence deserves our attention for yet another reason. Presence helps the preacher pastor negotiate the split between form and content in preaching. Influenced by recent language studies, it is almost a homiletical truism that form and content are inseparable. Form and content together convey meaning. Homileticians have argued that this is true for the sermon just as biblical scholars have argued the same for scripture.[28] Nevertheless, in actual practice preachers often find themselves approaching sermon preparation in a two-step process: What to say (content)? How to say it (form and style)? Preachers sometimes think of this two-step process as

---

[27]Weaver, "Language is Sermonic," 211.
[28]See Don Wardlaw, ed., *Preaching Biblically: Creating Sermons in the Shape of Scripture* (Philadelphia: Westminster Press, 1983).

moving from text (the what) to sermon (the how). Perelman's work suggests that such a distinction between aesthetics and reasoning is false. For example, would Martin Luther King, Jr.'s, "I Have A Dream" speech still carry the power it does had King committed the same ideas in different form? Perelman's presence is a concept that helps the preacher capture the dynamism of form and function. "Questions of form and questions of substance are intermingled in order to achieve presence."[29] Or again, "We refuse to separate the form of a discourse from its substance, to study stylistic structures and figures independently of the purpose they must achieve in the argumentation."[30]

What does this mean for the pastoral preacher? To achieve maximum presence in the awareness of the hearers, she will attend equally to form and content. Presence, though considered an element of the speaker's style, is in fact determinative of meaning. Brilliant insight does not shine when dimly conveyed, just as linguistic pyrotechnics may cause a sermon to waft away into thin air. Presence within the sermon requires a solid union between structure and content. This does not mean that even the most conscientious preacher attending form and content in sermons will necessarily achieve presence for the concern at hand. Listeners will respond with "variable intensity."[31] But by closely attending to presence in the sermon, the preacher enhances the possibility of establishing a caring community through care-full preaching.

Let's turn now to other linguistic elements that play key roles in pastoral preaching.

Images and Symbols in Pastoral Preaching

Sermons traffic among an array of linguistic symbols from scripture, the Christian tradition, the common life of the people, the particular congregation, and the world at large. The preacher's use of these symbols has persuasive intent, whether to instruct, criticize, support, challenge, or confuse the congregation. They are the rhetorical elements (gestures, cues) by which the preacher signals to the congregation any number of notions of care. She may be communicating to the congregation that care is the shared responsibility of every person within the hearing of the gospel. Or she may be communicating that care is the sole prerogative of the officially trained pastoral counselor. The preacher may signal that he or she doesn't really care. Or she may be saying through the language of the sermon that she feels overwhelmed by the human needs within the congregation and doesn't really know how to care effectively. My point is that because of the

---

[29]Perelman, *The New Rhetoric,* 120.
[30]Ibid., 142.
[31]Ibid., 511.

way the preacher uses the language, persons will make some sense of how the preacher understands care in the sermon.

At the deepest levels of the sermon, preachers build upon constitutive images of the way things are among human beings and God in the church and world. According to theologian Edward Farley, these images "guide the everyday activities of the religious community, its worship and liturgy, its institutional and canonical ordering, its…witness and preaching."[32] When we peer deeply enough into the swirling word pictures of our sermons, we find these baseline images that subtly though powerfully shape preacher and congregation. For example, the preacher sees the church as an ark, a safe haven amid the storms of life. Around this image cluster other representations of the church—sanctuary, hospital, shelter, retreat. Whether conscious or not, as he preaches in a congregation over time, the preacher routinely plays variations upon this symbolic theme of the church. After a while the actual congregation begins either to think of itself as sanctuary and retreat, or it will begin to resist the constitutive image that the preacher presents. Consequently, the congregation may begin to form over against the preacher's image of the church. Maybe the preacher understands the church as an ark upon the troubled waters, but the people understand the church as a chalice poured out for the city. The deep metaphors that inform preacher and congregation will conflict. So it will be necessary for the preacher and the congregation to adjust their constitutive images, live with the tension, or seek a pastoral change. In reality, congregations form around some combination of constitutive images. "Individuals and congregations may hold two or more of these images, and usually do, even though they might appear to be in theological contradiction."[33]

If we dig carefully through a body of our sermons, we find the root images or metaphors that are guiding our selection of texts, stories, examples, quotes, and allusions. The alert pastor knows that preaching helps establish, reinforce, challenge, or alter the constitutive images within the congregation. As Denham Grierson explains the connection between imagery and congregational identity, "Within the associated images of a congregation many of its core meanings reside. The total configuration of images can embody a fundamental vision. That is why attention to the imagery living within the people's language is so critical."[34] Since pastoral preachers wish to form the congregation as a pastoral community, we must continually ask ourselves whether the foundational imagery of our sermons supports this intention.

---

[32]Edward Farley, *Ecclesial Man: A Social Phenomenology of Faith and Reality* (Philadelphia: Fortress Press, 1975), 118.

[33]Dudley and Johnson, *Energizing the Congregation,* 97.

[34]Denham Grierson, *Transforming a People of God* (Melbourne, Australia: Joint Board of Christian Education, 1984), 109.

Joseph Webb offers another way to consider how language shapes congregations. He says that individuals and groups [congregations] construct meaning and value around "hub symbols."[35] Hub symbols are those internal images that are the most emotionally charged for persons and groups. They are the internal representations that highly excite us. When others criticize these hub symbols, we become defensive. For one person a hub symbol could be a particular sport, basketball say; for another it may be a family farm or a beloved novel or poem. So profound is the person's loyalty to this symbol that it occupies center stage in his world. He organizes his life around it. He draws connections between it and all other persons and events that he knows and encounters. It is the hub around which meaning spins.

Groups, like individuals, organize around hub symbols. When individuals enter into the life of a group, they "assume, at least to some extent, that group's hub; and if that group becomes very important in one's life, then that group's hub becomes a hub symbol within the individual for whom the group is intensely important."[36] You can see why this is significant for congregational preaching. The preacher articulates from week to week the hub symbols of the Christian faith that are embodied within the congregation. These symbols recur in the preaching, worship, and mission of the congregation. Some preachers emphasize cross and empty tomb. Some highlight broken bread and wine. Others turn the spotlight of preaching upon the anxiety of contemporary existence. Some preachers turn the focus on themselves, while others preach sermons that revolve around hot-button issues in the news, such as abortion. The possibilities are endless. The point is that every preacher and congregation rotate around these hub symbols like the solar system moving around the sun.

You may say that for every Christian church the core symbol is the crucified and resurrected Christ. Maybe it ought to be, if we are speaking normatively. But the fact is, until we carefully explore the sermonic language of the preached sermons (and other events within the congregation), we do not know what the actual hub symbols are. On the surface of things, congregations may place Christ at the center, but underneath, all kinds of loyalties actually compete for the winner's circle. Congregational members become deeply attached to these hub symbols and are shaped by them as they move toward the center of the congregation. In short, the preached word reinforces hub symbols that help create the identity of the congregation.

So congregational identity revolves around a core set of images and symbols. The congregation expresses and receives this identity in many ways, but one of the chief expressions comes through the sermon. Again,

---

[35]Joseph M. Webb, *Preaching and the Challenge of Pluralism* (St. Louis: Chalice Press, 1998), chap. 3.
[36]Ibid., 57.

the preacher and congregational leaders may not be intentionally aware of these core images. Indeed, Carl Dudley claims that most church leaders are not aware of their central congregational images. Rather, we hold these images intuitively, which in turn "guide and inform the lives of our members."[37] But preachers will be better prepared to preach pastorally if we become aware of the core images that do guide our preaching. While we may think that our sermons have pastoral content, close examination may reveal ill-defined notions of the pastoral community. For example, our symbolic representations of the church may have more in common with a drugstore than with the body of Christ. We may be painting a picture of the church as an outpatient clinic rather than as a covenantal community. Sometimes we think our sermons are inviting people into a fellowship of redeemed sinners, but the imagery of the sermons depicts a vague amalgamation of nice people who know neither sin nor redemption. Forming pastoral communities through preaching necessitates that we look carefully at how our sermons actually name the congregation in the symbolic world of the sermon. We want the constitutive images and symbols of the sermons to bring into focus a pastoral community that cares for the world. It was Peter Bohler who said to John Wesley that for those preachers who do not have faith, "preach faith *till* you have it."[38] Likewise, if we wish to shape pastoral communities, we will preach until they are.

Examples

Perhaps a few positive examples from sermons will help at this point as we forge the connection between the language of the sermon and the reality of the congregation as a pastoral community. While it would be better to look at sermons in their entirety, which we will do in chapter 6, I think that we can see in these excerpts how the concrete, foundational imagery of these sermons identifies and names into reality a pastoral community.

James McClendon preaches a sermon entitled "Food Enough for All," based on Exodus 16:4 and John 21:9–17. The sermon rests upon the theological conviction that God provides for the people of Israel and for the Christian church. A certain kind of church emerges, he claims, whenever the people trust in God's faithful provision.

> Why do members of this community care about others having enough to eat? Why are some of us cooking for the local shelter for the homeless? Why is it that not even a crafty beggar will be turned away hungry from one of our households? Oh, that's easy,

---

[37]Carl Dudley, "Using Church Images for Commitment, Conflict, and Renewal," in *Congregations: Their Power to Form and Transform*, ed. C. Ellis Nelson (Atlanta: John Knox Press, 1988), 90, 112.

[38]W. Reginald Ward and Richard P. Heitzenrater, eds., *Journal and Diaries* (1735–1738), vol. 18 of *The Works of John Wesley* (Nashville: Abingdon Press, 1988), 228.

you will say. Because it's right! Well, but how do we know it's right? Other people don't seem to know that. Other people in our society say, in effect, "Let 'em starve; it's not *my* family." So how do we know it's right? We know it is right because that is the way God treats us. God provides. Ever since the day of the manna, God has been providing. God *never* quits…Is it not God's church, into which God has called you, rather than the other way around? And will God who sends the manna not continue to provide?[39]

Notice the constitutive imagery of the congregation that this sermon rests upon. The church is like a *family* (community) who eats (breaks bread) together. Only it is a family with very wide arms. In fact, the arms extend to embrace the homeless and the beggars of the world, who have seats around our own *household* tables. The church communicates care for others beyond the walls of the church because that's how God is. The church is *the people of God* because God creates and sustains the church. This church lives in some tension with the world insofar as certain parts of the world will turn a cold shoulder to God's homeless family members, but the church knows that it can offer itself to others because God provides.

The language of this sermon, through its explicit and underlying imagery, presences an abundant pastoral community. McClendon holds the mirror up to the congregation and says, "See who we are," while at the same time reminding them of how they have become who they are through the provision of God. He preaches in the indicative voice rather than the imperative. The sermon avoids identifying the church as a thrown together group of activists or do-gooders by locating their identity in God, who is the primary hub symbol of the sermon. In looking at a series of McClendon's sermons, we might find that these constitutive images surface again and again. Or we might reasonably expect to find other variations of the congregational image in different sermons. But this quick look would indicate that such preaching will go a long way toward building up a pastoral community.

Let's take another example, this one from a sermon by Susan Newman Hopkins entitled "The Unexpected Possibilities of God." The sermon is based on Luke 1:26–38, 46–55, which includes the annunciation and the Magnificat. Hopkins interprets these passages as revealing the unexpected activity of God, who chooses Mary, a woman, to be the bearer of Jesus Christ, God's good news for the world. While she applies this interpretation to the call of women to preach, she grounds the sermon in an expansive pastoral vision of the Christian and human community.

---

[39]James William McClendon, Jr., *Making Gospel Sense to a Troubled Church* (Cleveland: Pilgrim Press, 1995), 13.

If I may take a flight of imagination, I see Mary "opening the doors of the church," inviting all women and men to come and follow a God of unexpected possibilities. I can see them coming down through the ages. Women and men who have accomplished things in spite of what others have called "the impossible." I see them coming from slavery–Sojourner Truth, Gabriel Prosser. I see them coming from the arts–Marian Anderson, James Baldwin, Todd Duncan, Maya Angelou...And yes, I see them coming from the church–Jarena Lee, Richard Allen, Martin Luther King, Jr. and Barbara Harris.

These are all lives filled with the unexpected possibilities of God. They said yes when others wanted them to say no. We too, like Mary, can magnify the Lord with our lives, for it doth not yet appear what we shall be...for eyes have not seen, ears have not heard, neither has it entered our hearts the things which God has prepared for them that love God.[40]

Two powerful consitutive symbols bear up this sermon. The first is the church as the *communion of saints* or *cloud of witnesses,* beginning with Mary, passing to Jarena Lee and Richard Allen, and running through to the very people in the pews ("We too, like Mary, can magnify the Lord"). The church is not an abstraction, a doctrine, certainly not a building, but a succession of men and women, boys and girls who follow God through concrete action in life. They do this at great cost and against seemingly impossible odds. Mary may be the symbolic mother of this church since she is the mother of Christ, but the congregation of this sermon is both maternal and paternal, receiving and acting on the call of God, saying "yes when others wanted them to say no." Those who are in the world, though not necessarily in the established church, merge with the heroes of the church as the preacher presences the whole company of the faithful in a "flight of imagination"(remember Perelman's definition of presence as making present those things that are actually absent but which the speaker deems important).

The second hub symbol of the sermon is *God,* the giver of *unexpected possibilities.* God is the one who gives purpose to the members of the communion. God is the one who sees beyond where the church can see and who offers to the church a glimpse (eschatological vision) of what is prepared for those who love God.

The pastoral community that this sermon seeks to evoke will not have shallow roots. It will draw its caring vision from deep within the soil of the communion of the saints. This community will not rest content in simply

---

[40]Susan Newman Hopkins, "The Unexpected Possibilities of God," in *Women: To Preach or Not to Preach,* ed. Ella Pearson Mitchell (Valley Forge: Judson Press, 1991), 129–30.

caring for themselves; it will listen for the unexpected call of God who wants to give birth through the community to new possibilities, even a new heaven and earth.

Similar images surface in Gardner Taylor's sermon "The Answer to a Riddle," based on John 14:12–13. Only for Taylor, the pastoral community forms even more closely around the work of Christ, who is both at the center of the caring community and on the edge of the community, calling it toward final consummation. In the sermon he wrestles with how the Christian community can fulfill the prophecy to do greater works than Jesus did.

> Look at the procession of "made-whole," "brought-back," and "second-chance" people who pass by where Jesus has been and whose lives He radically and gloriously altered: Simon and Mary Magdalene, the widow from Nain, men born blind, hustlers and extortioners like Zacchaeus. Then hear Jesus say, "Greater things than these he shall do…"

> The force and fire of Christ Jesus do not belong in any past, recent or remote. "Greater works than these shall he do." The mightiest preaching of the dear risen Lord has not yet been heard, the most moving music has not been sung, and the most powerful and prevailing prayers have not yet been prayed. "Greater works than these shall he do." Our highest peak of Christian believing has not yet been attained, our holiest state of grace has not yet been reached, our dearest communion with God has not yet been experienced, our fullest vision of God has not yet been beheld, and our noblest service to the slain and risen Savior has not yet been rendered…

> We have a friend at court; Christ is gone…and has sat down on the right hand of God…We may call on Him for He says, "Whatsoever ye shall ask in my name, that will I do." He can do: He sits at the right hand of God. He can help in our needy hour for He sits at God's right hand. He can heal us when we ask, for He is at God's right hand. We have but to ask Him, to call Him, to talk to Him, and to plead with Him.[41]

The sermon's guiding imagery paints a church composed of the walking wounded, a motley crew of *"second-chance"* human beings whom Jesus redeems (Simon, Mary Magdalene, hustlers, extortionists, Zacchaeus, you, and me). Taylor's symbolism calls to mind Luther's theological conviction of *simul justus et peccator* (simultaneously justified yet sinners). Yet the sermon doesn't stop with a crowd of redeemed sinners congratulating themselves on their homecoming. The journey of the church isn't complete. The

---

[41]Gardner C. Taylor, *Chariots Aflame* (Nashville: Broadman Press, 1988), 154, 158–59.

constitutive symbol is of the *church on the move* doing the work that Christ has handed over. The church cannot stop caring or worshiping, praying or serving the risen Savior.

Right in the heart of the sermon, at the hub, sits the resurrected Christ at God's right hand. He is the one who redeems this lot of sinful saints, and he is the one who makes it possible for the church to be the church. The church isn't stuck with a Jesus past his prime, sitting around remembering how good it was to save old Simon and Mary. The resurrected Christ goes before the church showing the way to God, interceding on our behalf. The church knows that through Jesus Christ it came to be, and in Jesus Christ it shall be. Taylor's use of repetition and alliteration, and a masterful arrangement of the material, beckons this pastoral community into existence. The core imagery of the sermon compels the hearers to become the people that the sermon says they are.

Summary

These are only three brief examples of how preachers use presence, constitutive images, and hub symbols to shape congregations as pastoral communities. I hope that they demonstrate this chapter's claims about the formative power of language in general and specifically about how preaching can mold pastoral communities. Preachers work with the language of the sermon like a potter shaping clay. It is true that the sermon is not complete until the congregation adds its own, "That's right," and "Amen." But on Sunday morning in the hour of worship, the congregation relies on the preacher to get the wheel spinning before it places its moistened hands on the clay. The vessel that becomes the sermon hopefully shapes the congregation as a pastoral community, even as the pastoral community calls forth a care-full sermon.

Clearly it is impossible for us to quantify or accurately predict the pastoral nature of the communities that form around our sermons. Too many other factors contribute to the unique character of the Christian congregation, including worship as a whole, the personalities of all constituents and the pastor, the social context of the church, its history, daily events that impinge upon the congregation, and most importantly, the activity of God through the Holy Spirit. Nevertheless, insofar as the preacher speaks words among a people of the Word, the formative and transformative power of language cannot be overlooked. If we wish to preach among a pastoral congregation, we will preach carefully, knowing that through our words God gives a caring shape to the people.

We move now to take a closer look at how pastoral preaching rests on the primary theological categories of anthropology and ecclesiology. In the first case, we will ask of our sermons, "Who cares?" In the second case, that of ecclesiology, we will explore the church that cares. It is these basic theological assumptions within our sermons that form the pastoral community through preaching.

4

Who Cares?

We are those addressed by God to become what God intends us to be: human beings, able to relate in love to ourselves, to others, and to God.[1]

—LETTY RUSSELL

It is one of our most common phrases: *Who cares?* Sometimes we say it to indicate our lack of interest in the subject at hand. "Big deal," we say, "Who cares?" Other times we say the words to show that we don't think others ought to care, or at least make such a big fuss. "Who cares about the snail darter or spotted owl anyway?" Spouses hurl the phrase at each other when arguing. "Who cares, Lindy? You think I give a rip?" Turning to the sad state of U.S. social welfare, wondering if government, private enterprise, and all the rest of us really are concerned about women and children in poverty, analysts ask our nation, "Who cares?"[2] We hear the phrase in one form or another almost every day.

Christian preachers have an answer to the question, Who cares? We know *who* cares, or at least we believe that we do. Who cares is written all over the notes of our sermons. Who cares tumbles around among the words and images of what we preach. Conscious or not, our sermons disclose to the congregation who we think cares, and who should care. This is one of the most basic elements of pastoral preaching. Every sermon we dare to offer to God and congregation proceeds upon some assumptions about who cares.

---

[1]Letty Russell, *The Future of Partnership* (Philadelphia: Westminster Press, 1979), 44.

[2]See John McKnight, *The Careless Society: Community and Its Counterfeits* (New York: Basic Books, 1995), 16.

How is this so? The theological anthropology of the sermon points toward who cares, at least in the mind of the preacher. All preachers base their sermons on some understanding of what it means to be a human being. In the case of Christian preaching, what it means to be a human being in relationship to God, Jesus Christ, the Holy Spirit, the church, and one another. How we view humanity, and how we present that view in our sermons, determines "who" cares. It sets up who gives care and who receives it. The view of the human being establishes who needs care and who is capable of offering care. For example, who is hurt, and who can offer healing? Who is lost, and who can guide the way? Whose life is in free fall, and who can extend the arms of support? Who is being oppressed, and who can untangle the oppression? Who is at odds with their neighbor, and who can bring them together? All of these are pastoral concerns that our sermons address through the pictures, images, descriptions, scriptural interpretations, stories, and symbols of the human being. We may not have noticed it before, but through our theological anthropology our sermons steadily signal to the congregation, like the bass notes of a musical composition, who cares.

Sermonic language constructs a congregational understanding and practice of care. As we saw in the previous chapter, the language of the sermon does matter. Words shape worlds. Who cares in the sermons will in no small way be reflected in who cares among the congregation, or who doesn't. It would be impossible to scientifically prove a direct correlation between the sermon's construal of care and congregational practice of care. But clearly the language and theology of the sermon will impact congregational theology and care just as congregational care and theology is mirrored in the sermon. As David Buttrick points out, "Though assuredly frightening, it is nonetheless true to say that congregational theology is largely a product of preaching."[3] Changing our theology and images of the human being who cares is one of the ways to shift congregational caring.

The Human Being in the Sermon

Theological anthropologies are numerous, complex, and diverse. Most preachers do not hold a systematic doctrine of humanity but rather "working doctrines." Informed not only by theology but also biology, psychology, sociology, and philosophy, preachers have an implicit understanding of the human being that draws from various sources. When it comes time to preach, we don't usually ask ourselves, Now what am I saying about human nature in this sermon? unless it comes up as a specific aspect of a biblical text (e.g., Genesis 1–3, or Psalm 8). Nevertheless, the theological anthropology is present in the sermons that we preach, and it orients the way the preacher communicates care within the congregation. So let's look

---

[3]David Buttrick, *Homiletic: Moves and Structures* (Philadelphia: Fortress Press, 1987), 19.

at several of the approaches to theological anthropology that crop up in pastoral preaching to discern how the sermon shapes who cares.

Individual Sinners in Need of Personal Salvation

Individualism

Well-worn tracks down the sawdust trail of Protestant revivalism lead to this first theological anthropology. Familiar to most North American Protestants, sermons that build on this view of humanity construe the primary human predicament of sin as inward and personal. Based on an individualistic understanding of the human being, each person is frightfully free to make his or her own decisions for or against God, for or against human sin. Isolated from God by our willful (mis)behavior, neglect, or ignorance, our guilt convinces us that we deserve nothing better than the wrath of God. We are each, as Jonathan Edwards' famous sermon proclaims, "sinners in the hands of an angry God." We cannot imagine any escape from the consequences of our own sin, which have already begun in the torment of conscience and self-loathing. As Roberta Bondi reflects on this view of self in relation to God, "I would try my best to flee from the wrath to come by believing that my heavenly Father loved me, sins and all–only I could not believe it. How could God love me in spite of my sins if they were bad enough to make God's own son die?"[4] Though we find it difficult to understand, somehow each one of us personally got ourselves into this mess with God, and somehow each one of us must get ourselves out.

Faith becomes a matter of personal choice, of getting ourselves right with God. The church as a corporate body formed by the power of the resurrected Christ fades away. Church is where individuals show up to get their needs met. Faith means making "up our deepest beliefs in the isolation of our private selves."[5] All that matters is the personal relationship with God. Never mind that the church is the Spirit-filled body that initiates and forms faith within the believer.

Since the individual thinks that each person is his or her own center, that individual cannot see how church or community participates in the formation of the self. Care means going deeper and deeper into one's own self to find solutions to whatever problems one has discovered. This subjective/objective split

> makes us forget that our private, experiencing selves, even our Christian selves, do not come unmediated from our own insides or even from God. Rather we are formed in very complex ways by our social experiences of family, church, school, and friends,

---

[4]Roberta C. Bondi, *Memories of God: Theological Reflections on a Life* (Nashville: Abingdon Press, 1995), 24.

[5]Robert Bellah, *Habits of the Heart: Individualism and Commitment in American Life* (Berkeley, Calif.: University of California Press, 1985), 65.

by our larger culture and its expectations, as well as by scripture, and by the Christian tradition. Failing to recognize the communal origins of our "private" selves makes us identify points of pain in ourselves as personal problems.[6]

When we define humanity in this way, and set up the problem so subjectively we squeeze care down to minor ministrations for the hurting individual. Whether the preacher points to God or to himself as the minister of such care, it is directed exclusively toward the private pains of distressed individuals.

Existentialism

Christian existentialism sinks its own taproots down into the same anthropological soil, though it recasts its views of humanity with philosophical sophistication. The riddles of human existence—who am I, who is God, what gives life meaning, what is death—are all anxiety-producing questions for the individual. We face life's toughest dilemmas alone. As Thomas Wolfe writes, "Naked and alone, we came into exile...Which of us is not forever a stranger and alone?"[7] If we find love at all, amid the wasteland of modernity, we find it "in the ruins."[8] We are, as Søren Kierkegaard imagined, like "knights of faith" who must seek the individual courage to embrace Christ with a "leap of faith." No one else can walk the excruciating journey of faith *for* us, and in most of the existentialist anthropologies, no one else walks the road of faith *with* us. The problem for humanity as Christian existentialism defines it is personal estrangement from God, self, and ideals. It is internal and personal. The isolated self wrestles alone in the dark like Jacob at the river. But whereas Jacob in Hebrew Scripture represents all of Israel, the human being of existentially oriented preaching is all alone with the despairing self. Proclamation of the gospel creates a "crisis event" for the listener who must independently decide for or against Christ.[9] A moment occurs for the angst-ridden individual in which she must choose once and for all either the life of sin or the life of salvation. The preacher stands by to offer the gift and await the response.

---

[6]Bondi, *Memories of God,* 16.

[7]Thomas Wolfe, *A Stone, A Leaf, A Door: Poems,* selected by John S. Barnes (New York: Charles Scribner's Sons, 1945), 1.

[8]Walker Percy, *Love in the Ruins* (New York: Farrar Straus & Giroux, 1971).

[9]This was Rudolph Bultmann's claim, which was picked up by the New Hermeneutics and influenced preaching as a "word event" throughout the past generation. "It is His [God's] Word as an event, in an encounter, not as a set of ideas, not, for example, as a statement about God's kindness and grace in general...but only as addressed to me, as an event happening and meeting me," Rudolph Bultmann, *Jesus Christ and Mythology* (Englewood Cliffs, N.J.: Prentice Hall, 1958), 79.

Psychotherapy

Psychotherapeutic psychologies retain the individual at the center, but once again reformulate the problem.[10] Individual human beings do not struggle with sin and salvation but with emotional and social adjustment. Our problem is not a matter of getting right with God but of gaining better insight about our own internal needs and motivations. In doctrinaire Freudian thought, the one who can gain sufficient insight (rational understanding) will have no need for God at all. Guilt, the driving moral and emotional force that compels us toward personal salvation (freedom from sin/guilt), will lessen as we understand more fully our own past, our family histories, and the forces of social constraint. The goal here is for the individual to find a way to reduce psychic pain and achieve a modicum of pleasure. The professional counselor and the couch replace the kneeling rail and the mourner's bench as the individual human being seeks psychological salvation.

The more optimistic psychologies promise refreshing showers of self-realization for the faithful, wherein the goal of life for the individual is to attain as much enjoyment as possible. The pathways to such a state of actualization are many, and our consumer-driven economy, piggybacking on an optimistic anthropology, always invents more. As recent commercials for the new Volkswagon Beetle tout, "It's about living, not about being alive" [paraphrase]. A full and happy life is within your individual grasp, this anthropology intones, so reach out and grab a fistful for yourself. Though often characterized as optimistic, the underside of self-actualization psychology is deeply pessimistic about the social order, and so it turns the believer inward to the self where some degree of happiness might be found.

The Winner's Circle

This orientation in preaching, with its tendency to stress self-actualization, health, and personal success, builds upon an idealized and individualistic image of humanity. The sermons project that humanity is created for success. Those who attain the fullness of humanity will enter the winner's circle, which is usually illuminated by spotlights, bedecked with flowers, and accompanied by cheerful attendants. We see this anthropology at work in the phenomena of the megachurches, whose entertainment-style worship and preaching all point toward the dominant value of success, at least success according to North American cultural standards. The entire worship experience, like a football game, shouts to the listener that bigger is better, and winning is what matters.[11]

---

[10]See Don Browning, *Religious Thought and the Modern Psychologies* (Philadelphia: Fortress Press, 1987).

[11]See Marva Dawn's assessment of contemporary worship, *Reaching Out Without Dumbing Down: A Theology of Worship for the Turn-of-the-Century Culture* (Grand Rapids: Eerdmans, 1995).

Rather than focusing on the pain of personal sin, this brand of individualistic Christianity suggests that sin is only a distant memory. Every now and then we need to remember how bad things can get, but overall God is happy with who we are and willing to bless us for our achievement. The church triumphant arises from this flooring. We are the winners, the victorious in God's eyes. On the extreme religious right in North America, this has led the church to identify almost completely with the nation, so much so that one leader of the religious right says, "The only way to have a genuine spiritual revival is to have legislative reform."[12] If winning is what counts for the Christian, conquering the nation is fair game. Sermons in such churches tout the victorious Christian lifestyle. Nobody really cares in the sermons because apparently the point of preaching and Christian faith is self-congratulation. Predicated upon an individualistic understanding of human nature, narcissism runs wild within the church. Sermons do little more than reinforce how good the winners feel about themselves. The irony is bitter: so much self-congratulation while following a servant savior, so much talk about winning rewards in life while Jesus loses everything on a cross.

Who Cares? The Pastor as Professional

Notice who cares in the sermons that we construct on these anthropological foundations. The pastor or some other helping professional is typically the one who offers care in these sermons. Why? Because the pastor holds the cure to the sickness of sin that plagues the individual. He or she knows what the sinner needs: for example, a trip to the altar to confess one's unworthiness and receive Christ, or the gift of the sacrament that only the priest can dispense. The pastor is the one who stands by patiently praying to offer consolation to the sick. The pastor is the one who listens deeply as the confused young adult puzzles over meaning in his or her life. The preacher is the one who can say with authority to the passive members of the congregation, "What you need to do is to meditate daily upon God's word, which will be a lamp unto your feet and a light unto your path." Trust me, the preacher is saying to the congregation, "I know, and I care."

Take, for example, the following story that a preacher might use to illustrate the importance of interruptions in Christian life. The sermon builds upon the many scriptural instances in which Jesus is interrupted by others.

It seems like we're always in a hurry to accomplish something. We've got our plans made out for the day, what we believe is important. Like the other day, I was leaving the office and was

---

[12]Cited in Robert E. Webber and Rodney Clapp, *People of the Truth* (San Francisco: Harper & Row, 1988), 10.

already late for a meeting downtown. I had just about made it to my car when this guy, sort of shabbily dressed, came up and asked me if I was the "preacher." I told him "yes," while wondering (I hate to admit) how much change I had in my pocket, and if that might not be enough to get him along the road so that I could get on to where I needed to go. He said he needed to talk for a minute. I glanced at my watch to indicate that I was in a hurry, but he ignored the signal. "I just want to talk," he said, "It won't take long." I looked around to see if anybody else was coming out of the church who could help me out, but no such luck. "All right," I said, "I've got five minutes. What do you want to talk about?"

And you know what? He didn't ask me for money. He didn't ask me for food. Didn't want a ride to anywhere, and didn't tell me a long story about how down on his luck he had been. He told me about how lonely he felt and how far away he was from his family. He said nobody wanted to listen to him because of the kind of person he was. Then he asked me to pray for him. Right out there on the side of the church with cars and buses whizzing by, he wanted to pray. So I took the man by the hands, and we bowed our heads, and I prayed for his life; I prayed for God to heal him, to touch him, to help him know that he was loved. And when we finished, he thanked me and walked on.

Now you know, interruptions are sometimes what is important in the Christian life. Like with Jesus...

In this example, the preacher sets himself up as the one who unwillingly cares for others. To his credit, he is not proud of his own busyness and attitude toward the other person. He is chastened by the discovery that in the middle of his own busy life he should still have time to care for another person. However, he is the one who finally cares. He is the one who prays for the other person in need. He is "the preacher" who is almost too busy to care, but when all is said and done can still pray for the homeless on the street. Care is almost completely unidirectional even though the other person in the story is offering the preacher an important gift of self-understanding. His prayer focuses abstractly upon the need for the man's inward healing, for "God to touch him." The sad fact is that the story tells us a whole lot about the preacher but very little about the man on the street. The preacher wants to show that we shouldn't be too busy to care about others, but he is the only one in the story who actually cares. While responding to the man's request for prayer, the care that he offers is an individual transaction between the preacher, the religious specialist, who does care and the man, down and out, who needs it. I'm not saying that he shouldn't have prayed with the man. I think that he should. But a fundamental individualism and inequality governs the exchange that denies mutuality in care.

The preacher could have taken a different direction if he had asked the other man to pray for him as well, but he didn't. The preacher actually aligns himself with Jesus in the story, albeit a reluctant Jesus. For the preacher, like Jesus, is the one who finds ministry in interruptions. With a steady diet of such examples in sermons, we wouldn't look for a pastoral congregation to form that would value mutuality and hospitality. Indeed, the church functions in the sermon only as a physical backdrop for the pastoral care of the preacher. He is departing from the church. He meets the man on the street beside the church. But the church as a pastoral community—a community of mutuality, hospitality, and compassion for the world—does not surface within the story. The church is actually absent when the pastor looks around for someone to bail him out of a tight situation. The preacher functions as an autonomous caregiver applying help to a lonely individual. This is how the story presences pastoral care in the sermon.

My point is that an individualistic anthropology and personal understanding of sin and salvation underlies this illustration. When we set things up this way in our preaching, the pastoral care will almost inevitably flow in one direction—down from the preacher to the individuals in the congregation, or down from God, through the preacher, to the congregation. There is theology in this anthropology: God acts solely through the ordained representative to distribute care to all who are in need. Pastoral care, therefore, depends on maintaining clericalism, wherein the clergy have the status and the power to fill what is lacking within the individuals of the church and community. The preacher is constantly reminding the listeners, "I know the way," or maybe even, "I am the way."

Robert Wuthnow, a religious sociologist, has analyzed the way narration in such sermons reveals the intent of the preacher to control the listeners. The preacher will frequently interject such personal stories as if he or she has learned something from them. But the preacher becomes "an intrusive object in his own narrative." The preacher hasn't really learned anything. The stories "show the speaker as one who has already found the answers, or who instantly recognizes them, or sees their applicability to others' problems."[13] When we engage in this kind of preaching, we crowd out the care of the congregation. Everything in the sermon suggests that the preacher is actually the one who cares.

Most of us have heard these type of sermons, and many of us have preached them. Our theological instincts are correct; something is badly broken within humanity. Theology and scripture have given us a name for this brokenness—sin. But we oversimplify matters when we say, as pietism has, that the problem resides only within the sinful human heart. When we do this, every act of pastoral care comes off looking like an attempt to fix

---

[13]Robert Wuthnow, "Religious Discourse as Public Rhetoric," *Communication Research* 15, no. 3 (June 1988): 332–33.

what is broken, since seemingly a little tinkering with the human heart will get things going right again. A utilitarianism inhabits our pastoral care and beguiles us into thinking that pastoral care is quasi-magical, with the ability to bring needed change now.

Notice how a pastor-centered, heroic drama builds up in these sermonic representations of care. The pastor prays by the bedside of a sick individual who gets better. The youth minister shows up just in time to help a confused adolescent avert suicide. The ordained deacon singlehandedly organizes a campaign to tighten fair lending laws. The priest teaches a group of inner-city kids how to program computers so they can find jobs. I'm not saying that these things don't happen from time to time as clergy carry out pastoral care. They do. But when we fill our sermons with these kinds of stories and images, it communicates that care comes from the official representatives of the church. The people who hear the sermon pretty quickly get the idea that they are the recipients of the pastor's concern, but rarely do they initiate the same. We presence care in narrow, clerical terms based on an anthropology that lodges sin only within the individual heart and then poses the pastor as Christ's stand-in, who can offer redemption.

The secular version of this kind of caring transaction happens within professional counseling. Transaction is the operative term, because care is a commodity, something that the needy client purchases from the expert counselor. The same goes for other "helping" professions such as medicine. "A dominant class of professionals earn their living by serving and caring for others. In order to create and maintain the need for their services, care professionals must convince consumers that they lack the knowledge about, and are unable to perform, what the professionals do for them."[14] All of this transactional care is premised upon an individualistic anthropology where individuals are supposedly free to pick and choose their own means of help but actually are highly dependent on those who set the terms by which help is offered. For example, How much does the care cost? Who can get the help and who cannot? What happens when the promised help fails? All you have to do is glance at healthcare in North America to see the state of confusion and sickness that our individualism has fostered. As long as we perceive human nature and its problems, sin or sickness, in such stark individual categories, we will need subjects who care and objects who receive care. But rarely will we attain mutuality within the community. Neither will we be able to experience genuine hospitality, because with such an anthropology guiding our preaching, we are always more intent on fixing problems in individuals than on sharing together the goodness of God.

---

[14]Roy Herndon SteinhoffSmith, *The Mutuality of Care* (St. Louis: Chalice Press, 1999), 13, citing John McKnight, *The Careless Society: Community and its Counterfeits* (New York: Basic Books, 1995), 16.

The pastoral perspective of such preaching often focuses on healing–healing of sin, healing of sickness, healing of despair or isolation. But the healing is inward, pietistic, emphasizing how God "touches me." The preacher pastor attempts to orchestrate an experience of God's healing grace for the individual believer, whether at the altar rail, in private prayer, or within the counseling room. The spotlight shines on the individual sinner, whom the priest will reach out and touch with a healing balm. The repentant sinner can then give testimony to what God has done for "me" while the pastor can tell how God is using him or her as "an instrument" for the other's healing. A certain level of pastoral care is certainly present in such interactions. But it falls far short of the pastoral care of the Christian community as a whole.

Who cares within the sermon based on a theological anthropology of individual sinners in need of personal salvation? The preacher pastor cares, that's who. If a community emerges from such preaching, the pastor will control the care. At least, he or she will control the care until collapsing under the burden of too much pastoral responsibility, too many helpless, individual sinners to care for, and not enough of a pastoral community to care with.

Social Sinners in Need of Justice

Social Liberation

Another theological anthropology that frequently informs pastoral preaching runs in the opposite direction from the one that we have just discussed. Here, preaching defines the human predicament as primarily external, social. The sin that plagues humanity is all bound up in corrupted social existence. Sin is manifested as oppression, racism, sexism, ageism, and classism.[15] Humans are highly determined by external social factors, many of which are seemingly beyond our control for good or ill. Evil is deeply embedded within these social processes and wreaks havoc among the human community. Indeed, we don't have to look beyond the suffering men, women, and children who populate all of our cities and towns to discover how much truth this theological anthropology names.

Based on these anthropological premises, preaching seeks to evoke a caring response within the church on behalf of those who suffer. The caring thing to do is for the church to identify with the poor among us, raise the cry of justice, and seek the welfare of those whom society (and the church) continually use and abuse. We understand this approach to preaching through the categories of liberation, social gospel, and the prophetic. But we should not thereby dismiss the element of pastoral care that is present. Pastoral care, as I have already claimed, seeks social healing and redemption. The impulse is prophetic, but the care is nonetheless real.

---

[15]See Christine M. Smith, *Preaching as Weeping, Confession, and Resistance: Radical Responses to Radical Evil* (Louisville: Westminster/John Knox Press, 1992).

Indeed, many who take this theological position will argue that exclusively individual care is not very caring at all, for without taking care of societal ills we can never develop an environment that will sustain healthy individuals.

Any thinking preacher can see the social dimension of Hebrew and Christian scripture. Those who base pastoral preaching here clearly remind the church of one deep element of our identity. Such sermons are vitally important for the church because they remind us of our founding social vision of the reign of God, a vision that we ignore at the peril of church and world.

Such pastoral prophetic sermons sound something like the following. The preacher is concerned about poverty and hunger within the inner city. She wants to motivate the congregation toward compassionate response.

> You've seen their faces a thousand times. They're standing on the street corners when you drive down Luden Avenue Day and night, children five, ten, twelve years old. They stare with empty eyes as the traffic passes, and you're not sure if it is drugs, or hunger, or abuse, or seeing too much too soon that puts the emptiness there. But there they are, haunting you, reminding you of how far we have to go before the Kingdom comes.
>
> It shouldn't be this way. It doesn't have to be this way. Not if each of us realizes what God is calling us to do—to feed the hungry, visit those in prison, clothe the naked. There is no reason at all that little children, women, and men should go hungry in our city, but they do. Why? Because good Christian folk like us haven't really taken the call of Jesus Christ as far as we should. Be honest. We'd rather talk about following Jesus than get in our cars and drive down there to Luden Avenue and actually follow Jesus.
>
> It's not easy to be a true disciple. I know that. But Jesus says that "those who lose their lives for my sake and the Gospel will find it. And those who would save their lives will lose it." So what about it, Christians? Is each of us willing to be a true disciple, or are we Christians in name only?

For all its persuasive pastoral intent, notice the problems that crop up in this approach. First, pastoral preaching that relies on this social anthropology fosters the same kind of split that occurs within individualistically oriented sermons. Now the problem is outside rather than inside—objective rather than subjective. The forces of evil are all out there running rampant through society—hunger, violence, drugs, and poverty. The task of the caring preacher is to point out the problems, and the task of the caring listener is to move out in faith and take up the causes that call for reform.

This subjective-objective split is heightened in this particular sermon example because it grounds the solution to the social problems within the individual will. Since we are aware of how much suffering goes on in our world, it's time for every person to decide to do something about it. We have to pull ourselves together, take Jesus' call to discipleship more seriously, and get out there in the world and do something for those who are suffering. It's up to every Christian to make this decision as a conscious act of will. How exactly we are supposed to make this choice, the sermon doesn't say.

What this anthropology leaves out is the tragic dimension of all of life. Suffering and injustice don't really seem all that difficult, because if we just make up our minds to face the problems, we can overcome them. In other words, the anthropology runs along the course of liberal optimism, assuming that Christians can participate in progressively making things better. What is lacking is will power. The sermon does not account for any limits on our freedom to act responsibly. As Douglas Hall convincingly argues, theologians throughout the history of the tradition have tended to gravitate to one side of this tension or the other as set forth in the Augustinian-Pelagian, Calvin-Arminian struggles. Hall believes that North American Christianity has gravitated into the Pelagian stream by aligning itself with enlightenment's progressive views of history. It belongs to the official optimism that we are trying to maintain that "tragedy is...an unpleasantness which might have been avoided by better social arrangements and an improved technology."[16] Sin in this anthropology is a failure of will rather than a fundamental flaw within humanity or an unavoidable response to the tragic dimensions of human existence.

Utilitarian Care

As with an individualistic anthropology, the socially oriented sermon imagines care as the act of fixing something or someone. Only this time what needs to be fixed is not the isolated individual, but corrupt society. Our chances are pretty good, the sermon says, of pulling the job off. Sin and suffering apparently do not have any compelling status of their own or any taproots within the world. Sin exists because well-intentioned Christians like us refuse to confront it. Sin exists because we haven't taken seriously enough Jesus' call to discipleship. If we did, we could change the causes of suffering within society. We could throw off the shackles of oppression.

Take another example from a sermon that focuses more specifically on social evil, specifically the violence of ethnic cleansing.

> Did you see the special program last night on the war? The picture on the television screen was horrific. I thought I was watching some horror show until I realized that this was a newscast. There were several bodies lying there dismembered. Dried blood was soaked into the ground. They switched to a couple of women who

---

[16]Douglas John Hall, *Professing the Faith: Christian Theology in a North American Context* (Minneapolis: Fortress Press, 1993), 232, citing Robert Langbaum, *The Gaiety of Vision: A Study of Isak Dinesen's Art* (New York: Random, 1964), 125.

were weeping and wailing, who said that the enemy soldiers had done this. The soldiers had forced them to watch.

It's evil I tell you. It's the power of evil that we are up against. How can the church stand by in the face of such wretched violence? How can we turn our heads when the crucifixion of Christ is happening all over again? When evil is hacking its way through whole groups of people in the name of justice? We dare not turn away. We dare not pretend that this doesn't matter.

For all its truthfulness, something like this in a sermon can overwhelm us. The sermon and the preacher ask us to care, but we don't have a clue about how we can begin to care about such massive atrocities as ethnic cleansing. There is no attempt to explain the reasons for this evil, though presumably it comes from somewhere. It is simply out there and is something that we in the church should fight. For instance, are the ones who are inflicting the evil deeds (them) different from those human beings who do not commit such violent deeds (us)? What will bring about the long-overdue transformation of this evil? Are there degrees of evil that we must meet with various weapons of goodness? If so, where does evil stop and goodness begin? How shall we resist the madness of evil in others if we have not gauged its height and depth within ourselves? Denouncing evil from the pulpit doesn't always help us know how to respond. Defining all social ills as the result of evil in the world doesn't necessarily show us how to care.

Please don't misunderstand. Ethnic cleansing is a social evil of vast proportions. Ethnic warfare in Serbia and Kosovo, Russia and Chechnya, as well as in other places around the world, is an atrocity. But the portrayal of it in the example above suggests a fundamental theological dichotomy between those who are good and those who are evil. The assumption is that Christianity is engaged in spiritual warfare between "us" and "them," usually explained in scriptural terms as "powers and principalities." But notice how easy it is, when we make this theological judgment, to separate human beings into good camps and bad camps. Out there are the evil ones. They live on the other side of town. They sit on the other side of the political aisle. They are the ones who speak a different language or worship a different God. Based on this anthropology, our care becomes selective. We care about those people who are not evil or sinful, at least as we define the terms. This is odd, given that the church proclaims that Jesus arrives to redeem the whole lost bunch of us.

Care as Moral Guidance

Pastoral care in this type of sermon functions as moral guidance of the believer. The normative demands of human existence take priority in the sermon, especially with respect to society. The sermon will guide the hearers in how they ought to live within the world. Usually such sermons are prescriptive. They inform the listeners of what we "must do," how we "should act," what we "ought to be willing to say," how we can "try harder" and "do better." The preacher bases this moral guidance on the aforementioned assumption that what we ought to do we can do. Never mind that most people find it very difficult, if not downright impossible, to do the things we "ought to do" because of the weight of human sin (Rom. 7:13–25).

Often preachers link such sermons to an understanding of Jesus as moral example. Jesus is the moral example who will show us how we ought to live in the face of social sin and suffering. Liberator, administrator, counselor, or teacher, Jesus looks a lot like us. If we embrace the radical love and nature of Jesus, we can overcome our own moral failings and those within society. Human responsibility rates high on the pastoral agenda of such sermons, but the crucified and resurrected Christ does not appear with much frequency or power. Demands are plentiful; the gift of grace is scarce. Jesus is present in these sermons, but usually as the perfect human one whom we are to follow. The sermons are like our children who wear arm bracelets that ask, "What Would Jesus Do?" (WWJD), as if the answer and response are patently obvious, even though the church has been trying for two millennia to do what Jesus would do. The optimism of such preaching wears thin.

Salvation turns out to be something that the church can accomplish on its own. We do not really need the presence of the resurrected Christ. As Christine Smith argues the point in her book *Weaving the Sermon*, "Salvation is something we do with each other in community…our commitment is to love ourselves into wholeness."[17] Such a position claims far more for human community than history would bear out. Most of our attempts to "love one another into wholeness" end in disaster, as far as I can tell, without the redemptive presence of the resurrected Christ. And even then, professing Christ among us by the power of the Holy Spirit, Christians have a hard time loving one another, much less those who are "outside" of the church. Most denominations, my own included, are presumably composed of people who love one another. Yet we are now fragmenting over concerns about homosexuality, abortion, and ordination of women. Loving one another into wholeness turns out to be more complicated than we first imagined. Moral guidance is hard to enact in preaching and pastoral care if we hang our hopes on willfully recreating what Jesus would do. Knowing all the suffering and sin in the world, and knowing how Jesus would respond, does not necessarily move us any closer to doing something about it.

---

[17]Christine M. Smith, *Weaving the Sermon: Preaching in a Feminist Perspective* (Louisville: Westminster/John Knox Press, 1989), 87.

Care without Christ

What is missing here is the power of the resurrected Christ to offer hope to the Christian community. Christian morality cannot be based on liberal or conservative assumptions that we know the right thing to do by following Jesus, our dead hero. This yields a pastoral preaching that expresses that humans have the power within themselves to right all wrongs, correct all self and social deficiencies, and usher in the kingdom of God. We must be wary of the pastoral call to build a better world given all the failed attempts at kingdom building throughout church history. Neo-orthodoxy's rejoinders to liberalism were a much-needed corrective to this shallow optimism within the church. Neither can we capitulate to the despair of passivity that cynically asserts that humans have no responsibility for one another at all–to each his own.

Pastoral preaching should present the resurrected Christ, who alone empowers the church to confront suffering and sin within the church and world. I will develop this claim more fully a little later on in the chapter. But I wish to signal here that a socially oriented anthropology often hangs on Jesus as moral example, a christology that will not be sufficient for the formation of a pastoral community.

Who Cares? The Prophetic Pastor and Weary Disciples

Who cares in such sermons? Pastoral care emerges in these sermons as the activity of the prophetic pastor and a few faithful-but-weary disciples. The sermon sets the pastoral care bar so high that few can attain the standard. Those who do, who take up the challenge to confront social sin with the militant gospel of righteousness, are like long-distance runners panting hard to attain the finish line. The scriptural image in Hebrews of the Christian life as a race does come to mind, except the grace of Christ does not usually buoy up the pastoral care runners in these sermons (Heb. 12:15). Slogging after social justice, without the grace of Christ, the activist clenches his teeth within a humorless jaw and struggles on to care for the downtrodden. As William Muehl puts it, "The reward offered for such self-denial is very often the sense of an onerous duty well done rather than an enriched and deepened experience of God at work in history."[18] In the illustrations above, the preacher knows how to care for those who suffer, and maybe a faithful few catch the vision, but most of the church stands by without knowing how to care. Through its theological anthropology and christology, the sermon consigns most everyone to the care-less role. Most of us simply do not have enough faith, enough will power, or enough compassion to take up the challenge of care. So we sit idly in the pews.

---

[18]William Muehl, *Why Preach? Why Listen?* (Philadelphia: Fortress Press, 1986), 43.

The specter of clericalism haunts this type of pastoral preaching, just as in the individualistic orientation. If anybody cares in the sermon, it is often the pastor returning from a trip to Guatemala, a visit to the AIDS hospice house, or a conference on the environment. She sees what needs to be done in the light of her firsthand experience of social suffering. In telling these stories from the pulpit, she becomes the one who identifies human need and the one who calls us to care. Or maybe the sermon will single out the dedicated effort of a handful of church members somewhere else who are "fighting for immigration rights," signaling that they are the ones who really care. Perhaps the sermon will recount how two or three valiant members of a student organization somewhere take a stand on animal rights. But everyone else is incapable of caring in this courageous fashion. We may not be morally corrupt. Rather, we are weak, timid, and indecisive. The sound of care coming through such sermons has the muffled thump of a few tired drummers marching off into the distance. The action is apparently out there in the field somewhere, but we've forgotten or have never known how to march.

Frequently, preachers will offer negative examples in sermons that tell the congregation how little they really do care. Preachers will use such examples as a form of prophetic challenge to the congregation:

> We've got homeless people sleeping on our sanctuary steps, but we sneak in the back door as if nobody is even home!

> Scattered all across this county are the leaking trailers and windowless houses of migrant workers who are doing the backbreaking and sweaty jobs that you and I wouldn't do. Their kids have nowhere to go to school, and most of them work for far less than minimum wage. But what do we do here at good old First Church? In the name of Jesus, who knew something about alien status, what do we do? We complain because we can't understand what they want when they come into our stores. Heaven forbid if these aliens should come into the church!

There is a time and place for such challenges of a complacent congregation. We intend for these direct statements to pierce the slumbering conscience of the congregation, to goad them into action. But we should be cautious about this approach.

For one thing, constant prophetic harangues from the pulpit will rarely create the desired response, at least not for the long haul. They begin to sound like the scolding parent who may force the child to pick up his or her room occasionally, but mostly the child learns to ignore the verbal chastisement. More than one layperson has joked after a preacher's prophetic diatribe, "Oh, he does that every now and then. He'll get over it." The fault does not reside with the hearer alone.

But more importantly, these negative examples tell the listener that the preacher is actually in charge of the pastoral care, social or personal. The preacher is the one who spots the problem, so the preacher is the one who will come up with some solutions, if there are any. The pastor apparently has some unending reservoir of care and compassion and can do the job better than all the rest of us, so why bother? The use of negative examples in prophetic preaching cuts both ways: It may stir the slumbering congregation or it may create resistance and reinforce the status quo. If the latter occurs, the preacher has only succeeded in buttressing that which she hoped to overturn. A hundred sermons later, the care-less, as the preacher sees them, remain care-less.

Basing pastoral preaching on a theological anthropology that defines humanity in exclusively social terms will probably not result in the kind of pastoral community outlined in the second chapter. We will offer hospitality begrudgingly, perhaps in response to the prodding of the preacher. Mutuality will be elusive, since the pastor and an avant-garde of the faithful control the terms of care. Our compassion for others within the community will bear the ruthless marks of legal obligation or of guilt-reducing works-righteousness. We may even wind up using others in society to fulfill our own compulsive need to care. Our care for the world will not ring true.

So let's consider an alternative theological anthropology that can inform pastoral preaching, one that attempts to avoid a strictly individualistic orientation on the one hand and an exclusively social orientation on the other. There does seem to be a distinctive way of understanding humanity redeemed by Christ that will help our preaching build up caring communities. We will explore this in a little more detail than the previous anthropologies, since I hope that these suggestions will offer some depth of insight for those who preach regularly and carefully.

People Who Care as God Cares

Theological Anthropology

Any attempt to isolate one element within theology is a lot like pulling on the proverbial ball of yarn: The whole thing comes unraveled. One cannot progress far into Christian anthropology without also addressing the other doctrines of God—creation, christology, incarnation, atonement, Holy Spirit, revelation, ecclesiology, and missions.

But we begin with theological anthropology because the human being before God is the primary concern of pastoral care and pastoral theology. For Christian believers today, God is not, as with the medieval theologians, the first cause of the natural order, but "inevitably presupposed in every act of human existence."[19] Though God originates humanity and creation,

---

[19]Wolfhart Pannenberg, *Anthropology in Theological Perspective,* trans. Matthew J. O'Connell (Philadelphia: Westminster Press, 1985), 12.

failure to take anthropology seriously makes our defense of God impossible.[20] We cannot erase, even if we wished to, the enormous contributions of the natural and social sciences to our understanding of the human person (biological, social scientific, psychological, historical). Hence, theology constantly returns to human experience and context in an attempt to correlate theological tradition and nontheological anthropological discovery.[21] Not surprisingly, and germane for our purposes, from pastoral theology we hear the insistent appeal to deepen our understanding of the human person, the central concern of pastoral care. But the reflections on theological anthropology that follow will necessarily touch on the other doctrines as well, sometimes, as John Douglas Hall notes when considering the Trinity, "willy nilly into soteriology, ecclesiology, ethics, eschatology— in short the entire 'story.'"[22] We will look at anthropology through several categories that theologians generally recognize as central to the task.

Human Nature and Sin

We are concerned about the human person within the congregation when we preach from a pastoral perspective. The pastoral sermon grows out of and speaks to the lives of the real persons within the congregation. Dietrich Bonhoeffer reminds the students at Finkenwalde that "just as the sermon grows heavily out of the pastor's work among the congregation, it also provides opportunity for work among the congregation to be developed out of it."[23] The preacher does not speak to generalized humanity but to particular persons in a particular time and place. We do not preach among isolated individuals with strictly personal needs but among people with whom we share an embeddedness in the wide world of families, congregations, communities, and nations. All these resources come to bear upon the preacher pastor's understanding of persons.

However, a plethora of nontheological wisdom (psychological, political, sociological, biological) often confuses our theological understandings of the human person. Preachers hold implicitly in mind some conglomerate view of the human person, "working doctrines" that function hermeneutically on our understanding of scripture, the situation of the community in the world, and the personal needs within the congregation. We want to minimize confusion and to deepen the pastoral dimension of

[20]Pannenberg's critique of Barth is insightful on this point. The theology of Barth "disdained to take a position on the terrain of anthropology and argue there that the religious thematic is unavoidable. As a result, it was defenseless against the suspicion that its faith was something arbitrarily legislated by human beings. As a result, its very *rejection* of anthropology was a form of *dependence* on anthropological suppositions. That is, when Barth, instead of justifying his position, simply decided to begin with God himself, he unwittingly adopted the most extreme form of theological subjectivism," *Anthropology in Theological Perspective,* 16.

[21]See David Tracy, *Blessed Rage for Order* (New York: Seabury, 1975).

[22]Hall, *Professing the Faith,* 164.

[23]Dietrich Bonhoeffer, *Worldly Preaching: Lectures on Homiletics,* ed. Clyde E. Fant (New York: Crossroads, 1991), 147.

the sermon. Therefore, preaching as a pastoral theological endeavor should be acutely aware of its own theological anthropology as it seeks to address the congregation.

A lack of clarity on this matter hamstrings the pastoral element of many sermons. For example, a socially oriented sermon can be weakened by the very anthropological claim that the preacher wants to make. Namely, preachers often argue for authentic (intimate and just) human relationship as the goal of preaching. They want the hearers to participate with them in the transformation of evil in the world into more just and loving human community. But they fail to show that this just and loving community is rooted in the image of God. In other words, to say in our preaching that just human relations is a good thing needs some kind of theological backing. We can't just toss out the statement in a sermon or show through a story that everybody should live together in mutuality. The sermon, without resorting to theological pedantry, must briefly indicate why mutality is the way of human beings in the world. Namely, because *God* makes us this way even though we spend a lot of time in friendships, with coworkers, spouses, and partners denying mutuality at every turn.

Next, we cannot make the claim for mutuality within community without being aware of that which thwarts it, specifically sin. The image of God is deeply distorted within human nature and relationships. This has nothing to do with our bodies, per se. For example, a child born with serious brain damage may reflect as much of the image of God as a child without such damage. Both are actually distortions of true humanity, not because of the body and its abilities, but because of the pervasiveness of sin within all creation. A fair amount of individualistic and socially oriented preaching simply ignores how sinfully distorted human nature is. So we get a lot of sermons that talk about how much we can each do if we just "try harder," or how we could overcome racism if we all "just got together."

Pastors preach among persons who are not simply choosing to live in disobedience to God, but whose lives are broken mirrors that only dimly reflect the image of God—not substantially, but relationally. Distortion of the human relationship with God is both act and condition, not because of any particular inferiority of human capacity—will, intellect, emotion (the essentialist argument)—but because we are bound by brokenness. At root, a certain tragic condition constitutes the human situation. Born into a situation that offers human freedom yet imposes limitation, we cannot help but respond out of our anxiety with idolatrous attempts to secure the self.[24] We do not have to accept Augustinian "concupiscence" as the biological transmission of sin that lays blame at the feet of women in order to grasp the power of sin within the tradition. We may even say that sin is not "original," at least in classical theological terms, but it is surely unavoidable.

---

[24]See Edward Farley, *Good and Evil: Interpreting a Human Condition* (Minneapolis: Fortress Press, 1990), chap. 6.

As Dorothee Sölle states the tension within the tradition between sin as act and sin as condition, "Sin is certainly my decision, my free will, my 'no' to God, but it is also the destiny into which I was born."[25]

The pastoral preacher will not be easily fooled into a shallow, optimistic read on human nature. Some socially oriented preaching derides the evil of humanity and then posits human response without acknowledging the depth of depravity that remains a part of the solutions. In the end, the care that emerges from such a homiletic will often have to address the unanticipated consequence of despair as persons flounder in their own inability to restore the image of God within the congregation and world.

Similarly, an individualistically based anthropology becomes overly optimistic. We human beings will somehow discover on our own the possibility of salvation as the antidote to human isolation (sin). This pietistic read of the human predicament suggests that each individual need only embrace an attitude of contrition or praise to slough off sin. But how we find such contrition or praise is detached from the struggle against sin.

Feminist and other liberationist approaches to preaching do help the preacher pastor affirm the relationality of human persons before God and with each other. As Letty Russell articulates so succinctly, we are created by God for one another (Genesis 1–2), not "lonesome but twosome."[26] This is precisely where feminist theology and other liberation perspectives turn to essentialist arguments about the human being even as they argue for the contextual factors that shape the human being. As Christine Smith claims, "Relatedness and attachment are at the heart and center of women's development and mode of being."[27] Such a claim, with which I agree if we extend it to include men, is that we are *essentially* created for each other. "Authentic humanity is humanity in relationship with the other" and "being means being with."[28] Preacher pastors work within a web of mutual interdependence that is sustained by and reflective of the divine human relationship. Pastoral preaching will seek to strengthen the threads within the web not simply by guiding the congregation into transformative action in the world but by sustaining and healing the congregation in its sinfulness and broken relationships.[29]

---

[25]Dorothee Sölle, *Thinking About God: An Introduction to Theology,* trans. John Bowden (London: S. C. M., 1990), 55.

[26]Letty Russell, *Human Liberation in a Feminist Perspective–A Theology* (Philadelphia: Westminster Press, 1974), 152.

[27]Christine M. Smith, *Weaving the Sermon,* 27.

[28]Hall, *Professing the Faith,* 321, 325.

[29]From psychology, object relations theory offers helpful dialogue with theology at the point of relationality as generative of religious sentiment and imagination. See Ana-Maria Rizutto, *The Birth of the Living God* (Chicago: University of Chicago, 1979); and Paul Pruyser's interpretation of D. W. Winnicott in *The Play of the Imagination* (New York: International Univ., 1983).

Douglas John Hall calls this essential relatedness of the person an "ontology of communion" in contrast to various existential ontologies that posit an isolated individual or a human being who is somehow hierarchically superior to the rest of God's creation.[30] We have seen how an existentialist anthropology bends the sermon inward as the preacher pastor addresses the private hurts of the individual in the pew. Yet our creaturehood consists of communion. Our sin is both our choosing and our being unable not to choose otherwise to live in broken communion. This disordering of relationships, what some would call radical evil, is what the tradition has meant by the fall. It is the human being who "alone can sin," but it is the entire creation that bears the scars of sin.[31]

Ed Farley, in a thorough explication of anthropology, claims that the sphere of the *interhuman* is the primary sphere of humanity. The interhuman designates that persons share fundamental relatedness. The human being is neither an autonomous individual (an enlightenment construct) nor a conglomeration of social influences (the organic and behaviorist model). Rather, human beings are marked from birth onward by relationality, interdependence. The term interhuman "describes a sphere of face to face relation or being-together in relation."[32] Being-together in relation permeates all other spheres of life, the personal and the social.

It is this interpersonal dimension of human beings that makes possible both the virtues and vices of human living. Compassion for the other, responsiveness to the needs of the other (hospitality), even surrender on behalf of the other all point toward the interhuman as the basic anthropological category. Likewise, suffering emerges from within the interhuman, either in benign or malignant forms, for suffering depends upon the presence of an other whose very relatedness to the self is both threat and promise. Malignant forms of suffering (evil) result from gross violations of the other and occur throughout the three spheres of human existence (the personal, the interhuman, the social). For Farley, evil has no ontological status. It is a response to the tragic situation of humanity as human beings in relation strive for security and elevate self or other things to the status of ultimate power, thereby victimizing others.[33] Evil deeds by individual agents become systematized within social institutions, just as social institutions that run awry spawn individuals who act malevolently.

Such an understanding of human nature and sin accounts for the bureaucratization of evil that socially oriented preaching wishes to counter. We have noted, however, that such preaching often poses an optimistic

---

[30]Hall, *Professing the Faith,* 73ff.
[31]Rosemary Radford Ruether, *Sexism and God-Talk* (Boston: Beacon, 1983), 88, cited in Hall, *Professing the Faith,* 322.
[32]Farley, *Good and Evil,* 33.
[33]I am following Farley in *Good and Evil,* esp. chaps. 1, 14.

solution to various social evils. This inadvertently bypasses the interhuman sphere wherein lies the possibility for redemption.[34]

On the other hand, an individualistic anthropology claims that the individual alone needs correction. It isn't clear just how the individual's healing is related to the health of the social world or to interpersonal relations. In Farley's analysis, the interhuman offers a central category that repairs the split in theological anthropology between the personal and social, subjective and objective that undermines many pastoral sermons. Bear in mind that the interhuman does not deny the personal or the social but weaves through them both. It is similar to what I think Jacquelyn Grant means when she refers to the African American saying, "I am because we are."[35] The *I* of the self is always based in the community that gives the self its identity. Robert Webber and Rodney Clapp make a similar point. "We *become* personal in relation to others...It is impossible to communicate and care if there are no others outside the self."[36] Admittedly the construct is elusive, and Farley's work is philosophically technical, but he suggests for preaching and pastoral care a way of understanding the human being that can refocus our answers to the questions, To whom are we preaching? Who cares?

Pastoral preaching that begins with these theological understandings of persons in communion with God, each other, and the created order, yet recognizes our distortion of this communion (sin), will open up avenues for pastoral care that begins among the people as community and moves outward from there toward care for God's creation. With respect to human nature, pastoral preaching will affirm our creaturehood, tragic yet redeemable. Whenever God's care for all creation springs fresh from the pulpit, persons will find strength for caring in the world. Preaching that focuses exclusively on the radical evil within the world gives too much power over to sin itself. This is one reason that, for all their vividness, some socially oriented sermons leave us passionless. The language of the sermon remains so focused on evil that nothing is left of the God-relatedness within humanity to confront the evil. I am not talking about the need to preach "positive thinking" or false optimism. Proclaiming the goodness of creaturehood does not mean refusal to confront sin in its many guises. Nor does it mean a retreat in Christian worship into the beauty of sacred aesthetics. Rather, proclaiming creaturehood asserts humanity's grateful dependence on the God of creation in whom we find our identity and purpose. For at the core of our humanity is God's goodness and our

---

[34]Farley states that "redemption originates in the sphere of the interhuman and is promoted by face-to-face communities," ibid., 282.

[35]Jacquelyn Grant, "Faithful Resistance Risking It All: From Expedience to Radical Obedience," in *Women: To Preach or Not to Preach,* ed. Ella Pearson Mitchell (Valley Forge, Pa.: Judson Press, 1991), 107.

[36]Webber and Clapp, *People of the Truth,* 11.

creaturehood. "To be a creature, to know oneself to be a creature, and to be glad in one's creaturehood: this comes close to the heart of the matter, for Christians."[37] In our embrace of suffering humanity, we dare not lose sight of the God who is not only with but also above humanity. As this past century's pastoral care tradition has insisted, *God is with humanity. But—God is not humanity.* To the contrary, God the Creator also stands over against humanity as judge and redeemer.[38] We cannot master ourselves, as much as certain psychological and social scientific paradigms would argue otherwise. That's good. For our humanity—in the image of God though laden with sin—we can express gratitude in preaching and pastoral care.

Perhaps an example of this kind of theological anthropology will help. In the movie *The Spitfire Grill,* the central character, Percy Talbot, is a young woman who is an ex-convict.[39] After release from prison, she shows up in the small town of Gilead, Maine, where she is hired as a waitress at the Spitfire Grill. The Grill stands at the center of this rural community, and much of the movie explores how the small township learns to accept Percy, the outsider. But one member of the community, Nahum Goddard, simply does not trust Percy. He is suspicious of her at every turn. Eventually, he sets up a plan to trap her in deceit so that she can be lawfully removed from the community. The plan runs awry, and Percy drowns in an accident.

The climactic scene occurs at the funeral. The sheriff presides, functioning as an unofficial lay pastor within the community. He asks if anyone would like to say something about Percy. Nahum, who is indirectly responsible for Percy's death, comes forward to speak. He confesses his sin and guilt to the entire community. And then he says, "I never knew Percy Talbot. I only thought I did. I thought she was a stranger that would bring no good to my aunt, to my family, and to this town...I thought I knew Percy Talbot, but I was wrong as wrong can be. I never knew Percy Talbot."

The scene dramatizes how integrally related every member of the community is; it is a "community of the face." The guilty member of the community does not make his confession privately to a pastor, a counselor, or a law enforcement officer. He confesses to the community as a whole. He confesses both the sin of not knowing his own relatedness to another human being and what that sin causes him to do. But in the confession he affirms the central relatedness of the community. Though broken, they remain in communion. It is no accident that the confession occurs within the church, although the service is not presided over by an official priest. The movie, as I understand it, illuminates what we mean as Christians when we claim to be members of Christ's body, broken yet reconciled by

---

[37]Hall, *Professing the Faith,* 337.
[38]Pamela D. Couture and Richard Hester, "The Future of Pastoral Care and Counseling and the God of the Market," in *Pastoral Care and Social Conflict,* ed. Pamela Couture and Rodney Hunter (Nashville: Abingdon Press, 1995), 52.
[39]*The Spitfire Grill,* Castle Rock Entertainment, 1996.

Christ to one another. Though sin gnaws away at our communion, in Christ we find reconciliation with God and one another. This is always a gift of God's grace, often experienced after confession and repentance. This is the kind of relational anthropology that can helpfully support our pastoral preaching.

Human Responsibility and the Grace of God

Pastoral preaching both forms *and* transforms the people of God in the world. As transformative, pastoral preaching does address the ethical demands of Christian discipleship. There is a guiding function to pastoral preaching as it focuses the life of the community on witness and service. No clear lines of demarcation separate the pastoral and prophetic within preaching. Preachers worthy of their salt will regularly find themselves asking God, the scriptures, the community, and the tradition's best thinkers, So what should we do? What should we do about a society that rushes headlong toward class warfare in the name of free enterprise? How can and ought we respond when the government reduces food and rent subsidies for our poorest women and children while many of our disenfranchised minority men kill one another in the streets trying to get a piece of some kind of action? What must these people in this congregation do whenever we discover sexual abuse or woman battering right here among us? What ought we to do when every couple of weeks someone in our society goes on a shooting rampage to intentionally kill innocent persons? Cries do sound night and day, and Christians should have a voice with which to respond in the name of God. The preacher pastor who is unable to speak with clarity about the reality of human need most certainly will, even if naively, give his or her imprimatur to unchecked human suffering. Preaching transforms the church again and again for responsible witness in the world.

Christian faith, if we take seriously the foregoing discussion on creation and sin, presupposes that "the world nor we ourselves have to be as we are."[40] Our goodness as God's creatures, just as our fallenness within creation, assumes that God desires more. If the world is not good, why "would God bother to redeem it?" And if the creation is not fallen, why "would God *need* to redeem it?"[41] The question is, given God's desire for redemption of humanity and all creation, what is our responsibility (vocation)? Preachers with pastoral concern want to help the congregation puzzle out an answer to the basic question, What are people for? As people of God, what is our human responsibility to participate in God's purposes for creation, a creation that will not return to original goodness but that moves toward something better in the eschaton?

---

[40]Hall, *Professing the Faith,* 239.
[41]Ibid.

Douglas Hall argues correctly, I believe, for recovery of the biblical metaphor of stewardship to designate the participation of the human being with God in creation. Against others who see the metaphor as hierarchical, implying forceful dominion, Hall poses a covenant-partnership understanding of stewardship (from Genesis 3 but also throughout the tradition).[42] Letty Russell is moving in this same theological direction when she claims that "partnership" names the relationship between God and humanity.[43] "Dominion" in Genesis 1 doesn't mean domination but *preservation* of that part of creation, the earthly domain, where humans dwell.

The problem is that humans choose self-preservation over preservation of the creation and thereby engage in "anticreational" activity that destroys partnership with God. Like Tom Wolfe's character Sherman McCoy in *Bonfire of the Vanities,* we attempt to be "masters of the universe."[44] Assuming mastery over the world, humanity unleashes powerful forces of evil and destruction. So when we assess in faith humanity's inhumanity, we are led to the very question that much liberation preaching wants to answer: What ought we (can we) do now?

It is here that we cannot dismiss preaching and pastoral care's normative concerns. But it is also here that an inadequate theological anthropology will create problems for preacher and congregation. The obvious answers are the ones that have riddled theological tradition throughout church history. One side says the steward can no longer do anything at all within creation, so preaching and pastoral care resorts to groping for restoration on the ladder of spiritual hierarchy, or in psychological parlance, "self-actualization." As I have already stated, sometimes we characterize such views as naively optimistic, but the underside of self-actualization psychology is deeply pessimistic about change within the social order, and so it turns inward to seek some dollop of happiness. On the other side, the social one, once convicted and repentant of sin we take up the banner of activism to purge the world of the evil that we (or often "they") have unleashed. These are the tensions of humanity often characterized as pessimism or optimism and within which preaching and pastoral care wants to offer some guidance for the believer's responsibility in the world.

My caution for pastoral preachers is that often we swing back and forth between these positions on human responsibility without ever admitting that some kind of solution is needed to address the tension. Hence, we condemn evil with a strong call to action. Yet we offer nothing more than a paean to human solidarity to confront evil. Care under such conditions may lead the church to collapse under the weight of its own

---

[42]For a feminist critique of "stewardship" see Mary Ann Hinsdale, "Heeding the Voices," in *In the Embrace of God: Feminist Approaches to Theological Anthropology,* ed. Ann O'Hara Graff (Maryknoll, N.Y.: Orbis, 1995), esp. 25–31.

[43]Russell, *The Future of Partnership.*

[44]Tom Wolfe, *Bonfire of the Vanities* (New York: Farrar Straus & Giroux, 1987).

busyness and the inadequacy of its theological anthropology. On the other hand, in existentialist preaching we sometimes assume that personal salvation from brokenness comes to us in the midst of life crises. But who knows from where? Such a theological anthropology places a tremendous burden on the individual for self-healing. The scope of salvation narrows down to the psychic struggle of the believer.

But preaching that affirms the world, and that pastorally guides human responsibility (care) in the world, speaks of the real world, not a utopia. It embraces a world where wheat and tares grow up together, where light and darkness struggle together (Mt. 13:25–40). Such affirmation is only possible, finally, through faith engendered by the grace of Christ. The only way for us to respond to the needs of humanity without perpetuating destruction is through the transformative grace of God offered in Christ. Preaching that jumps too quickly to a plan of action, on the one hand, or never risks requiring any action at all, on the other, is preaching untouched by the grace of the crucified and resurrected Jesus; it is unable to offer the fullness of Christian care. Caring Christians seek not only personal health but the healing of creation, not only social reconciliation but interpersonal forgiveness, not only individual spiritual guidance but communal vision.

It is God's gift of divine grace to human creation through the death and resurrection of Christ that makes human responsibility possible. In Christ, we know what we "ought" to do, and we find the wherewithal to do it. Jesus Christ, God's care for the world, makes possible the human resistance to evil that pastoral preaching proclaims in its guiding function.

The purpose of human beings is the realization of just and loving community with God and one another. The final reign of God beckons the Christian forward. Wherever sin and evil reign, communion does not exist. And wherever persons fail to praise God, Christian community is absent. But communion is offered in and through the God who comes near in Jesus Christ. This is God's choice, not our own. The otherness of God should not be sacrificed to an undialectical immanence that informs liberationist preaching nor to a personal piety that undergirds individualistic preaching. Much pastoral preaching that seeks to express care errs in either of these directions. The homiletic expression of this undialectical immanence often comes out as over-identification by the pastor with the congregation, or the devolution of narrative preaching into sermons as autobiography. Just "being yourself" in the pulpit, while pretending to gain listener contact, gets preachers into all sorts of trouble.

Preaching that nurtures care for creation needs the Christ of God who saves us, not for heaven, but for creaturehood. Since the God who creates is the God who saves, God through Christ frees us not from but *for* the world. We must reckon with this Christ in pastoral preaching. Pastoral preachers will necessarily reexamine sermons for their christological content. For in the Christian preaching tradition, Christ is the bearer of grace that makes human responsibility possible.

Just who Jesus Christ is and how he is present for the believing community is of course the question that has exercised theology from the early church on. Shall we begin with the identity of Jesus and then move to his effect on humanity? Or do we start with Christ's effects on humanity and then move to the identity of Jesus?[45] It is clearly the latter that has informed contemporary theology and preaching, whether conservative or liberal. The human problematic frames the theological response. That is, christology ascends from below. The other option, of course, is acceptance of Barth's early insistence on a descending christology that defines the human problem.[46] Yet there is no way, this side of the Enlightenment, to return to a literal reading of scripture and a dogmatic reassertion of the historicity of Jesus' identity as "the Christ" as the key to christology. We will continue to define Jesus in relation to humanity, though not necessarily as a self-constructed answer to individual or communal need.[47] Jesus Christ is clearly more than our own best representations of self (the liberal construal, Jesus as moral example). Christ does stand over against us even while standing with us. But an alien Christ who is always and forever other than us has no more power to save than a Jesus made in our own image. The real problem with much pastoral preaching is not the beginning point in human need, but the fact that our sermons have no christology to define and respond to human need.

Pastoral preachers always have in mind some construal of the human situation in relation to Jesus Christ. The sermon would not be pastoral, that is caring, without it. The Christ who addresses the human situation through the sermon and by the work of the Holy Spirit does so not as a Jesus of Nazareth stepping out of the pages of scripture to take up our causes or calm our anxieties. Neither does the sermon simply retell the story of Jesus to rewrite the hearers into the script of God, as if God's script can be cleanly presented unsoiled by human interpretation.[48] No, Jesus

---

[45]For a succinct summary of the issues, see Walter Lowe, "Christ and Salvation," in *Christian Theology: An Introduction to Its Traditions and Tasks,* ed. Peter C. Hodgson and Robert H. King (Minneapolis: Fortress Press, 1994), 222–48.

[46]This direction is now receiving renewed attention in homiletics through the work of Charles Campbell, building upon Hans W. Frei, *Preaching Jesus: New Directions for Homiletics in Hans Frei's Postliberal Theology* (Grand Rapids: Eerdman's, 1997), especally pp. 39–40, 60–61.

[47]David Buttrick observes, "There is no such thing as a pure, disembodied gospel free from the taint of cultural influence. Because we must speak the gospel in language, it is always entagled in all kinds of cultural assumptions...The gospel is always spoken to the mind of a particular age," *Preaching Jesus Christ* (Philadelphia: Fortress Press, 1988), 26.

[48]For critique of this direction in narrative preaching, articulated by Charles Campbell, see David J. Lose, "Narrative and Proclamation," in *Papers of the Annual Meeting of the Academy of Homiletics* (Oakland, Dec. 4–6, 1997), 22–45.

Christ becomes mysteriously present to the worshiping congregation by the power of the Holy Spirit through word and sacrament. Despite our discomfort with the idea, God does not depend on our literal, figural, mythical, or symbolic reading of the scripture to show up in the world. How we read scripture is an important consideration for every generation. Hermeneutics is here to stay. But the truth of the matter is that God in Christ, precisely because of being *extra nos*, does not wait around for us to find the key to unlock the doors of scriptural interpretation. We will not find security in biblical interpretation any more than in a well-adjusted self. Thank God. Mysteriously, Jesus Christ present to church and world is the "presence of God–in God's own freedom."[49] We heed the words of Bonhoeffer, audacious as they seem, that "the proclaimed Christ is the real Christ."[50] Because God is in Christ through the preached word, God, whose ways are grace-full, addresses human need. But because God who is in Jesus Christ is God, this One will not be limited or determined by our human need. Pastoral preaching can't help but speak of Christ to human need, and it can't help but speak of human need before God. When the human community knows itself as known by God in Christ, it enters responsibly into the free exercise of caring for others.

What are people for? The preacher who cares will hear the question with the same seriousness that she will reply: "People are for caring for each other in the world by the grace of God in Jesus Christ."

Freedom and Limitation

Preachers who attend to the pastoral dimension of the sermon help form a congregation whose members live faithfully within the paradoxical nature of human personhood–between freedom and limits. A caring preacher pastor will in sermon and pastoral care enjoin the hearers to explore the outer reaches of their freedom through responsible use of their own gifts of ministry on behalf of the world. Liberation of the self within community and the community within the world is not too grand a hope; indeed, the whole creation, awaiting freedom, groans like a mother giving birth (Rom. 8:19–23). From whatever bondage enslaves the people of God in the world (psychological, economic, ecclesiastical, biological, political), Christ offers freedom ("For freedom Christ has set us free" [Gal. 5:1]). "The promise of Christian salvation is the hope of being set free not simply from inner compulsions–error, depression, binding fantasies, and foolishness–which are problems enough, but of liberation from the systems, social attitudes, customs, and oppressions that hold us captive."[51] Freedom

[49]Lowe, "Christ and Salvation," 247.
[50]Dietrich Bonhoeffer, *Christ the Center*, with an introduction by Edwin H. Robertson, trans. John Bowden (New York: Harper & Row, 1960), 46.
[51]David Buttrick, *A Captive Voice* (Louisville: Westminster/John Knox Press, 1994), 109.

moves us toward health (salvation) and away from sickness (sin). Preaching that liberates is preaching that heals and reconciles.

Yet care-full preachers know the other dimension of the human person, the limits of freedom. Movement toward freedom sometimes results in further bondage. Witness the snares of poverty within the African American community even as some African Americans gain greater political and economic freedom. Persons can seemingly become healthy spiritually and emotionally while becoming sick physically. Witness some persons with terminal illnesses.[52] Unfettered freedom is finally nonhuman. We cannot, Icarus-like, soar to the sun. We are bounded by finitude, and within these bounds we learn to live in love and seek human justice. This much seems to be the actual dimensions of human persons among whom the preacher speaks.

The problem is that into our boundedness and freedom, as already discussed, enters sin. Preacher pastors who are theologically aware cannot care for long without discovering, as Dorothee Sölle so aptly phrases it, that "people are somehow wrong right through."[53] We are neither fully free nor fully secure within our limits. So we seek to free and secure ourselves. We forget that the possibility for final consummation does not lie within the creature but within the Creator. We seek to secure our existence against the tragic vulnerabilities of life itself; in short, we sin. The Hebrews and the Reformers, especially in the Calvinist tradition, called it idolatry.

Therefore, preachers who care will want to de-center the congregation from itself and re-center the congregation in Christ, where the paradox of humanity coheres. Pastoral preaching will lovingly challenge the church's attempts at securing identity through ratcheting up church programs, membership drives, entertainment worship, and hodgepodge social crusades. Self-adjustment preaching will not do. Neither will the pounding rhetoric of *ought* and *should* that funds moralistic preaching. Preaching will care-fully uphold the freedom and limits of human personhood that can only be redeemed by the God in human flesh—Jesus Christ, who is both fully free yet humanly bound. As Douglas Hall says, "Jesus saves us from the awful habit we have of saving ourselves."[54]

Once we get that straight, and preaching pastorally will do everything possible to accomplish that, we can lay hold of Christian freedom in care for the world. We preach, not to instill pessimism over human caughtness, but rather so that we may recognize Christ as the source of human freedom. Christian proclamation is not just for individual comfort nor solely for raising human cries from the margin. It penetrates into the ambiguities of

---

[52]For an insightful description of illness that elaborates this paradox, see Arthur W. Frank, *At the Will of the Body: Reflections on Illness* (Boston: Houghton Mifflin, 1991).

[53]Sölle, *Thinking About God,* 56.

[54]Hall, *Professing the Faith,* 552.

the human persons in community, who need and give God's care. We do not, as Luther reminds us, "preach to people who are perfectly whole or hopelessly corrupt, but only to those who are being healed or getting sick."[55] Luther, like Paul before him, insists that we are paradoxically sinners who are justified. Open-eyed honesty from the pulpit about our freedom and limits may be one of the most caring things a preacher pastor can do. For this may help us realize that God's care is the only real basis for our care in the world.

Preaching among the People Who Care

So how does this theological anthropology actually impact our pastoral preaching? What difference will this sort of theological anthropology make in the sermon, in the way we handle scripture, in the choice of stories, images, and symbols that constitute the sermon?

Our Togetherness in God

For starters, we have to find a way for our sermons to address our togetherness in God, Jesus Christ, and the Holy Spirit, rather than our isolation. To whom do we preach? Not to the lonely individual nor to the nameless crowd. As preachers we do not ask, What does the text say to me? or even, What does the text say to me as a representative human being? but, What is the text saying to *our* faith-consciousness?[56] This is no easy task, because in preaching, especially in pastoral preaching, we usually center on individuals with personal problems or triumphs whom we intend for our sermons to address. Yet we have already explored the many pitfalls of such an approach. First and foremost, we want to preach to the relatedness of the gathered body of the congregation, our communal identity that is given by Christ.

Barbara Brown Taylor insightfully explores the need to preach out of and toward a more relational anthropology.

> One thing I notice when I listen to sermons—including my own—is how often they treat a congregation like a collection of individuals, addressing individual behavior, individual faith, individual fears…[But] our business is relationship, which does not stop with relating individuals to God. Our good news is that God has related us to one another and that the least act of love has infinite consequences. We are one body, whether we act like it or not… What if we could, through our preaching, support that sense of belonging to a body that is more than its parts, that has a life and a purpose of its own, in which people do not feel like individual atoms but like members of a whole?…This shift of perspective

---

[55]Richard Lischer, "Luther and Contemporary Preaching: Narrative and Anthropology," *Scottish Journal of Theology* 36 (1983): 500.
[56]Buttrick, *Homiletic*, 277

will take place first in the mind of the preacher, who will begin to notice the personality of the congregation as something more than the personalities in the congregation…Based on what you see when you observe these things, you may begin to offer the congregation images of themselves in community—not a collection of individuals but a body with a word to say and a job to do.[57]

The challenge, as Taylor recognizes, is to develop pastoral sermons that in image and story present the congregation as an interrelated body. In the final chapter, we will see an example of how Taylor does this in her own preaching. Unaccustomed to preaching in this fashion, the preacher must consciously strive to make a shift in the anthropological perspective. Sermons will help the congregation see themselves as a people, a body, the way God sees them.

To be even more specific, stories and examples in our sermons should focus more on human beings together before God and less on individual and personal experiences of God. If we believe that the human person is "not lonesome but twosome,"[58] our sermons will give priority to those events, scenes, and symbols of human experience and scripture that present us in our togetherness rather than our aloneness. The constitutive imagery of the sermon will revolve around the mutuality, hospitality, and compassion of the pastoral community. Obviously, we will avoid sermons that, under the guise of therapeutic concern, take us on journeys of psychic self-exploration (of preacher or member). Personal dreams, a favored sermonic content of some preachers, are probably not helpful and are rarely meaningful except to the one who relates them. We need to root out individual epiphanies that seem to crop up like weeds in today's preaching (I stand guilty with all the rest) and sow anew the sermon with revelatory moments of God among *us*. Preachers will be cautious about intruding themselves too much into the story of God with *us*. We can usually recast accounts of how *one* person overcomes adversity or how *an* individual encounters God's healing.

For example, take this story that focuses on an individual who overcomes a tragedy.

It had been months since he had set a foot upon the ground. Lying there in the hospital bed for weeks on end, he had had all the time in the world to think about what really mattered. The wreck had left him unconscious and drugged for days. A blessing, too, because his legs were a twisted mess. When he finally came around, and the pain began to subside, the odd thought struck him that this

---

[57]Barbara Brown Taylor, "Preaching Into the Next Millennium," in *Exilic Preaching: Testimony for Christian Exiles in an Increasingly Hostile Culture,* ed. Erskine Clarke (Harrisburg, Pa.: Trinity Press International, 1998), 95–97.

[58]Russell, *Human Liberation in a Feminist Perspective,* 152.

was what everybody at church meant about faith. It is the ability to hang on, to believe that there is some reason, God knows why, not to succumb to the meaninglessness of it all, not to put his pain off on God or anybody else, but to grapple with how all the pieces fit together. When he finally hobbled out of that hospital, and took the first barefooted steps upon the good, green earth, a lump caught in his throat. He could feel it coming and couldn't stop it. Like Lazarus back from the dead, he croaked, "Thank you, God. Thank you."

Notice that the story unfolds out of the interior experience of the individual as he wrestles with God and life. As listeners we learn what it feels like for this individual to recover from a tragic accident. We know his inner thoughts. We hear how out of the tragedy he comes to renewed faith in God.

But we could set the story up from another angle, with a different anthropology, introduce a few more characters, and achieve a different perspective. For example,

People hovered around his bedside day and night after that gruesome accident. "It was a miracle he survived," they said. Even though he was mostly unconscious for days, they kept coming by to sit with him. They were, as one of the old-timers said, "Praying him through." His parents, church members, even the guy from the emergency squad who got to him first, would come by and watch him breathe, hold his and each other's hands. Even though he didn't respond, they would call his name. The hospital staff didn't seem to mind their being there. The nurses helped eat up all the peanut butter cookies (his favorite) that he was too sick to eat, and that kind of helped those hospital people get through their job. It was touch and go for quite a while, and they weren't sure whether they were going to have a funeral or a homecoming. But then the day finally came for him to walk out of the hospital. He was holding onto his Daddy on one side and that big Trimble boy on the other. The first time his bare feet hit the green earth, he kind of choked up. And you could hear that whole congregation say with him, "Thank you, God. Thank you."

It is the same story, but in the imagination of the preacher the story is reshaped to bring out the experience of God within the entire community. In the second telling of the story, the relationships of the community move to the center. The community, not the individual, functions as the central symbol of the story. Their relationships, their faith in God, and their love of each other and the wounded member all come into view. While the individual does suffer, the preacher chooses not to make this the focus of the story. The preacher wants to highlight communal belonging and communal faith because she wants to point toward communal pastoral care. Yes, the individual still undergoes an existential crisis of faith as a result of the accident, but because he is embedded within a community, his interior experiences are still related to the community as a whole. The Christian community and its care is the precondition for the individual's rediscovery of faith.

It is the preacher's responsibility to decide how to tell the story. The preacher chooses to give presence to the experience of the individual or of the community in which the individual is grounded. This decision determines who cares in the sermon. Notice in the first telling of the story that the individual seemingly comes to faith on his own. There are no caring agents in the story. Out of nowhere he seems to develop faith in God. If there is any care, it is self-care. But in the second account, the community members actively participate in the ministry of care. Their faith stands as the foundation for his faith. Their care makes it possible for him to walk out of the hospital and to join them in praising God.

Over time, many such decisions paint a picture of the world of care that the preacher and the congregation will or will not inhabit. The sermon helps constitute the world of care of the hearers. Either the individual will be stuck alone with his pain and somehow come to faith, or the community will surround the individual with communal pastoral care, reminding him of God's sustaining power and the Christ-given promise of new life that calls him and the entire church up out of the grave. Preaching is a matter of emphasis, and the choices about who cares are finally the preacher's to make. As Walter Brueggemann explains, "Nobody can switch worlds unless an alternative world is made richly available with great artistry, care, and boldness."[59] It's up to the preacher to decide whether the world of the sermon will be populated by a collection of individuals or a communal body full of care. It's up to the preacher to determine which caring world she will hold before the people.

A whole cast of characters accompany an individual's trip to Jerusalem. Why not speak of how the one leper who is healed praises God because he is restored to human communion rather than lifting him up as a hero of faith over against all those who do not have faith (Lk. 17:11–19)? Pastoral preaching begs for concrete, vivid imaging of the way we are persons together before God in all our human wonder, bound yet free, broken yet connected through Christ. Sure, we do have our moments of introspection, and these are not always inappropriate to the sermon, but a preponderance of such sermonic fare becomes too privatized. It reduces God's pastoral word for the entire human community to a pastoral secret for "me" alone. We shall move much further toward a truly pastoral community if our sermons presence persons bound together in Christ.

---

[59]Walter Brueggemann, *Cadences of Home: Preaching Among Exiles* (Louisville: Westminster John Knox Press, 1997), 35.

Given Western cultural assumptions about human beings, it is difficult for us to see the interdependence of humanity. We still believe that the rugged individual writes the scripts that matter within our society. Recently public radio aired a program that discussed the "great explorers" of the past century. They noted how the stories of these explorers usually leave out the equally heroic contributions of their native guides, many of whom actually accompany the explorers to the summits or the remote places on the globe that they are attempting to map. So in 1953 Edmund Hillary becomes the first person to ascend the summit of Mount Everest, when in fact, Tenzing Norgay, a native of Nepal, accompanied Hillary all the way.[60] Of course, such accounts of culture are now being steadily revised by feminists, persons from other cultures, and minority members of Western society. Pastoral sermons should write all of humanity back into the script. They will replace the heroic individual with the interdependent human community who within the church is formed in Christ. Importantly, many African American preachers have not lost this sense of human relatedness. Their preaching still gives voice to a people who cares. They know that "I am because we are."[61]

Christ at the Center of Pastoral Preaching

But we shall go farther than images of *human* togetherness, all our messy loves and deceits, hopes and failings. Yes, as pastoral preachers we will fill our sermons with children, youth, adults—old, young, and middle— from every station of life, together. But in our togetherness, preachers must name the incarnate presence of Christ who lives, dies, and is resurrected among us by the power of God through the Holy Spirit. Christ is the central symbol and reality of all Christian preaching. The human family is capable of remarkable acts of compassion and atrocious acts of cruelty. The family table may be now a table of joy and later a board of enmity. That's why Christian sermons will name Christ at the center of the human table, the one who promises to redeem our broken togetherness and who offers himself as a foretaste of the love feast of plenty. At Christ's table there will be no more bruised faces, no more hungry children, no more enemies.

Pastoral preachers cannot afford to assume that the congregation will add Christ to the sermon if we inadvertently leave Christ out. We are the ones whom the church has called to preach in public worship. It is our responsibility to do more than tell tales of human kindness and evil. Finally, as Christian preachers we must disclose Christ among us or reexamine our call. It was a rude awakening to me, a number of years back, of just how far my own preaching had drifted from a christological center when a person

---

[60]National Public Radio, *Morning Edition,* Alex Chadwick (May 10, 1999), Washington, D.C.

[61]Jacquelyn Grant, "Faithful Resistance Risking It All," 107.

who had been worshiping within the congregation for several weeks came up and said, "Well, it sounds like you are a Christian after all." Bending over backward to discover meaning within the messiness of human life, I had obscured the presence of Christ, who defines and redeems our humanity. Christian preaching is always rooted in and centers on Christ, for Christ is the Word in our words, the Spirit in our spirits, the One who calls preaching forth in the first place, and the One who is disclosed within the pastoral community. The imagery, stories, symbols, and biblical interpretations of our sermons do constitute the pastoral community. But more importantly, they disclose Christ, who ultimately is the One who through word and table constitutes us.

Does this claim mean that every sermon must be overtly christological? Must the preacher do double-somersaults to reinterpret Hebrew Scripture through christology? The answer is again, No. Christian preachers can faithfully interpret Hebrew Scripture without the compulsion to "go to the cross." For the God of the Hebrews is the God of the Christians, the God of Christ. Sermons may bring into focus humans hearing the promises of God together, receiving the guidance and forgiveness of God, and living faithfully unto God, without forcing Jesus into every sermon. For example, it is enough for Christian congregations to hear the call/covenant between Abraham, Sarah, and God (Genesis 12) without also needing to reflect in the same sermon on New Testament interpretation of the covenant. In this case, God offers full disclosure to us without need for the mediation of Christ. But notice, God remains central to the telling of who and how we are in the world together, just as in many sermons Jesus Christ becomes central as disclosure of God with us. The larger point, with respect to pastoral preaching, is that the divine initiative forms and transforms human beings together. We know our truest selves in relation as God knows us–created for love of God and one another.

Pastoral Correction of the Social in Preaching

Pastoral emphasis on the interpersonal should correct the tendency of our preaching to become overly social just as it abridges our tendency toward the personal in preaching. Constant reminders from the pulpit about the starving masses do not really offer pastoral guidance to the congregation. Prophetic denunciation of environmental despoliation does not necessarily motivate us to clean up our act. By all means, pastoral preaching will address the larger social world, and at times it will serve the prophetic function of rebuking the faithful who chase after false gods.

But what we wish to presence in our sermons is the relational world at the heart of the social. This is the central sphere of human life, the interpersonal, or the interhuman. For example, one might in preaching on confession and forgiveness turn to the story of John Plummer, the Vietnam War pilot who was responsible for the napalming of the village of Trang

Bang in Vietnam. This bombing resulted in the severe burning of nine-year-old Phan Thi Kim Duc. A photographer captured the event on film, and it became one of the enduring images of the Vietnam War. Years later, Phan Thi Kim Duc and John Plummer met and were reconciled. They actually greeted each other as a sister and brother in Christ.[62]

As we presence this story in the sermon, why not focus on the strangely interpersonal nature of guilt and forgiveness that emerges from the larger social phenomena of war. War is a horror—period. It has immense social significance. But the destruction of war—the people who are no more, the pillage, rape, and cruelty—occurs between persons.[63] It occurs between people named John Plummer and Phan Thi Kim Duc. The story will achieve greater presence if told within this interpersonal framework than as an illustration of how bad war is and a call to march on the Pentagon. We may in fact decide as a people to march on the Pentagon because we are convicted of our complicity with human warring. We may desire to witness to the nation in the name of the God of peace. But we are more likely to arrive at such action-response through drawing close to the interpersonal suffering and redemption of those involved than through listening to accounts of war in general. As Robert Webber and Rodney Clapp remind us, "Amid genuine suffering, the preacher will not be allowed to reduce the gospel to an abstract, cold formula. In this sense, visits to jails and hospitals may do more to foster good preaching than the finest homiletics course."[64]

This means, especially with respect to social themes in preaching, we should be cautious not to overwhelm the hearers with shocking stories of violence or devastation. We saw this mistake in the earlier example about ethnic cleansing. Concreteness is generally desirable in preaching. But hearers are not sure how to handle too much personal intimacy or too much social horror from the pulpit. The impact is visceral. By the time the preacher gets around to linking image and idea, a necessary move in every sermon, the congregation is lost in the shock waves of the story or image. Maybe this would be a good strategy if the preacher wished to lose the congregation, but we are proceeding on the assumption that preaching saves persons through Christ in and for the world. We can leave the tear-jerking intimacy and gruesome world stories for other occasions in the life of the church. This is not to avoid emotion or important global concerns within our preaching. Rather, such caution is needed precisely because the pastoral preacher wishes for the congregation to care deeply about issues

---

[62]The story of their reconciliation appears in the *Wesleyan Christian Advocate* 161 (14 February 1997).

[63]I am claiming with Edward Farley that the interhuman or the interpersonal is the primary sphere of redemption through the criterion of the other or the face that makes redemption possible within the personal and social spheres of human existence. See *Good and Evil*, 250, 288.

[64]Webber and Clapp, *People of the Truth*, 73.

that matter. If we create too much emotional catharsis from the pulpit, the congregation leaves the sanctuary confused or spent, with nothing left to share with the world.

The pastoral preacher will search life, congregational events, the Bible, news stories, films and novels, snatches of conversation, and theological works for those images that speak of our social world known through human relations. Those interpersonal relations that we give presence to in the sermon help the congregation understand its own place in the world. For the interpersonal dimension of human life runs right through church and world.

Here are a few examples:

- Picture for the congregation two clowns weeping before a show rather than a circus in general.
- Allow the church to overhear a brief conversation between a gay man, his mother, and father rather than preach about gay issues. Or recall a scene from a movie like *Philadelphia* that sensitively treats persons who are gay.
- Picture the first time children fight on a school bus or playground rather than discuss the violence of our society.
- Recreate in vivid imagery and sound the shared exuberance of those who tore apart the Berlin Wall rather than discuss the hope for peace on earth.
- Recount the bittersweet joy of a particular family whose dying youngster is granted a last wish by a community foundation rather than discuss terminal illness in general.

Novelists and poets understand that particular images, specific conversations, and the local open the reader up to general understandings. So, too, the interpersonal opens up to the social and the personal. Relation is the primary category, though it is difficult to see this when we view life either as social (out there) or personal (in here). In pastoral sermons, we want to concretize the relationships within church, community, and world so that the congregation will begin to see themselves and the world in a new light. Discovering how to be concrete in sermonic imagery without too much detail is more a matter of skilled practice than hard-and-fast homiletic rules. But preachers who are pastors will make the effort because they care deeply for the people among whom they preach. They want to help form a caring people, an interpersonal community, for care in God's world.

Let me be clear. I am not saying that pastoral sermons will only name God and Christ present within the church community, though I think that we need to make frequent efforts to do so. The pastoral sermon will also presence God *among* humans together in the social world. But naming God in the larger world is no easy matter. We should question those sermons that uncritically point to social activist movements in our communities, conservative or liberal, and say, "See, there is God." Caution is in order before we pronounce divine approval on any mass social action. The liberal has no higher theological ground on which to stand than the conservative when it comes to social causes. The fact that the new religious right has now figured out how to lobby Congress for partisan issues such as anti-abortion legislation or family values disturbs the liberal mainliners because "they" (the conservatives) have now figured out how "we" (the liberals) have played the game of politics and religion. But we should be wary of identifying God with our issues—social, political, or otherwise. That road can lead to idolatries of many stripes—nationalism, denominationalism, sexism, racism, materialism, to name a few. God is surely active in human history if creation and revelation mean anything in the Christian tradition at all. But how we shall name the action-presence of God in the world is a tricky problem indeed. People imagine themselves and so become compassionate because they see other persons in need, not because the preacher looks around at the world and says God is present in this or that social agenda.

Suffering and Resurrection

The pastoral preacher will help the congregation see the world through the redemptive christological motif of suffering-resurrection. Wherever in our world we see human beings suffering yet struggling, longing for resurrection and redemption, there God is present through Christ and the Holy Spirit. As we engage the social world, wherever persons taste the sweet freedom of resurrection that comes from a loosening of the chains that enslave humanity—tyrannical governments, abusive households, economic sweatshops, environmental degradation—there Christ is present in the power of the resurrection, freeing humanity from the bondage of sin. To bring alive in the sermon such redemptive social occasions taxes the theological and rhetorical acumen of the preacher pastor. We inevitably risk identifying Christ too closely with human activities on the one hand. And on the other, we risk no symbolization of Christ within creation at all.

Again, what the preacher hopes to presence in the sermon is the interpersonal within the social wherein the suffering-resurrected Christ is at work. A case in point: For thirty-five years now, many preachers and theologians have cited the civil rights struggle in the United States as evidence of the redemptive presence of Christ at work in the world through the empowerment of the poor and minorities to overturn the social conditions that perpetuate injustice. The movement clearly achieved a degree of social redemption for millions of persons in the nation. Its liberating impact is still unfolding. It may be true according to our theological criteria of suffering-resurrection that Christ was and is present in the civil rights movement. But such a general statement in a sermon either receives nodding approval by those who agree or bemused tolerance by those who disagree but aren't threatened enough to strenuously object. So what? both might ask. Who cares?

The preacher pastor who wishes to move a congregation toward recognition of Christ in the civil rights movement, and thereby to engage the congregation's active care in that social arena, will need to freshly imagine persons in relation who are caught up today in the push and pull of this monumental social struggle. We will need to be alert to those unique experiences that are identifiably Christ-shaped, that are characterized by suffering-resurrection. Sadly, our most enduring symbols from this period of social ferment are now being co-opted by other interests, especially economic ones. For example, the advertising industry now uses the image of Martin Luther King, Jr., to promote car sales. So we need to look at new images that can help the congregation identify where God may be at work in the world.

Here are some further examples of what I am suggesting:

- Help a U.S. congregation hear a recent immigrant girl try to explain to her teacher that she doesn't comprehend the instructions because she doesn't yet understand the majority language, wondering all the while what language God speaks.

- Recreate for the congregation a daily drama from office politics in which persons are passed over for promotions because of their gender or race, assigning to the characters names and faces and situating in their midst the rejected Christ.

- Highlight the recent international campaign to ban land mines by painting a picture of a small town whose old and young are now free to stroll and run outside their homes without fear of death. Imagine Christ there overcoming the power of death.

- Paint a picture of a group of high school students planting trees for a reforestation project. Listen to three or four of them discuss God and creation as they give themselves lovingly to care of the earth.

Pastoral sermons will give presence to the suffering-resurrected Christ among persons together in the middle of our social world and thereby draw the pastoral community toward compassionate care for the world, where Christ is present.

Summary

I will be the first to admit that it is a difficult task in mainline churches to reorient pastoral preaching to a relational anthropology, a theological anthropology that affirms that Christ gives us our common humanity and calls us together for care of each other and the world. We'd rather stick to our personal experiences of Jesus, what God through Christ is doing for me. Or we'd prefer to align Jesus with our own causes, liberal or conservative, and seek to declare our way the winning way. This makes pastoral preaching fairly easy, because the preacher controls the terms of care, whether that means helping individuals adjust to personal problems or rallying a faithful few to carry the banner in the next social crusade. While pastoral care does emerge from such preaching, it is limited in nature. It lacks the fullness of care that we would hope for if the sermon brings forth caring relationships among persons in Christian community.

Often the preacher can presence a relational theological anthropology in the sermon (once convinced that it is needed) simply by recasting biblical interpretation, everyday stories, conversations, and images to create the world of care within the sermon. It boils down to seeing self in relationship to others with new eyes, through the eyes of Christ among *us* and then helping the congregation see, hear, touch, taste, and experience the caring presence of Christ within human community. We need not force Christ on the congregation. Christ is already here among us. He is the unfailing gift of God's grace disclosed in preaching and the breaking of the bread. Christ is the one who through care-full preaching forms us into a caring, pastoral community.

So we move now to discuss a theology of the church that can be the basis of pastoral preaching. Just what are the characteristics of the church that can enliven our pastoral sermons? What is the nature and purpose of this reality that we call church, and that we always assume when we stand in the pulpit to preach? Practically speaking, how can we preach in such a way that this church will actually emerge as the basis for a pastoral community?

5

The Caring Church of
the Care-full Sermon

"The Word is incarnate not just in worship or in the gathering of the community, but in our presence in the world. Jesus did not preach the church; he preached the coming of God's reign on earth."
—KAREN LEBACQZ[1]

Every Sunday when we stand to preach, we stand before a gathered body of people that we routinely refer to as church. This church is composed of all kinds of people who lead ordinary human lives. They are not perfected saints, though some would say, especially in the Wesleyan tradition, that they are on the way to perfection. What we see is not some kind of hyped-up, super-spiritual group of human beings, even though at times the church falls into such heresy. What we see in the faces of those who are church are the faces of God-created humanity. The church, whatever else it is, is a very human institution.

Here's who you might see from the front of the sanctuary where the church is gathered. Bob and Sylvia Davis, a middle-aged couple without children who moved thirty miles away, but every Sunday they get in their car to drive here and sit in the center section, halfway back. They smile constantly. Over there is Mr. Tribble, close to eighty years old, handing out bulletins at the front entrance to the sanctuary. When he comes down the aisle to receive the offering, he sort of leans to one side, becoming more

---

[1]Karen Lebacqz, *Word, Worship, World, & Wonder: Reflections on Christian Living* (Nashville: Abingdon Press, 1997), 75.

119

wobbly on his feet with each passing week. The two sisters, Bernice and Clara, are in their regular spot, looking a little tired from coordinating last Sunday's women's mission project. Everybody agreed it was a huge success. James, on the left side, just got some bad news from his doctor, but he hasn't told anyone but you and his wife. You keep hoping he'll be able to tell the members of his Sunday school class. One pew holds five kids, all under ten years old, from various families in the congregation, and two parents sit on either end, bracketing the children like overworked bookends. The kids draw, color pictures, play tic-tac-toe, and whisper while the parents pretend to listen attentively to the sermon. Up in the sparsely populated balcony, three teenagers perch next to the railing and survey the heads of the whole congregation. Two of them are active in the youth group, but the other one you only see from time to time, and you never can remember his name. Near the front and off to the right is Bruce Wilkins. When his wife committed suicide, he struggled for over a year. You know that he isn't through grieving yet. Close to the back is Lou Anne Thompson and her four-year-old son, Jason. Randy Thompson, the husband, rarely ever attends worship with Lou Anne and Jason, but everybody in the community likes Randy. He occasionally participates in special projects. Here they are, the church.

It is for them, and among them, that you have crafted the sermon. You see their faces. You know significant details about many of their all-too-human lives. In fact, their usually messy, sometimes joyful lives remind you constantly of your own humanity. They put down newspapers and coffee to arrive at worship. They set aside home-improvement projects and hobbies. They leave toys and telephones, dirty dishes and gardening to come to this meeting place. Some arrive willingly, eager to join with friends and strangers in the worship of God. Others come by the sheer force of habit. And some show up under protest. But here they are, a gathered congregation—the church. They expect to hear a sermon, a caring word from God that they, the church, have entrusted you to preach.

But who are they theologically? Who is this body of people? These people who gather weekly around word and table to sing hymns, offer prayers to God, and tell one another the stories of the Christian faith, who are they? And how do we preach pastorally among them? The pastor knows them personally, but we have already said that pastoral preaching doesn't focus therapeutically on the private aches and pains of individuals in the pew. As preachers we do not preach at or to Bruce Wilkins or Lou Anne Thompson, even though we are familiar with their personal needs. Yes, individuals do arrive at the sanctuary. Each is a unique person biologically, psychologically, and socially. But they are persons-in-relation, as discussed in the previous chapter. And they come together because they share a unique corporate identity. They are human, to be sure, and they gather like all other humans. But their gathering is decidedly distinct.

In short, we preach among a people called *church*. How we as preacher pastors understand the living theological reality of this human church, and how our sermons construe the church, is a crucial element of pastoral preaching. For God extends care to the world in and through the human gathering called church. And preaching, in no small part, helps to form or not form the church as a caring community. Preachers need to be clear about the nature and purpose of the church if we want to help shape caring congregations in deed and truth.

The Caring Church

We call this peculiar gathering of human beings a church, the *ekklesia*. This means, in New Testament terms, that the church is the people called out by God for God's purpose. "Once you were not a people, but now you are God's people," says the writer of 1 Peter (2:10). God calls the church, like Israel, into covenant with God and fellowship with one another to show forth the marvelous acts of God, that is, to show forth in its life together God's loving compassion and liberation for all creation. The preacher does not speak to individual listeners but to members of the covenantal community, or the *ekklesia,* whose lives God shapes through Christ and the Holy Spirit.

Now it is the work of the Holy Spirit through preaching and the celebration of holy communion that constitutes the people as a church and not simply an audience. Reformers Calvin and Luther insisted that wherever the word of God is preached and the sacraments duly offered, there the church is present. This is why preachers dare not take lightly the task of preaching and worship, because through the sermon and the sacraments God knits together a corporate body that is united in Christ. "One body, many members," Paul calls the church (1 Cor. 12). So those who gather around the sermon and the communion table do not come together as a civic association, friendly group, players on a team, or individuals in a crowd. We come together as God's people being built up as the body of Christ for care in the world.

The amazing thing is that many preacher pastors do not often picture the church as a living people *in the sermon*. This dawned on me when I sat down and looked at notes of my own sermons. I discovered that if I had any theology of the church in mind, it wasn't evident in the sermons themselves. The people who are the church, sitting together in pews, or standing around a coffee pot, are left to figure out for themselves the theological significance of their togetherness. That Christ is really present among the church, through Word, sacrament, and Spirit, which is a foundational premise of ecclesiology, usually comes as bewildering news to mainline church folks, because as preacher pastors we have consistently reinforced the inwardness of religious experience to the neglect of the corporate reality of the church. Preacher pastors might find the people more deeply interested in the church if in our sermons we were willing to explore the theological nature of our togetherness in Christ. A little later we will look at how the sermon can help establish a caring church, a pastoral community. But before we do so, we need to look in greater detail at the theological dimensions of the caring church.

The Image of the Church in Pastoral Preaching

Our understanding of the church, its purpose and identity, always guides preaching and pastoral care. Avery Dulles, Paul Minear, and Susan Thistlethwaite all show that one's image or model of the church underpins the various ministries of the church.[2] As Minear explains,

> [The church's] self understanding, its inner cohesion, its esprit de corps, derive from a dominant image of itself, even though that image remains inarticulately embedded in subconscious strata…The process of discovering and rediscovering an authentic self-image will involve the whole community not only in clearheaded conceptual thinking and disciplined speech, but also in a rebirth of images and its imagination, and in the absorption of these images into the interstices of communal activities of every sort.[3]

How the pastor understands the church in the world fundamentally shapes the sermon. Over time, because of the relationship between language and community, it helps form the congregation. For example, if a therapeutic community governs the preacher's image of the church, over time he or she will preach to a community of individuals with psychological needs that the sermon will attempt to address. Or if the preacher sees the church as herald of the good news of Jesus Christ, preaching will aim to impart the gospel to the hearers, who are then urged to speak up about the good news (evangelize) in the world.

As stated earlier, congregations and preachers usually retain several images of the church within their collective understanding. Bear in mind, we are not talking about formal, doctrinal understandings of the church, but about the foundational images that persons in Christian community hold of themselves as church. These images are what Edward Farley calls "constitutive images," which I discussed earlier.[4] They are the images that orient the life of the Christian community, from worship to education, mission to administration. Preaching over time helps establish, reinforce,

---

[2]Avery Dulles, *Models of the Church* (Garden City, N. Y.: Doubleday, 1974); Paul Minear, *Images of the Church in the New Testament* (Philadelphia: Westminster Press, 1960; repr. 1975); Susan Thistlethwaite, *Metaphors for the Contemporary Church* (New York: Pilgrim Press, 1983).

[3]Minear, *Images of the Church*, 45.

[4]Edward Farley, *Ecclesial Man: A Social Phenomenology of Faith and Reality* (Philadelphia: Fortress Press, 1975), 118.

challenge, or alter such constitutive images of the church within the congregation. In the practice of ministry, church conflicts often occur because congregants hold differing images of the church, even though unacknowledged. Conflicting constitutive images of the church cause members to tangle over matters large and small–from building programs to public prayers. The wise pastor will spot this dilemma when it emerges and seek to guide the congregation toward some sort of clearer church image or synthesis of images that can nourish vitality in worship and mission and that can help the congregation form as a caring church.

The People of God

The theology of the church that will sustain a caring community draws from one dominant biblical image–the people of God–and adds to this another–the church for others. People of God retains the association with the Hebrew tradition of those persons called out by God for covenant (a nation, a people, a holy race). But in its New Testament interpretation, especially through Paul, the image broadens out to universal inclusion of all who are incorporated into Christ (Rom. 9:25–26; also 1 Pet. 2:1–10). As Peter Hodgson summarizes, Paul's use of the image extends it universally to include Jews and Gentiles without losing the specification of a "temporal, historical, political reality."[5] The church as people of God are those whom, within and beyond the walls of the organized church, God is calling through Christ and the Holy Spirit to communion with God and one another. The people of God, therefore, exist within the church *and* world, though within the institutional church they are visibly present. *People of God* has particular expression within the concrete congregation yet universal dimensions, since God is the God of all creation.

Among the people of God we would expect to find a caring fellowship, since God through Christ and the Holy Spirit binds the body (the people) together in mutual love and affection. Members care for one another not because it is natural or easy but because Christ stands at the center of the fellowship and makes pastoral care possible. When we attend to one another's concerns within the Christian fellowship, we are attending to the very body of Christ, in which each member needs the other (1 Cor. 12). Many Christians intuitively understand the caring nature of the church as a fellowship of believers because somewhere along the way they have experienced the loving support of a congregation. They have been nurtured in the hearts of fellow believers. They may even have been held accountable to the ethical demands of the fellowship.

One of the primary ethical demands of the people of God is that of hospitality toward the stranger. We explored this category in the chapter

---

[5]Peter Hodgson, *Revisioning the Church: Ecclesial Freedom in the New Paradigm* (Philadelphia: Fortress Press, 1988), 29.

on the pastoral community (chap. 2). Here we affirm that hospitality is more than a pastoral ideal within the community. Hospitality is a theological and ethical reality of the church as the people of God. The covenantal community moves outward from Israel, to the Christian fellowship, to the stranger beyond. The people of God realize that exclusive inward fellowship defies their own nature. God, known through Christ, is a hospitable God, who welcomes Jew and Greek, slave and free to the banquet table of grace. If the holy communion of the people is to remain holy, then it will remain open to those who are near and far. The church as communion is open to friends and strangers. God initiates the covenantal community, but God is not exclusively bound within it. The church, as God's people, will remain open to the stranger, for thereby they may host "angels unawares" (Heb. 13:2, RSV). This opens the image of the church in pastoral preaching to a second and equally important theological theme.

The Church for Others

The church courts disaster when it primarily understands itself as an intimate fellowship of believers who care for one another. Why? Because the impulse of the gospel is outward toward "all nations" (Mt. 28:19). To remain huddled together around the warming fires of our own fellowship is, finally, a denial of God's care for all creation. To be sure, the temptations are great in our post-Christian culture for the church to withdraw from the world at large, a world that we often perceive as full of threat to the good news of God or a world that looks upon the church with benign neglect. But without commitment to the world that God creates in love and redeems in grace, the church has no particular theological mission. We would be a people without a purpose.

We could say with Calvin that our purpose is to worship and love God forever. But worship means service of God. We rehearse our service of God in the sanctuary, but we eagerly practice our service of God in the fields and streets, offices and restaurants of our cities and towns. The caring fellowship of the people of God generously spills over into the wider community because God cares for the whole world.

The movement of the church beyond the confines of its own fellowship is not for the purpose of forcing Christianity upon the rest of the world (the colonial missionary model of evangelism). Our aim is not to win souls for Jesus but to witness to the resurrection of Christ, to point toward God's ongoing care for the world through the resurrection of Christ. Christ's resurrection is good news for all creation, not just for the fellowship of believers. It is particularly good news for those whom the world despises and rejects–the poor, the outcasts, the hungry, the powerless. The gospel means that their liberation is at hand. The church enacts the witness to that liberation. As Susan Bond says, "The vocation of the church is to risk its own corporate identity and life (to risk institutional death) in pursuit of

God's beyond-the-church future."[6] We cannot fully live the gospel by holding one another's hands and singing hymns of joy, as meaningful as that may be for many Christians. God does call "the people" together, but it is for the purpose of sending us out into God's world for others. The church, formed by Christ and Holy Spirit through word and sacrament, is the church for others.

Self-giving Reexamined

The image of "the church for others" suggests Christ's self-giving as the basis for the ministry of the church as *diakonia,* or servanthood. There are problems here, however. Servanthood is a difficult image to sustain in our era given the ways in which it has been associated with slavery and servitude. Christians and non-Christians have used servanthood and slavery to perpetuate oppressive racist, classist, and patriarchal structures within church and society. Feminists, liberationists, and black theologians have strong reasons to oppose servanthood, or servant community, as a way to imagine the church in our day. Perhaps Elisabeth Schüssler-Fiorenza is correct to propose an alternative image, such as "discipleship of equals" as a way to retrieve a similar emphasis in the tradition, yet cleansed of patriarchal dominance.[7] But what is important is that the church be able to realistically imagine itself today as connected to the self-giving motif that lies at the core of the central symbol of the faith, Jesus Christ. Christ lives in the world not to be served, but to serve, and Christ is host (server) of the banquet meal for all humanity.

I believe that the servant theme can still guide the church. But we must recognize its various misuses in the tradition. As Letty Russell suggests, we must reinvigorate servanthood as "honor and responsibility to take part in God's work of service in the world."[8] If we imagine the church as "for others," perhaps we can remain open to the stranger and the other in need, which characterizes the core meaning of the *ekklesia* from its beginnings without stumbling over the oppressive associations of the term *servant* in the Western Christian tradition.

Giving oneself for others doesn't necessarily mean that we become submissive doormats for others to use and abuse. Nor does it mean that we offer care for others out of our own need to be needed or to control those who receive our care, though human motives are usually all mixed-up.

---

[6]L. Susan Bond, *Trouble With Jesus: Women, Christology, and Preaching* (St. Louis: Chalice Press, 1999), 177.

[7]Elisabeth Schüssler Fiorenza, *In Memory of Her: A Feminist Theological Reconstruction of Christian Origins* (New York: Crossroad, 1983).

[8]Letty Russell, *Human Liberation in a Feminist Perspective–A Theology* (Philadelphia: Westminster Press, 1974), 142. Russell is in tension with other feminist and womanist theologians on the question of "servanthood." See Jacquelyn Grant, "The Sin of Servanthood: And the Deliverance of Discipleship," in *A Troubling in My Soul: Womanist Perspectives on Evil and Suffering,* ed. Emilie M. Townes (New York: Orbis, 1993), 199–218.

Self-giving can mean that the church as a people willingly aligns its care with the care of Christ, who embodied the paradoxical truth that we find ourselves by giving ourselves away. In the upside-down world of the reign of God, lost is found, and the last is first. Surely in a culture that hawks personal self-fulfillment as *the goal* of human life, the church can strive to present the countercultural value of self-giving as the way of the people of God in the world. The church will see no benefit from such a mission, at least not in a world that calculates cost and benefits on accounting ledger sheets. The church will probably grow no larger in numbers nor more influential in guiding public policy. But in self-giving for others, the church will bear witness to a way of life in God's world that is distinctively Christ-shaped and that offers a glimpse of a new heaven and earth. The church is not in charge of bringing about God's new creation—God is—but in our care for others, in our self-giving as the people of God, we at least try to point in the right direction.

Many other images cluster around the theological picture of church as "the people of God for others." To the people of God we might add "priesthood of all believers," "body of Christ," "household of God," "community of saints," "mystical communion," and "covenant people." In accord with the church for others, we might also understand church as "sacrament," "disciple community," or "exodus community." Letty Russell has explored the evocative metaphor of "church in the round." This image brings forward the communal dimensions of the church. Its table imagery invites inclusion of those on the margins of church and society.[9]

My purpose here is not to nail down one theological definition for the church today. This would be undesirable given the creative theological and cultural ferment that now stirs the church. Rather, with these two images I am suggesting a broad range of understanding of the church in which to ground pastoral preaching. Pastoral preaching occurs within a church that is distinctively communal by its God-given nature. Simultaneously, the church has a clear vision of its responsibility for others in the world.

Christ and the Pastoral Community

As discussed in the previous chapter, a pastoral community rests upon an anthropology of communion rather than hierarchical understandings of the human being. We are relational rather than frighteningly free individuals. The biblical tradition insists on freedom from bondage to self that we might live in community with others. Yet Christian interpretation of the self in community is always through Christ, who is the basis of the church's existence. Explaining this mysterious relationship between Christ

---

[9]Letty Russell, *Church in the Round: Feminist Interpretation of the Church* (Louisville: Westminster/John Knox Press, 1993). For homiletical explorations along these lines see Lucy Atkinson Rose, *Sharing the Word: Preaching in the Roundtable Church* (Louisville: Westminster John Knox Press, 1997), and John McClure, *The Roundtable Pulpit* (Nashville: Abingdon Press, 1995).

and the church, Bonhoeffer says, "It is the mystery of the community that Christ is in her and, only through her, reaches to men [humanity]. Christ exists among us as community, as church in the hiddenness of history. The church is the hidden Christ among us."[10] When we look at sermons for their pastoral perspective, we look for this crucial link between church and Christ that is the basis for human togetherness in the Christian community. For it is through Christ that pastoral preaching occurs within the church. Pastoral healing, guiding, sustaining, and reconciling is only possible within preaching if we preach among a community that finds its being in Christ, through whom God cares for us all.

Sermons lose their pastoral dimension when the connection between Christ and church is severed. Sometimes we see this separation in sermons that stress the intimacy of human community but fail to recognize the formative claims of Christ on the community. Noting this tendency in some incarnational christologies, Susan Bond points out that, "God's love is more than the desire to be connected and in relationship."[11] Somehow in our sermons we must present Christ as the basis of the Christian community. Out of this Christ-centered community grows the church's compassionate care for others.

Church and World

We need to maintain both sides of the church as a pastoral community, its inner formation in Christ through word and sacrament, and its outward care for creation, where God is already present. The church needs preaching that will guide the community into redemptive action in the world (pastoral guidance and reconciliation). Simultaneously, the church needs preaching that will form and nurture a distinctively Christian body of communion as preparation for engagement with the world (pastoral healing, and sustaining). As the literary critic Robert Detweiler says, "the destiny of community is not merely to provide its members with a place to belong. It is also to give them a context where, and a structure of how, they can constantly plot their lives."[12] The plot of the Christian story is always much bigger than the church that it forms. It is God's redemption of all creation that calls the pastoral community beyond mutuality into compassion and hospitality for others. Bonnie Miller-McLemore suggests that we can view church congregations as both "holding environments" and "communities of prophets and visionaries."[13] Most of us, if we are honest, do not need one or the other, fellowship or worldly self-giving, but we need both all the time.

---

[10]Dietrich Bonhoeffer, *No Rusty Swords* (San Francisco: Harper & Row, 1965), 68.

[11]L. Susan Bond, *Trouble With Jesus,* 114.

[12]Robert Detweiler, *Breaking the Fall: Religious Readings of Contemporary Fiction* (Louisville: Westminster John Knox Press, 1995), 190.

[13]Bonnie J. Miller-McLemore, *Also A Mother: Work and Family as Theological Dilemma* (Nashville: Abingdon Press, 1994), 185–91.

Letty Russell's definition of the church holds together this dynamic: The church is "a community of Christ, bought with a price, where *everyone* is welcome" [emphasis mine].[14] Formed in the self-giving love and grace of Christ, the church as community fulfills its purpose through care of all persons because God desires health (salvation, liberation) for all creation. As Russell elaborates,

> It is a community of Christ because Christ's presence, through the power of the Spirit, constitutes people as a community gathered in Christ's name (Matt. 18:20; 1 Cor. 12:4–6). This community is bought with a price, because the struggle of Jesus to overcome the structures of sin and death constitutes both the source of new life in the community and its own mandate to continue the same struggle for life on behalf of others (1 Cor. 6:20; Phil. 2:1–11). It is a community where everyone is welcome because it gathers around the table of God's hospitality. Its welcome table is a sign of the coming feast of God's mended creation, with the guest list derived from the announcements of the Jubilee year in ancient Israel (Luke 14:12–14).[15]

What is noteworthy in this definition of the church is the balance between Christ, who forms the community, and the community as responsible in and for the world. Such a definition may seem obvious, but many attempts to understand the church collapse the tension. For some, the church represents the ideal human community in internal relations and external moral action, yet it overlooks concern for the centrality of Christ. For others, the church centered upon Christ becomes the only reality that matters, so the church understands itself in sectarian fashion as always over against the culture. Pastoral preaching, however, seeks a view of the church that remains grounded in Christ, the basis of Christian community, yet attentive to the world to whom God offers Christ. Christ did not come to save the church, but the world. Therefore, the church as the ongoing embodiment of Christ does not exist to save itself, but to participate in the healing of the world.

In one sense the revelation of God through Christ is a word/story entrusted to the church through scripture and tradition. Yet in another sense the Word of God runs before the church throughout all creation where the Spirit blows. The church is the community where believers learn the language and action of Christian faith, as Stanley Hauerwas and William Willimon insist.[16] But the church must also clearly recognize and name

---

[14]Russell, *Church in the Round,* 14.

[15]Ibid.

[16]Stanley Hauerwas and William Willimon, *Resident Aliens: Life in the Christian Colony* (Nashville: Abingdon Press, 1989). See also Stanley Hauerwas, *In Good Company: The Church as Polis* (Notre Dame: University of Notre Dame Press, 1995).

God's graceful presence in the world, as Mary Catherine Hilkert claims.[17] Hauerwas and other proponents of postliberalism propose a church that will only be renewed by focusing on the distinctiveness of the gospel as revealed in scripture, tradition, liturgy, and the moral practices of the Christian community (the identity of the church). The model weds Protestant concern for revelation and Catholic concern for sanctification. But in its churchly focus, it equally misses the Protestant desire for redemption of the creation and Catholic insistence on the world itself as sacramental, a mediation of God's grace. A church that obsesses about its identity over against the modern world runs the grave danger of not hearing the cries of those outside the walls of the church.[18] Hauerwas argues that only within the church can Christians develop the virtue to hear and respond to the needs of the world. Underneath this argument is a Christ-against-culture view of the church that finally insists that there is no salvation outside the church.

Where Hauerwas and others accent the necessity for re-formation of the church in the contemporary world, I agree. Clearly the church, at least the old mainline church, struggles for identity and purpose in our society. We grasp management models, therapeutic models, entertainment models, triumphalist models (church as winning team), and social gospel models (conservative and liberal) because, unsure of its purpose and place within Western culture, the church grabs anything available for survival. In large part, postliberalism is correct that the church has forgotten the language of faith and has become a people without a name or voice. Whether church or culture is responsible for this state of affairs is a misleading question because church exists within culture; each shapes the other as it always has throughout church history. Nevertheless, postliberals aid the church by calling us to consider anew our identity as the people called out by God and shaped by Christ and Holy Spirit. Such consideration does give rise to political response. Postliberalism correctly considers the church a political body, that is, a public with vested interest and authority. That interest and authority is of Christ, who quite often puts the church at odds with the world.

The purpose of preaching in the postliberal model, as explained by Hauerwas, is its power to form a people who "use their language rightly." Hauerwas cautions, however, that the preacher is not the one responsible for such formation. "Rather, for the preached word to be God's word the Holy Spirit must make us a body of people capable of hearing the word rightly...The preached word's power is its capacity to create a people

---

[17]Mary Catherine Hilkert, *Naming Grace: Preaching and the Sacramental Imagination* (New York: Continuum, 1996).

[18]This is James Gustafson's critique of Hauerwas in "The Sectarian Temptation: Reflections on Theology, the Church and the University," *Proceedings of the Catholic Theological Society* 40 (1985): 83–94.

receptive to being formed by that word."[19] Preaching does indeed shape and edify the people of God in the world. The language of preaching, by the presence of Christ through the Holy Spirit, helps create the community we know as church. As Charles Campbell clearly states, "The preacher's task must be seen not as that of creating experiential events for individual hearers, but rather as that of building up the church…God in Jesus Christ is…the active subject who gathers and builds up the eschatological people of God in and for the world."[20]

This church-forming dimension of preaching is pastoral, given the preacher pastor's concern for the health of the congregation. Preachers speak and act among a people, a relational community. Preacher pastors are concerned for the health of the whole congregation, its caring *ethos,* not just for the health of each individual. Pastoral preachers will look seriously at how the theology and language of preaching shapes the church as a caring community. In large part language shapes our worlds.

But we need to be cautious here when we define the church and pastoral preaching in such fashion. Pastoral preaching dare not envision a church that takes a rigid stance against the culture as it carries out the work of formation. When Hauerwas and others within postliberalism look at the world, they see total corruption, the rotting fruit of modernity and liberalism. In their view, the best hope for church renewal is through a distinctive return to the biblical narrative in preaching, worship, and education. But their reading of the biblical narrative renders a Jesus whose incarnational presence is restricted to the church alone. Ultimately, the hearer of such proclamation "is confronted with the distinct possibility that God is at work in no place outside of the narrative" or the church formed by the narrative.[21] According to postliberalism's claims, when in dialogue with the world, the church always retains privilege, for the church has no other way to understand itself, no other place to stand, than on the Jesus uniquely revealed in scripture. Jesus, whom God offers to the world in love (Jn. 3:16), becomes instead Jesus for the church. The church, a fleshly sign and embodiment of God's love for the world, becomes a people who study their own "grammar." This results in the odd image of the preacher pastor as head grammarian. Yes, the church is Christ-centered, but the church does not fully contain Christ. Renewal of a sort may come to this church, but it is doubtful that this church will engage in the transformation of the world that God is already bringing about, sometimes through the church and sometimes despite the church.

---

[19]Stanley Hauerwas, *Christian Existence Today: Essays on Church, World, and Living In Between* (Durham, N.C.: Labyrinth Press, 1988), 60.

[20]Charles Campbell, *Preaching Jesus: New Directions for Homiletics in Hans Frei's Postliberal Theology* (Grand Rapids, Mich.:Eerdmans, 1997), 221.

[21]David J. Lose, "Narrative and Proclamation," in *Papers of the Annual Meeting of the Academy of Homiletics* (Oakland, Dec. 4–6, 1997), 38. Lose continues, "The assertion that the storied world rendered by the biblical narrative is the one, true world, suggests an insidious denigration of created reality, a disposition clearly at odds with the Incarnation" (39).

John Cobb points out that we have here two different understandings of the church's task at hand, "renewal or transformation."[22] Both are needed–renewal *and* transformation. We cannot afford to discount the church's participation in God's transformation of creation any more than we can pretend that the church isn't in serious need of renewal. We need to pay attention to both the *ethos* (character) and the *telos* (purpose) of the church. We cannot determine the nature of the church apart from its mission and relationship to the wider world. I have found no better expression of the relationship between church and world, though it is now a generation old, than that of H. Richard Niebuhr. He says that the world is "companion of the Church, a community something like itself with which it lives before God...The world is the community to which Christ comes and to which he sends his disciples."[23]

The Prophetic Pastoral Church

The church takes up the liberating task of care in the world. Even more, the church hears those voices within the world who offer transformation to the church. Pastoral preaching paints a picture of the church whose members care for one another and the world and–this is crucial–who by caring for the world recognize the validity of the world's claims upon the church. When women, minorities, the poor of the world–those whom the mainline Western churches have largely ignored–call for emancipation of the church from the forces that exclude and divide, it is not an alien impingement upon the church. Rather, this is often the voice of God speaking from within the world as a corrective of the church.

Pastoral preaching sounds the overtones of prophecy that serve as a caring internal critique of the church and a transformative orientation toward the world. Charles Gerkin captures this balance in his work *Prophetic Pastoral Practice.*[24] Pastoral preachers want to preach into existence a compassionate, hospitable, communal church in which the focus is on being together with other women, men, and children as a manifestation of the humanity of God. But this church in the world is based in the *koinonia* made possible because of Christ's presence among the people. Without this faithful christocentrism, the Christian church does not exist. Other meaningful forms of human gathering and action do exist, but we cannot call them Christian. Pastoral preaching, if it hopes to form and transform the church as a truly caring community, must learn to see the church and the world from the perspective of those "on the margins." But this is so because "the ultimate

---

[22]John Cobb, *Reclaiming the Church: Where the Mainline Church Went Wrong and What to Do About It* (Louisville: Westminster John Knox Press, 1997).

[23]H. Richard Niebuhr, *The Purpose of the Church and Its Ministry* (New York: Harper & Row, 1956), 26.

[24]Charles Gerkin, *Prophetic Pastoral Practice: A Christian Vision of Life Together* (Nashville: Abingdon Press, 1991).

goal of God's household is to do away with the margin and the center by joining the one who is at the center of life in the church [Jesus Christ] but dwells on the margins where he lived and died."[25] The conservative who reads the liberal out of the church is no more tenable than the liberationist who casts out the progressive.[26] The church forms around a table with seats enough for all to hear a word transformative of all.

Incorporation into this community of care in the world is present now and also an eschatological possibility. Pastoral preachers hope to form such pastoral communities, while realizing that the present community is a sign of that deeper communion with God and creation that is yet to come. The nature of this community that pastoral preaching seeks to help bring into existence is one of mutual concern among members, hospitable relations, and compassionate practices. Persons within this pastoral community seek to guide, heal, sustain, and reconcile one another to God and neighbor as each carries on the work of pastoral care within and beyond the congregation proper. As Luther said to members of the church at Wittenburg, drawing out the pastoral care conveyed through the eucharist, "For this bread is a comfort to the sorrowing, a healing for the sick, a life for the dying, a food for the hungry, and rich treasure for all the poor and needy."[27] The Lord's supper stands as the means and symbolization of God's great creation banquet, in which God's care for those who gather around the table extends outward to embrace the world.

Just why participation in such a Christ-centered community is pastoral should be clear. Indeed, care cannot be experienced (given or received) except through interpersonal means, whether between two persons or among many. The failure of many primary relationships, for example within marriages and families, results from the unrealistic expectation that the nuclear family alone will provide sufficient community. Pastoral concern for others occurs among those in communion. Such concern moves with tender toughness out into the world to embrace the presence of God that is not confined to the institutional church.

The formation of prophetic pastoral communities in which people care for one another and the world broadens the scope of pastoral preaching to encompass the church as a whole. Prophetic pastoral preaching seeks to nurture the entire community, which shares the task of pastoral care within church and world. John Patton nicely sums up this contemporary pastoral care turn to the church as a pastoral community. "It is the caring community,

---

[25]Russell, *Church in the Round,* 92.

[26]"It is only patriarchal either/or thinking that leads persons to assume that if God is for the poor, God is against everyone else," ibid., 121.

[27]Martin Luther, "The Sixth Sermon, March 14, 1522, Friday after Invocavit" in *Luther's Works,* vol. 51, ed. and trans. John W. Doberstein (Philadelphia: Fortress Press, 1959), 95.

inclusive of both laity and clergy, that provides pastoral care."[28] Historically speaking, this ecclesiology emerges from a Lutheran emphasis on the priesthood of all believers and a Calvinist-Methodist-Catholic emphasis on sanctification within community that leads to works of love and justice in the world. Though a great gulf opened between Calvinists and Methodists in the eighteenth century over sin and salvation, I think that the founders of both movements would agree that the people of God exist for care of others.

The hunger for community within the Western world is a truism. In response to the fragmentation and individualism of postmodern culture, contemporary desire for community suggests an opening for Christian communities who care deeply for the world. This longing for community runs through all persons if we take our theological anthropology seriously. Community is not a women's or men's issue, a first- or third-world concern, a black or white privilege or problem. As Christine Neuger states, "It is a human issue to be related in community, not a woman's issue."[29] Judaism and Christianity have specialized in the forming and transforming of community throughout their history. The grace of Christ is manifest in Christian community, yet this community is not defined by persons intent on internal nurture but as a people who actively care for all creation. As Teresa Fry Brown writes, "The role of the church is to meet people where they are, help them when we can, and let God use them as God sees fit."[30] Pastoral preaching will address the real people before us here and now, not presuming to know everyone's needs in advance. Yet such preaching is confident that the care of God in Jesus Christ that speaks in the sermon will form "the people of God" who live "for others" in the world.

Now that I have sketched out these general outlines of a theology of the church, a Christ-shaped church that we understand as the "people of God for others," we can move ahead to look at a few suggestions for how our preaching can actually help fashion this pastoral community. Just how might this theology of the church actually inform the sermons that we preach? From the pulpit, when we look out at the faces of "the church," how can our sermons help the members of the church recognize themselves as church and be guided by their theological self-understandings into care for others in the world?

---

[28]John Patton, *Pastoral Care in Context: An Introduction to Pastoral Care* (Louisville: Westminster/John Knox Press, 1993), 3.

[29]See Christine Cozad Neuger, "Gender: Women and Identity," in *The Treasure of Earthen Vessels: Explorations in Theological Anthropology: In honor of James Lapsley,* ed. Brian Childs and David Waanders (Louisville: Wesminster/John Knox Press, 1994), 234.

[30]Teresa Fry Brown, "An African American Woman's Perspective: Renovating Sorrow's Kitchen," in *Preaching Justice: Ethnic and Cultural Perspectives,* ed. Christine Smith (Cleveland: United Church Press, 1998), 59.

From Sermon to Caring Community

The central characters of John Updike's satiric novel *Couples* wrestle with the absence of Christian community in the postmodern world. The sermons of their preacher, Reverend Horace Pedrick, strain pitifully to make connections between the Jesus of scripture and the lives of the members of the congregation. Pedrick preaches,

> The man Jesus does not ask us to play a long shot. He does not come to us and say, "Here is a stock for speculation. Buy at eight-and-one-eighth, and in the Promised Land you can sell at one hundred." No, he offers us *present security*, four-and-a-half per cent compounded every quarter![31]

Little wonder, with such hackneyed preaching and such attempts to translate between gospel and a money-driven culture, that the people within the congregation do not find genuine Christian community. The preacher fails to paint a picture for the members of the Christ-shaped church that will sustain their lives together and challenge their vision for the world. The sermon does not help the hearers see themselves any differently than the culture in general. So they turn from the church and attempt to build a substitute community, a kind of erotic fellowship that replaces the language and rituals of worship. They preach their own sermons to one another. They seek to lose and find themselves in the mysticism of passionate sexual relations. Their experiment falls apart, of course. Without the sustenance of the sacred, their community collapses on itself. But this only heightens the failure of the original church and its preacher to incorporate the believer into a caring community. Perhaps Updike is too harsh with the church in his work, but his stinging fictional critiques seem born from deep disappointment and from the desire to hold the church accountable to its own theological nature and purpose.[32]

All along I have stressed the crucial link between preaching and the pastoral community of the church. The sermon is not something that the church can take or leave. It is not something that the preacher can pick up or put down like an optional task—"I know it's Sunday, but I don't think that I'll preach today." The sermon is one of the primary ways that God forms and addresses the people. Without Word and Sacrament, there is no church. Insofar as human words become a sermon, by the power of the Holy Spirit the preached word has immense power to shape the church. If we seek to preach well through prayerful preparation, thoughtful attention to theology and culture, and scriptural interpretation, the church may form as the people of God for others, a pastoral community. But if we preach poorly without careful thought for the church, as Reverend Pedrick does in

---

[31]John Updike, *Couples* (New York: Alfred A. Knopf, 1968), 26.
[32]I have followed Robert Detweiler's commentary on Updike, *Breaking the Fall*, 91–121.

Updike's story, the consequences can be disastrous for the church and the members of the body.

Preaching among the Church That Cares

Pastoral preaching stirs up the vision of a caring Christian community. The congregation needs to see in the sermon what such a church looks and acts like in order to know themselves and their purpose in the world. The pastoral sermon, like powerful fiction, can "cause a community to rethink its identity—to consider whether it is, in fact, a community."[33] I do not mean that the sermon or its contents is fiction. Rather, the sermon works like fiction on the imagination of the congregation, helping them to see themselves within community, and the community within the world, in the ever new and enlivening light of the gospel. If all that the people see is their own disconnected lives when the preacher paints word pictures from the pulpit, they will leave the sanctuary as fragmented as when they arrived. But if in word and image the preacher amply imagines for the congregation the shape and details of a caring, pastoral community, centered in Christ, they may leave the house of worship with a greater awareness of their own communion with one another. They may step into the sunlight enlivened enough to care for others whom God loves in the world.

This means that pastoral preachers will seek every occasion in the sermon to give full presence to the core image of the church as the people of God for others. Obviously, every sermon will not be *about* the church. But every sermon will grow out of some consistent pastoral theological understanding of the church. Whether references in the sermon to the church are explicit or implicit, by what we say or what we imply, the sermon will point the people toward who they are as God's people and what their purpose is—to love God and neighbor.

On a practical level, the pastoral preacher will intentionally lift out of the common life of the gathered community those experiences of worship, fellowship, education, and service that re-present to the church their central identity and purpose in Christ. For example, a very small urban church has become the distribution center every Christmas for more than ten thousand toys for homeless children and impoverished families. That this congregation of twenty-five persons each year coordinates such a massive relief program expresses and reinforces their identity as God's people with a vital mission in the city. The preacher pastor would be wise to occasionally recall in sermons this unique feature of congregational witness, even as she expands their vision of love and justice. Pastoral preaching at times holds up a mirror to the people of God and says, "Look how Christ is among us." The intent is not to foster ecclesial works righteousness but to deepen the church's vision of itself as an agent of care in the community.

---

[33]Detweiler, *Breaking the Fall,* 117.

If we fail through the sermon to help the congregation see itself as a pastoral community, we should not be surprised that they do not act as a pastoral community. How can we expect the congregation to understand the theological nature of communal hospitality without pointing to examples of hospitality in our sermons and saying, "Take a look at yourselves? You are the people who share bread with others?" We want to be sure to pick up the actual instances of mutuality, hospitality, and compassion that occur within the congregation and, like a mirror, reflect these back to the congregation in the sermon. If all our sermonic examples of pastoral community come from other congregations, ones that we have heard about or know about firsthand, we are probably signaling to the actual listeners that we do not really discern their own pastoral nature. Such a mistake will breed either contempt or apathy on the part of the church. Take a little time. Listen and look for the signs of the caring community that is already emerging within the congregation. Then remind the church through the sermon that you know who they are. You see and value their caring for one another through Christ.

Such pastoral preaching gives presence to congregational life (*koinonia*) *and* to the church's caring ministry in the world (*diakonia*). Themes of mutuality, fellowship, bread-breaking, sustaining one another in prayer, disciplining one another in love, healing, and reconciliation among the body will make up these inner-church elements of the sermon. I stress *inner*-church, not inward, for the church is present among the people of God in relation, not as an inward experience. Sermons will hold up to the congregation the simple acts of kindness and celebration that speak of communal pastoral care. These are obvious, but we sometimes overlook them because they are so mundane, and because preachers tend to scan the horizons of church and culture for the dramatic story. Congregations usually express pastoral care simply, but nonetheless effectively, and it varies from one congregation to the next. Here are a few examples:

- Someone prepares a chicken casserole for a family returning from the hospital.
- A children's Sunday school class makes and delivers cards to the congregation's homebound members.
- Someone places a phone call to a lonely teenager at just the right time.
- The entire congregation quietly takes a special collection for persons who are on a labor strike.
- Hushed conversations in the sanctuary are mutual prayers of support among families who have experienced tragedy.
- The congregation spontaneously applauds when a parent and child are baptized.

The preacher can highlight in sermons the various acts of pastoral ministry that go on in churches all the time. Again, this is not for the purpose of congregational self-congratulation, but to help the people remember who they are. When the preacher does this, she speaks a pastoral community into being. The way that the sermon shows how the people care for one another forms the caring community itself. The caring church of the sermon cues the congregation in its pastoral ministry, even as the pastoral ministry of the congregation finds presence in the sermon.

Such presencing of congregational care in the sermon is much more than positive reinforcement. I am not suggesting that the preacher is a cheerleader urging the congregation on to pastoral victory. Indeed, there may be some congregations that are care-less, and the preacher would be hard-pressed among a mean-spirited people to point toward any shred of mutual affection. What I am referring to is the constitutive power of language itself. The images of care that we offer in the sermon become embodied in the church. This is so not only because language shapes communities, but because the Holy Spirit infuses our preached language. The Spirit of God gathers in the body of Christ through the sermon. Caring sermons form caring communities; caring communities find themselves in caring sermons.

Caring Community Realities (and Cautions)

Pastoral preaching that builds up the church as a caring community does not idealize human togetherness. Christian communities often lapse into instrumental or utilitarian relations. Persons within congregations can inadvertently begin to treat one another as means to personal ends in the same way that we often relate to one another in the wider culture. To use Martin Buber's famous phrase, our relations become "I-it" relations rather than "I-Thou." Tragically, we see one another as objects rather than as subjects. The church becomes a place (rather than a people) where individual believers gather to garner personal gain or to have their own needs met. In this scenario, we view the church as a filling station where each believer comes to fill up. We forget that Christ is the host of this pastoral community and that Christ sees us all as beloved members of the family of God. In Christ and the Holy Spirit, we gather to worship God, enjoy one another, and remember our calling in the world. When in the pastoral community we treat one another as means to our own personal ends, we have succumbed to the very cultural myths that are destructive of God-given community in the first place.

Preaching will also help the pastoral community be alert to the threat of the demonic. Loving communities can become seething cauldrons of hatred. Despite our best efforts to live as a reconciled people, sin is yet present within church and world. In its most aberrant forms, sin erupts as violence within the community. Where we wish to sow love, we sow hatred. Where we desire to offer pardon, we inflict injury and harm. It is appropriate to occasionally remind the congregation of its own potential for harm. The occasional negative example of community destructiveness can serve to awaken the pastoral conscience of the congregation. This can be done without lobbing pulpit stones on the heads of the unsuspecting congregation or chewing the hearers out for their faithlessness. Perhaps the negative example should come from another congregation, or from within the imagination of the preacher, or from scripture. There is certainly no shortage of conflict and violence in the scriptures. But these images will remind the pastoral community that the work of confession and reconciliation is ongoing. And it will help us to recall that Christ is the one who overcomes the pastoral community's potential for harm.

Some congregations actually experience occasions that approach ideal fellowship, where "we are one in the Spirit, we are one in the Lord."[34] But these moments are never perfected and always fleeting. Preacher pastors will recognize the need to account for the broken nature of all communities, Christian and otherwise, because of the presence of human sin. This recognition will allow the preacher to image the church of the sermon as broken yet whole. Broken because the church is composed of broken people. Whole because Christ reconciles church and world to God (2 Cor. 5:16–21). Even if not physically violent, church people can be downright mean to one another. We can be care-less. A good preacher pastor will allow this warts-and-all church into the sermon as well, holding before them the pastoral call to confession and the promise of forgiveness.

A perfectly caring church would clearly not be the church that Jesus comes to heal, for Jesus stakes his claim among sinners. But many of our sermons dress up the church so much that the people who compose the church cannot recognize themselves. We hold up false pictures of the church as a people who are always kind and charitable with every wrinkle pressed and every collar buttoned down. When the preacher paints these unimaginable portraits of the church, you can almost hear someone in the congregation whisper to her neighbor, "Who's he talking about?" Preacher pastors can air things out a little bit with respect to the church. Pastoral preaching can help the congregation by being honest about the church's nature. Some examples that are fairly common within our churches might be the following:

- A good committee conflict, once resolved, ought to show up in a sermon every now and then, though never to shame or embarrass congregational members.
- A story or two about the way the church botches its own best efforts at worship can actually raise the level of pastoral integrity of

---

[34]"They'll Know We Are Christians," *Chalice Hymnal* (St. Louis: Chalice Press, 1995), #494.

the congregation as they are led to a deeper understanding of God with us.[35]

- The church's tendency to worship itself, its programs, its buildings, its status, ought to be named in preaching, not to harangue the congregation for its falseness, but to remind the members of who they are as children of God.

- A congregational setback or defeat can become an opportunity for nurturing "holy irony," such as Joseph saying to his brothers, "You meant it for harm, but God meant it for good."

- Whenever actual violence or deep emotional harm erupts within the community, this can be handled with care in the pulpit, though it should properly be addressed outside of the pulpit as well.

In these and similar ways, pastoral preachers will cast light upon the many faces of care within the church as the pastoral community forms. If we want to construct a pastoral community through preaching, we will show the community realistic pictures of itself now even as we paint hopeful pictures of who they are becoming by the grace of God.

Preaching among the Church That Cares for Others

Despite everything said thus far about pastoral preaching within the congregation, the inner care of the congregation is not the real telos of pastoral preaching according to our theology of the church. Pastoral preachers hope to form pastoral communities whose purpose is care for others in the world. We hope to fashion communities that express ongoing compassion for those outside of the congregation. With the systematizing of care in the twentieth century, authentic communities whose members care deeply for one another and the world may be one of our last hopes of seeding the culture with care. As Walter Brueggemann says, "The church at its most courageous and its most faithful, deliberately and intentionally makes its claims for the sake of the nonchurch public."[36] Unlike the many other systems designed for care "delivery"—health care systems, government, criminal justice—who routinely fail to deliver care, churches remain uniquely voluntary with a vision and capacity to respond informally and directly to the needs of those inside and beyond the church.[37] In short, the church sociologically and theologically retains community reality when much of culture does not. Since care characterizes community, the surest sign that a church is a true community formed in Christ is shown by its caring activity in the world.

---

[35]See Annie Dillard's hilarious yet reverent take on Christian worship in *Teaching a Stone to Talk: Expeditions and Encounters* (New York: Harper, 1982), 17–52.

[36]Walter Brueggemann, *Cadences of Home: Preaching Among Exiles* (Louisville: Westminster John Knox Press, 1997), 79.

[37]See John McKnight, *The Careless Society: Community and Its Counterfeits* (New York: Basic Books, 1995).

From the beginning, the church has claimed its mission within the world to proclaim God's good news of liberation, feed the hungry, clothe the naked, and stand among the poor. Through Christ's mission the church understands its own purpose as an emptying on behalf of the world so that the world might be filled in Christ (Philippians 2). The church as a pastoral community realizes its true calling not only in communal comfort and health but in active living for others in the wider world. As David Buttrick coins it, the church is the "being-saved-community-in-the-world."[38] Part of the church's being-saved (being healed) is that the church participates in the healing of the world and so discovers, by the power of God, how its own salvation is linked with the salvation of the world wherein God is "making all things new." Therefore, the mission of the church can be helpfully understood in terms of "care." In answer to the cynical quip frequently tossed off today, "Who cares?" the church responds, "We do."

Congregations need to hear sermons that picture the church as a care-full presence in the wider world. They need to imagine themselves engaging culture care-fully. Churches will be able to do so when our sermons bring such caring action alive in story and imagination, in scriptural interpretation and theology. Some preachers easily bring to congregational awareness the caring ministry of the church within society. But other preachers rarely point to the caring work of the church in the world, either that of their own congregation or another's.

What we are after are concrete images of the church engaged in care for others. In the background we wish to see an empty church with the front doors wide open; in the foreground, the people of God caring in the world. The possibilities are not difficult to imagine. Here are a few examples that come to mind:

- An intergenerational group of church folks walking down the side of the highway wearing orange vests, scampering in and out of the ditches to collect trash

- An adult church group that volunteers regularly at a battered women's shelter

- A whole congregation standing together at a vigil for persons who have died with AIDS

- A small group of church members who tutor children who fall behind in their schoolwork

- A church such as one in New Mexico that several years ago constructed their new sanctuary on a defunct site for intercontinental ballistic missiles

- An ecumenical body of churches that supports a community health clinic that provides affordable health care for the poor

---

[38]David Buttrick, *Homiletic:Moves and Structures* (Philadelphia: Fortress Press, 1987), 41–42, 254–55, 260.

- A church meeting with local bankers to inquire about enforcement of fair lending laws

The possibilities for highlighting the care of the church for others are almost endless. Each of these examples is pastoral and prophetic in one way or another, though clearly none of these caring ministries is perfect or without complications. These examples obviously reflect a middle-class congregational perspective. Issues of economic, political, racial, and environmental justice impinge on each of these scenarios, and pastoral communities that engage the world with care will quickly find themselves drawn into the irresolvable tensions between love *and* justice.

The crucial point is that pastoral preaching projects on the screen of congregational awareness realistically imaginable scenes of the church actively caring for others in the world. If the church is already engaged in such ministry, stories of these ministries should appear regularly in sermon and liturgy. We can hold up the caring ministry of the congregation without being self-congratulatory by remembering that the mission of the church rests on the self-giving of Jesus Christ.

The pictures of the church in the sermon should not be beyond belief. This does not mean that the ecclesiological images shouldn't challenge the congregation. But a challenge is something imaginable, within the realm of possibility. Dismissed, our sermonic images of the church cannot do the work of congregational formation and transformation. We want to be cautious. Congregations "out there" who seem to be doing something "incredibly important" may not speak to the congregation that gathers in the sanctuary. The work of that congregation "out there" may be true, but the image of the church doesn't function effectively in the sermon to draw the congregation toward care in the world.

Notice that the rather commonplace examples above involve active participation of church members and not simply financial support. Care is interpersonal. True, congregations are significant funding bases for others who minister care on behalf of the global church. This is necessary, and images from such ministries will engage the caring capacity of the congregation. But I am persuaded that in our care-less society of today we most need pastoral communities who live carefully in word and deed. Yes, we will collect money and send it to the local hunger agency. But better yet, we'll find congregational representatives to stand side by side in the soup kitchen and see the faces and hear the stories of those who hunger and thirst for righteousness' sake. It's the pastoral thing to do.

Communion in Pastoral Preaching

One further comment about the use of language in preaching may assist us in the actual building of pastoral sermons. We have already discussed the importance of presence in preaching. Presence refers to how the sermon brings into focus those images, symbols, scriptural narratives, and cultural concerns that the preacher wants to highlight for the congregation. I have claimed throughout this chapter that how the preacher gives presence to (or does not give presence to) the church in the sermon will help shape the formation of a pastoral community. And I have offered several examples of ecclesiological images that can bring the caring church into view in the sermon. But preachers can also deepen the pastoral perspective of preaching through the use of communion.

Communion is what establishes the relationship between the preacher and the congregation that allows the preacher to draw the congregation toward the desired aims of the sermon.[39] Preaching assumes the reality of a community, the congregation, who with the preacher work together in preaching and worship through cooperation and understanding. The preacher and the congregation may achieve communion through references to a common culture, tradition, or past. Or the preacher may take the congregation into her confidence, inviting the congregation's help and identification. In many African American congregations, for example, the preacher and congregation are building communion when the preacher seeks help with the sermon by saying, "Help me now," or "Can somebody say, Amen!" But many preachers, aware or not, seek to develop communion with the congregation as a way to make the sermon more effective. The closer the speaker and audience are drawn together in communion, the more probability exists that persuasive communication will occur. In our case, the preacher pastor hopes to move the members of the congregation toward an understanding of themselves as a community centered in Christ whose purpose is care for others in the world.

Here we move toward the impact of the preacher pastor as a person. Interpersonal dynamics necessarily affect the sermon event. The preacher is not a mechanical communication tool. She is a living person who knows that her own loves, desires, hopes, failures, abilities, and limits all participate in creating communion within the congregation. She stands not above but among the people, inviting and, yes, persuading them to see themselves as agents of God's care in the world. At a minimum, this calls on a preacher to empathetically enter the lives of others. Effective pastoral sermons show the preacher's cognitive and emotional ability to establish communion through appropriate expression of shared tradition, communal wisdom, shared worldviews, and the use of the self as representative person to speak on behalf of the public.[40] Interestingly, the penchant today for many

---

[39]I am drawing from Chaim Perelman's *The New Rhetoric: A Treatise on Argumentation,* trans. John Wilikinson and Purcell Weaver (Notre Dame: University of Notre Dame Press, 1969), esp. pages 177–78.

[40]"Empathy...is the ability to find, in public or private, the words which so fully appreciate the reality of another that heart-to-heart contact is made. For instance, prophetic preaching, at its best, begins in an experience of empathy between the preacher and the congregation–an expression of the way that we are human beings together." Pamela Couture, *Pastoral Care and Social Conflict,* ed. Pamela Couture and Rodney Hunter (Nashville: Abingdon Press, 1995), 65.

preachers to begin or end sermons with personal stories is probably based on the desire to establish communion. Unfortunately, the personal in the pulpit is often not communal but private and idiosyncratic. I once heard an incredulous parishioner comment about her preacher's personal stories, "How can any one person have so many unusual things happen in his life?" Here, the idiosyncratic stories of the preacher have blocked out communal participation in the sermon. In this instance, while the preacher's goal of establishing communion is important, the end result is loss of communion.

We should not think of communion as the preacher speaking about his or her own life as a way to establish pastoral contact. What I mean by communion is that the preacher's sermonic language and imagistic content clearly communicate to the hearers that she or he shares their world and some notion of what the world seems like to them from the inside out. The preacher is able to foster communion with the congregation primarily because he or she is embedded in that same world through congregational and communal ties, and secondarily because she or he hones the art of human understanding and applies it to the task of pastoral care and preaching.

Many preachers with innate pastoral sensitivity communicate empathetically. But others can learn to develop the empathic imagination.[41] While no single quality of the preacher pastor will necessarily form the congregation as a pastoral community, empathy at the service of the Word is surely one of the most important. Used well, the preacher weaves empathy into the caring language that establishes congregational communion. None of this ever closes the door on the active participation of God through Christ and the Holy Spirit. Rather, it recognizes that the preacher pastor's ability to establish communion with the hearer is one means whereby God does the work of grace through preaching.

Note well, however, that communion is for the purpose of the formational goal of pastoral preaching–to form the church as a people of God who care for others in the world. Our theology of the church and the kind of people that our preaching forms are what matter. Communion in preaching is not for its own sake. Preacher-congregation identification is not to massage the ego of the preacher (We just love his stories!) nor to take the congregation on a sermonic roller-coaster ride of emotional catharsis through identification with the preacher as tragic hero. A certain distance is necessary between congregation and preacher for communion to be effective. The goal is for preacher and congregation to know that they

---

[41]See Fred B. Craddock, *Preaching* (Nashville: Abingdon Press, 1985), 84–98, for examples of how preachers can develop empathic understanding of the congregation. Also, David Buttrick's use of tightly crafted imagistic systems works off of the empathic imagination of the preacher seeking connections (establishing communion) with the congregation, *Homiletic*, 113–25.

stand side by side in pastoral care and that they are moving outward together for care of others.

Communion in pastoral preaching, therefore, is a preaching strategy that helps a congregation envision a common future of care-full action in the world. It draws not only upon shared meanings from the past but shared anticipation of the future. For example, the preacher might say,

> We get awfully callous around here sometimes. We pick at each other and fuss over the color of our hymnals while the neighbors go hungry at night.
>
> But we know there's a better way. We know about the New Community in Christ, where no one hurts or destroys, where we care for our neighbors with the love of God.

In this simple exchange the preacher establishes communion when he identifies with the congregation ("we"), draws on the common life of the people ("around here sometimes," "pick at each other over the color of our hymnals"), and paints a recognizable vision based in scripture and theology of who humanity and church really are ("the New Community in Christ, where no one hurts or destroys, where we care for our neighbors"). The dialogue is faithful to a pastoral theological anthropology that sees humanity in brokenness together before God and to an ecclesiology that approaches the worldly mission of the church with utmost concern.

In the following example, notice how the preacher draws from the common life of the congregation (choir, hymns, sermon) and their lives in the world (budgets and bills). He establishes communion with the congregation even as he draws on the communal imagery of the eucharist. The sermon points toward Christ at the center of the congregation, Christ who is the basis of the Christian community.

> But even when we fail to be one with each other, Christ is still one with us in the breaking of the good bread. When the budget is quivering for relief and we strain to pay our bills, he is with us. When the hymns sound unfamiliar, the choir is off, and the sermon stinks, quite literally, to high heaven, he is with us. When all else fails, when our spinning world is shattering into a million fragments, he is still with us piecing us together around his holy table. When we've got nothing left but our hunger, we still have a loaf and a cup through which we are united: with Christ, with each other.[42]

Efforts like these to establish communion will hopefully bind preacher and congregation to the understanding of the church as a pastoral community—the people of God for others. Congregational members turn

---

[42]R. Mark Giuliano, "Good Bread for a Hungry Age," *Pulpit Digest* (Jan./Feb. 1996): 61.

toward the world with the same tender concern that they share for one another formed in Christ. In turning care-fully to others in the wider world, the church most fully recognizes itself as a pastoral community–a community of mutuality, hospitality, and compassion. This pastoral community seeks to guide, heal, sustain, and reconcile the world and all its people to God and one another.

Summary

The pastoral preacher understands that formation of congregational identity around the image of the church as the people of God for others occurs gradually as preacher and congregation move toward one another in theological understanding. Simply standing in the pulpit each week and repeating that "we are the people of God who care for others" will not get the job done. The ethos of any congregation is highly complex. It is formed over time and rooted in the history of a people in a concrete place. The many persons and events that touch on a particular congregation shape its character. Nevertheless, there is clear evidence that regular preaching over time may be one of the most consistent ways that a people come to understand themselves as a Christian congregation with certain theological commitments and a distinctive mission in the world.[43] The preacher pastor must move through all the events of parish ministry, and especially the preaching and liturgical events, with clear views of the human being and the church in heart and mind. Opportunities will naturally occur to speak about the nature of the church as "the people of God for others" or one of its attendant images–covenant community, household of faith, servant community–without forcing this anthropological and ecclesiological understanding on the congregation.

The possibility exists that through preaching, the pastoral community will gain greater awareness of how they are God's people bound together by common faith and practices and united by the power of the resurrected Christ and the Holy Spirit for worship and care. They will awaken to the transformative power of God's care within their midst. They will be energized by discovery that this local gathering of the people of God is related by creation and redemption to the whole human race as God's people. For if the congregation actually coalesces in its understanding of self and purpose as a pastoral community, it becomes a sacrament for all humanity, signifying in its patterns of interaction, its values and commitments, and its life together the possibility for all people to perceive themselves as the people of God for others.

---

[43]For actual sociological data on this point, see Robert Wuthnow, "Sources of Doctrinal Unity and Diversity," in *Views from the Pews: Christian Beliefs and Attitudes,* ed. Roger A. Johnson (Philadelphia: Fortress Press, 1983), 33–56.

6

Pastoral Sermons

I hope that preachers and pastors who have read these pages have become convinced, and if not convinced, at least willing to consider, that whatever else pastoral preaching may be, it is necessarily a theological endeavor. I hope that preachers will want to take a second look at the pastoral theology of their own sermons, especially at the anthropology and ecclesiology that guides their preaching. Some sermons are more pastoral than others because in their theology, regardless of the text, theme, or topic, they beckon a pastoral community to life. Such sermons paint vivid pictures of the church as a pastoral community for the listening congregation. They invite the congregation to see themselves within the pastoral imagery and theology of the sermon and to live as a pastoral community in the world.

The following sermons and analyses can help preachers think more concretely about their own sermons from a pastoral theological perspective. Using them as examples, preachers might learn how to sort through their own sermons to see the kind of human beings and churches that their preaching seeks to construct. I hope that this will help preachers become more proficient at pastoral preaching.

I consider each of these examples to be pastoral sermons, although the preachers may not have thought of them in such terms. They are diverse in content and preaching style. Each preacher was engaged in pastoral ministry when he or she preached the sermon, and each sermon occurred in distinctive congregations. By carefully exploring such diverse sermons, we get a glimpse of the various ways that pastoral theology occurs in all preaching. But more importantly, perhaps these representative sermons and the pastoral theological analysis of them will assist preachers in the ongoing task of pastoral preaching within the congregation.

Whatever Happened to the Golden Rule?[1]

James A. Forbes, Jr.

Dr. Forbes is senior minister at the Riverside Church in New York City. He was professor of homiletics at Union Theological Seminary in New York City from 1976 to 1989. He preached this sermon on April 30, 1989, at the Riverside Church.

The sermon for today was born beside the hospital bed of one of my friends with AIDS. He was disturbed about God's attitude toward people who are dying from AIDS and wanted to know whether the fact that he was gay would put a barrier between himself and the love of God. He wanted to know, Will God affirm me, celebrate the uniqueness of my being, my affection, my relationships?

Now I suspect you would like to know what I told him. And I would like to know what you would have told him if you had been there. Before I tell that story, let me say this sermon comes at a time when our entire community is attempting to respond to the brutal attack on the woman jogger in Central Park, while we as a people reflect upon what to do about the issue of AIDS and the increasing violence that we are experiencing in our times.

Back to the story of my friend. I came to discover that the church had in some way affected his sense of whether God could really be for him. His church, in this case, was a sensitive and caring congregation, but the wider community had made it difficult for him to trust even a biblical perspective of love and mercy and graciousness from God. Somehow the church and our society had not done what they could have done to make the passage through the perilous waters of pain and isolation more gracious for him.

It was while I was sitting by his bed that I started asking, What should the church do? And a response suggested itself like a word sent by Federal Express: The church should live by the Golden Rule. Do unto others as you would have others do unto you. I thought, "That's right." But let me confess something—I did not know where in the Bible the Golden Rule was found. And I'm a theological professor! Now don't laugh at me, brothers and sisters. Do you know where the Golden Rule is found?

I have not heard a sermon on the Golden Rule for a decade or so. As a matter of fact, I really think that rule is not the current policy of our citizens. For a period of time, it has seemed to be more and more appropriate for folks to look out for themselves—that a kind of narcissism has come to the fore in which I look into the mirror and I find myself focusing on what is

---

[1]Used by permission of Dr. James A. Forbes, Jr. First printed in Eleanor Scott Meyers, ed., *Envisioning the New City: A Reader on Urban Ministry* (Louisville: Westminster/John Knox Press, 1992), 90–97.

good for me, what will secure me, my family, my crowd, my caucus, my group. The rule about doing unto others as we would have them do unto us has not been the major motif in our time. So I am happy to tell you where it can be found. You can find the Golden Rule in the Gospel According to Matthew, chapter 7, verses 7–12:

> Ask, and it will be given you; search and you will find; knock and the door will be opened for you. For everyone who asks receives, and everyone who searches finds, and for everyone who knocks, the door will be opened. Is there anyone among you who, if your child asks for bread, will give a stone? Or if the child asks for a fish, will give a snake? If you then, who are evil, know how to give good gifts to your children, how much more will your Father in heaven give good things to those who ask him! In everything do to others as you would have them do to you; for this is the law and the prophets.

Now, two observations. Did you notice at the end of the Golden Rule—"In everything do to others as you would have them do to you"—that was not the end of the sentence? That there was a semicolon? And, following the semicolon, these words: "for this is the law and the prophets"? This suggests that the Golden Rule is not just some optional extra, added to the Ten Commandments. It is not just some voluntary principle of reciprocity; it is at the heart of the gospel. The core of Christian conduct is found right there in these words: "Do unto others as you would have them do unto you." I think it is such a strong admonition that persons who call themselves Christians who do not at least attempt to live by the Golden Rule might, on one day of harsh judgment, be required to turn in their membership cards.

What? You don't live by the Golden Rule? That is not the principle by which you order your relationships at home, in your workplace, at the church, and in the wider community? This is at the heart of it. This is almost a one-sentence requirement upon which Christian education programs are built: that we might learn how to treat other folks as we would wish to be treated ourselves.

Now there is a second thing about this text that helps to make the Golden Rule shine more brightly as we face our Christian responsibility. Notice that it was introduced with what I think is a rather staggering claim: Ask and it shall be given; seek and you shall find; knock and the door shall be opened unto you.

This text is introduced by a promise that the things we need in order to survive will be provided for us. What is this business? I think what you need to be aware of is the preceding chapter, chapter 6, where Jesus makes it clear what he is talking about: "But strive first for the kingdom of God" (Mt. 6:33)...what we now often call God's realm, the commonwealth of love. Seek God's kingdom and God's righteousness and all these things shall be yours as well.

In other words, Jesus is talking about a new community, a new arrangement that will obtain when God's reign has become the order of the day. In that time, people who have needs because of the quality of life in the beloved community would ask and it would be given; they would seek and find; they would knock and doors would be opened unto them. It is Jesus' projection of what it will look like when the church configures its life, or when society configures its life, according to the dream in the mind of the Creator. It is Jesus' way of saying, "This is where you learn to incline towards the inevitability of God's great reign, the beloved community." That is what Jesus was talking about: when God's reign and the principles of justice and mercy and equality have become the Magna Charta of the people of faith, when you could ask and it would be given.

It is within this kind of projection of a caring community that Jesus then says, "Do unto others as you would have them do unto you." Jesus compares God with our parental instincts: If you, with your shortcomings, based on your human frailty, know how to show special love and care for your children, then you are like God, who will provide the things we need. I think this gives deeper meaning to the world of the Golden Rule: Those who have entered the realm of God's tender, loving care will be set free from inordinate preoccupation with their own security and their well-being. One of my colleagues in the preaching class this week spoke about the problem of people being willing to extend graciousness to others who are unlike themselves. She said, it is as if people think that if God is gracious and merciful to somebody who is quite different from us, that the mercy and grace will run out before God gets around to our needs. But she said, "Not so." God can love somebody other than you and still have quite an abundance of love and grace for the likes of you and also for me.

So I tried my best before I answered my friend's question to see if I could get my spirit right with the principles of the Golden Rule. I guess I tried to put myself in his place: I tried to make my response on the basis of if I were gay, if I had AIDS, or if I happened to be a victim of the tyranny of drugs, if I had been despised, if I had been rejected, and if I had been denied a sense of comfort, if folks who used to touch me would not touch me anymore, if people were ashamed of who I was as I tried to be what I knew myself to be, what would I want somebody to say to me?

This is what I told him. I said, "We are all God's children." That is what I said. I said, "We are not the same, for God in creation was much more risk-taking to make differences. On the spectrum even of sexuality, if we'd line up, it would make an interesting rainbow coalition." I told him, "God loves us just the same. God celebrates the uniqueness of each one of us and calls us to discover the path of our own fulfillment in ways characterized by the integrity of our being." I said, "God bends from where we are and lifts us up in service of others. God forgives us when we fail to be faithful to who we are, and then God rejoices in our freedom to be who we are and encourages the community to celebrate with all people the integrity of their being. And if the beings are significantly different, then God's glory is in the diversity of creation itself."

And I said, "That does not mean we don't have problems to work through, brother; there are a lot of things I don't know, a lot of problems in the social fabric that have not been figured out yet, and I don't know how to work through them." I said, "But man, God loves and celebrates you. You don't have to wait in dread of death, thinking that God shuts the door on you." I said, "God, in fact, has a *special caring* for those who have been despised and rejected and abused and oppressed, and maybe you'll get a more royal welcome than some who think they deserve to enter before you." That's what I told him.

But it was not immediately clear to me that I had broken through the barriers built during the days of ostracism, so if, perchance, you are not yet able to see how the Golden Rule gives us the principles by which we respond, I wish to give some pointers to help us with what I call a case study: the Golden Rule as it was lived out by the Good Samaritan.

You know the story: A man on his way from Jerusalem to Jericho falls victim to robbers. The illustration is introduced by Jesus in response to a question from a lawyer wishing to put Jesus to the test. Desiring to justify himself, he asked Jesus how he might find eternal life. And I think a clue is right there. Let me tell you this, brothers and sisters, that if you—a preacher, or a deacon, or a lawyer, or a schoolteacher, or a doctor, or whatever your profession or your vocation may be—if you constantly find yourself trying to test other folks about who they are and what they ought to be doing, if you find yourself inordinately invested in that, or if you are like the text says, always trying to justify yourself—if you find that every day you get up you are conducting a referendum as to whether you are a worthy character—it means that you have not yet entered fully into the realm of God's tender, loving care. Everybody in the realm of God's love and tender care is already somebody. You don't have to make a case for being there. By God's grace you're already in. You don't have to go around testing folks all the time, judging other folks; *you're in!*

But between Jerusalem and Jericho, hear what it says. Fell among robbers who stripped him and beat him and departed leaving him half-dead. This is a description, and I think of it in two ways. I think of patients with AIDS and I think of that young woman jogging through Central Park. In the whole analysis, a victim falling among robbers who rob you of your dignity, of your personhood, who violate your very body and your spirit and your soul. This victim fell among the robbers; they stripped him and they stripped her; and beat him and beat her, and departed, leaving him and her half-dead.

Now let me ask you this morning: In light of this story, who is the victim? In the case of AIDS, is it the person with AIDS? Or the group to which the person belongs? Or the family? Or the total society? In Harlem, in Manhattan, it's the whole community that suffers every time there is an AIDS patient, for in a sense everybody has AIDS. All of us are going to die—

there are just those that require specialized attention. They are the victims, but I am also a victim; you, you too, are a victim. Is the victim the young woman in the park? You know it is. There is nobody that can smooth over that dastardly deed. But again, who is the victim? Are those kids victims? (Bless their hearts—I still cannot seem to identify them as a "wolf pack"; they're human beings!) Is the victim the kid who devised it from some kind of demonic impact or the other guys drawn in? Is it the mother of the victim or the mothers of the kids? Who is the victim? Is it the community itself? Is it the low-income housing project where those kids lived—the Schomburg Plaza apartment area? Who is the victim? In fact, the reason we are all so upset in this case is that we have not yet been able to identify with the attack. Was it because of poverty that they did it? The problem is we can't figure it out.

I think, brothers and sisters, that it may very well be that it is HIV—hearts infected with violence—which has broken out. I think the reason we are all upset is because there has been a break in the social contract. That you can't walk through the park, you can't walk down the street, you can't live. Something is coming unglued. And I think what is becoming unglued is *whatever it was that God had in mind* about how people ought to deal with each other as they would love to be dealt with. The Golden Rule is tarnished; some kind of acid has been poured on the Golden Rule that is strong enough to tarnish the gold. I think you and I are aware that whatever might hold our community together is coming unglued. And I think we have a right to be worried about it. A right to be frightened!

Of course, let's lay a wreath of flowers, let's have a prayer vigil, let's do the parade to show that we are together—black and white, gay and straight—and that sacred and secular organizations are working together. That's right. Let's do all of that. But you and I, looking at this story, understand that we need more than a temporary response, more than outrage. Somehow we have to recover the Golden Rule and thank God there was this person, after the preachers passed by, and after the deacons, too—after we all passed by—there was this person who came upon the fallen man and instead of bypassing him, poured oil and wine upon his wounds. He picked him up and put him upon his own horse, took him down further and put him in an inn. And the text says, "took care of him." That's the word: took care of him! And this is the part that is really exciting to me: After he took care, he took out two silver coins and gave them to the innkeeper, saying, "Take care of him."

Riversiders, this is for us! Namely, we are a congregation where we do not simply take care. We do our charitable bit, but we are also people who, as we take care, find a way to engage the system in taking care. In the moving beyond charity to the analysis that leads toward system change, not only are we taking care, we are creating a take-care system that will allow us once again to live, to walk freely in our streets, and to enjoy jogging in our parks.

The question in this case study that held me up was, Why did that man stop and do that? And I think I know the answer. Why did this good Samaritan stop and give genuine care? I think I've gotten onto it! I believe he did it because he had been on that road. I suspect—it doesn't say so in the Bible, so please forgive the homiletical imagination—I suspect that he might have experienced, in one form or other, that assault on his person; he was a Samaritan, you know. He knew what it felt like to be despised and rejected, to be robbed, assaulted, and called names. He had been there. It was that capacity that I think makes possible movement into the realm of God's tender, loving care, and I think that's where I ought to end.

Jesus the Christ invites us into the realm of tender, loving care. Jesus' invitation is to the young woman, and all young women, black and white, Hispanic, Asian, and Native American. Jesus says, I know what it is like. Jesus has been in Central Park—they called it Gethsemane. Assaulted, even by his friends. He had been there. He knew what it was like to be called names.

So Jesus is with our sister. Yes, and as they at the vigil stand and pray the prayer, Jesus is there. He says, "I know what you have been through; I know what it is like." And yet, Jesus says, maybe something redemptive can come from it.

So I say to my friend, "Hey, brother, in your bed of AIDS, Jesus has been there. He knows what death will be like. He knows what it's like; he's been there."

The purpose of the church in this time is to create a group of people who understand that this God created us out of the same batch of divine creativity, that we've all been there. And when you recognize in my sister and brother that we've all been there together, it will become increasingly impossible for us to engage in various forms of assault against each other.

My prayer is that we in this congregation, slowly maybe, sometimes kicking and screaming and debating and shouting about it, will become a congregation where, when we look at one another and see into the eyes of a brother or sister, we will understand their suffering and pain; we will be able to say, *I've been there,* so let me do unto this person even as I would have him or her do unto me. Amen.

Commentary

This sermon begins with the preacher's recounting a pastoral care visit with a man dying from AIDS. The preacher is disturbed by the questions that the man is asking: "Will God affirm me, celebrate the uniqueness of my being, my affection, my relationships?" With such an opening, the hearer might think that the whole sermon will focus on the difficult matter of the Christian response to those with AIDS. This would certainly be a worthy topic for a pastoral sermon.

But Forbes quickly signals that the sermon will attempt more than to develop a response to persons with AIDS. The entire community is wrestling with another problem: the brutal assault on a jogger in New York's Central

Park. He asks the Riverside Church congregation to consider not only the pain of those who are dying with AIDS but the church's answer to the overall violence that infects society. What should the church do? It is a huge undertaking for a sermon, but one that Forbes is ready and able to address.

Yet for all the pastoral contextual material in the sermon—AIDS, assaults, violence in society—it is also pastoral because of its theology. Forbes grounds the sermon pastorally by the way that he understands humanity and constructs the church. As we look at these pastoral theological emphases in the sermon, we will see how the pastoral intent of the sermon is to reconcile and guide the hearers as God's people in the world.

Theological Anthropology

Human Nature and Sin

The opening lines of this sermon indicate that theological anthropology is foundational for the entire sermon. In some sermons, theological anthropology is more implicit than explicit, but in this sermon, the preacher gives it direct consideration. The friend with AIDS poses straightforward anthropological and theological questions. Does God love him even when society rejects him? Does God affirm him even though he is gay? Does God celebrate his uniqueness? Can God really be for him? Right away, Forbes indicates to the listeners that this sermon will wrestle with what it means to be a human being in relationship with God. This theological concern, as I have claimed throughout the book, is one of the ways that sermons develop a pastoral perspective.

The sermon answers yes to the man's questions about God's love and acceptance. It grounds this affirmation in a biblically informed understanding of the nature of God ("love and mercy and graciousness from God") and in the image of God within all humanity. "We are all God's children…God celebrates the uniqueness of each one of us." Deep down within humanity resides the goodness of God, who creates us for love of one another. The Golden Rule is not simply telling us how we ought to live. It indicates that our very purpose, the reason God creates us, is for care of one another. The sermon embraces the theological norm of God-given mutuality in human relationships. This is what the Golden Rule indicates. "It is not just some voluntary principle of reciprocity; it is at the heart of the gospel." God does not create us as solitary individuals nor as nameless faces in a crowd. God creates us for one another.

The problem with humanity, however, is that "we fail to be faithful to who we are," the caring sons and daughters of God. Instead, we become preoccupied with ourselves. Narcissism comes to the fore, "in which I look into the mirror and I find myself focusing on what is good for me, what will secure me, my family, my crowd, my caucus, my group." We cannot see, much less respond to, the concerns of others because self-interest blocks our compassion. There is a fundamental "break in the social contract" that is causing human society to become "unglued." And "what is becoming unglued is *whatever it was that God had in mind* about how people ought to deal with each other as they would love to be dealt with." Though God creates us for one another, sin distorts our relationships and causes us to elevate ourselves above others. We constantly seek our own justification. This sinful distortion is so deep within the human family that we cannot pin it on any one person or situation. "Who is the victim?" Forbes asks. And by implication, Who is the perpetrator? But he finds no easy answer because we all are "infected with violence," unable to deal lovingly with one another as God intends. The human family does not divide into sheep and goats, the good and the bad. Even the boys who attacked the woman in Central Park cannot be condemned as a "'wolf pack;' they're human beings" whose humanity is brutally marred by sin.

The first pastoral intent of the sermon, therefore, is to effect reconciliation between persons and between God and humanity. By being reconciled to God and one another, the human community can fulfill its primary purpose of caring for others in the name of God. The sermon does not, however, individualize this traditional Protestant pastoral emphasis on reconciliation. We are not individual sinners who need to get our lives right with God. We are members of a broken human family whose violence toward one another signals our deep need for interpersonal reconciliation in God. The sermon beckons the hearers to realize the gift of God to restore us to human mutuality. Pastorally, the sermon wants to bring about such reconciliation within the lives of the members of the congregation and within the wider community.

Human Responsibility and the Grace of God

The second pastoral emphasis of the sermon is moral guidance. Forbes repeatedly calls for the congregation to live by the Golden Rule. "Somehow we must learn to live by the Golden Rule," Forbes says. We must learn to "face our Christian responsibility." The church must go beyond works of charity, as important as they are, to help create a "take-care system that will allow us once again to live, to walk freely in our streets, and to enjoy jogging in our parks." Like the Good Samaritan, the church should "stop and give genuine care." Clearly, the sermon calls for human responsibility within the wider community, doing unto others as we would have them do unto us. Notice, however, that though the sermon offers pastoral moral guidance, Forbes avoids moralism. The sermon does not enlist the hearers into social crusades for any particular cause, liberal or conservative. The sermon does not chastise the congregation for irresponsibility, nor does it suggest that Christian faithfulness is an easy road to walk.

Rather, God's grace offered in Christ empowers Christian responsibility. Faithful Christian living, doing unto others as we would have them do unto us, is possible because of the grace-filled goodness of God. "God forgives us when we fail to be faithful to who we are, and then God rejoices in our freedom to be who we are." Christians do not have to justify themselves through any kind of moral action at all. We belong to God first. Our responsible action follows. In one of the most persuasive moments of the sermon, Forbes preaches, "Everybody in the realm of God's tender care is already somebody. You don't have to make a case for being there. By God's grace you're already in. You don't have to go around testing folks all the time, judging other folks; *you're in!*" This theological priority on grace allows Forbes to develop the Golden Rule as an indicative within the Christian community, not simply an imperative. Christians live by the Golden Rule because, as members of the "realm of God's tender, loving care," we are set free from inordinate preoccupation with our own security and well-being. By grace, we are free to live according to the values indicated by the Golden Rule.

The sermon might have stopped with the grace-empowered call to seek systemic change, but it doesn't. Forbes lodges the grace in Christ. "Jesus the Christ invites us into the realm of tender, loving care." If there is any doubt about God's commitment to humanity, the sermon offers Jesus Christ as evidence. Jesus enters human suffering and endures human violence just as the man with AIDS and the woman jogger did. And to the violated and the suffering, Jesus says, "I know what you have been through; I know what it's like." In its moral intent, the sermon doesn't so much call us to be like Jesus as to recognize that Jesus suffers with humanity. Christ's suffering with us is the redemptive bond that makes it "become increasingly impossible for us to engage in various forms of assault against each other." With the suffering Christ between us, and recognizing one another as fellow sufferers, we are free to do unto others as we would have them do unto us.

Freedom and Limits

As you might expect of a sermon grounded christologically in the suffering of Christ, there is a healthy respect for human limits. Yes, the sermon calls the congregation to fulfill humanity's purpose of mutual love and care. But Forbes knows that it is difficult for the human community to implement the Golden Rule. The maximlike nature of the Golden Rule belies the complexity of actually putting into action such distilled wisdom. The church usually knows what it ought to do, at least in a general sense. Yet the church struggles to live by its own vision because of various limitations within human existence. Without such awareness, Forbes's sermon might have collapsed under the weight of generalities. But Forbes is wrestling theologically with real people in life and death situations, from AIDS patients to victims of random violence. When he guides the congregation to "Do unto others as you would have them do unto you," it is with the awareness of the many human limits that impinge on freedom.

This awareness comes out clearly when Forbes is speaking to his friend in the hospital. After reminding him of God's full acceptance (offering reconciliation), Forbes says, "'That does not mean we don't have problems to work through, brother; there are a lot of things I don't know, a lot of problems in the social fabric that have not been figured out yet, and I don't know how to work through them.'" The sermon does not offer complete freedom to the man in the hospital or to the hearers. The social fabric is torn; our understanding is cloudy; barriers remain. We might dreamily wish for all human difficulties to go away so that we might live in a world of perfect freedom. But this is not the world in which Forbes is preaching.

Forbes's pastoral theological response to the limits of human life, as to the sin of violence, is to remind the congregation of Christ, who through suffering identifies with the whole human race. Using the familiar biblical story of the Good Samaritan, Forbes interprets that the Samaritan cares for others because he has experienced suffering and rejection. He knows how to care for another's needs because he has known the same needs. "He knew what it felt like to be despised and rejected, to be robbed, assaulted, and called names. He had been there." Forbes gives strong rhetorical presence to the phrase "He had been there," using it or slight variations of it eight different times at the end of the sermon. Forbes claims that "Being there," knowing suffering, allows us to care for one another. "Being there" makes it possible for Christians to act responsibly even when our freedom is limited. "It was that capacity [to know suffering] that I think makes possible movement into the realm of God's tender, loving care." Here again, we note that Forbes doesn't exhort the congregation to "do better" or "love more," as if humans have no limits to responsible action. Rather, he says that Christ identifies with suffering humanity. That identification empowers us to care for one another as members of the suffering yet redeemed human family.

Ecclesiology

Forbes preaches this sermon within the Riverside congregation in New York City. The congregation is in focus throughout the sermon as Forbes wrestles with the church's response to suffering and violence in society. Early on, he says, "I started asking, 'What should the church do?'" He addresses the congregation as "brothers and sisters." Toward the end of the sermon, he speaks directly to them, "Riversiders, this is for us." This is not a general sermon that is marked "To whom it may concern." Nor does the preacher focus on particular individuals who are sitting in the pews. Forbes has moved beyond his predecessor at Riverside, Harry Emerson Fosdick, to see the congregation as a whole. He does not preach the sermon as counseling on a group scale but as a pastoral theological endeavor to build up the people of God. At least that is how I interpret the sermon's understanding of its hearers.

The church that the sermon envisions is based on the reign of God, which Forbes calls "God's realm, the commonwealth of love." Forbes claims that the church should live by the values of God's realm. These values are the basis of the community that forms around God and Jesus Christ. He does not preach that the church is the realm of God. Rather, the realm of God infuses the imagination of the church and offers it a picture of how Christians ideally live as God's community.

> In other words, Jesus is talking about a new community, a new arrangement that will obtain when God's reign has become the order of the day. In that time, people who have needs because of the quality of life in the beloved community would ask and it would be given; they would seek and find...It is Jesus' projection of what it will look like when the church configures its life, or when society configures its life, according to the dream in the mind of the Creator. It is Jesus' way of saying, "This is where you learn to incline towards the inevitability of God's great reign, the beloved community." That is what Jesus was talking about: when God's reign and the principles of justice and mercy and equality have become the Magna Charta of the people of faith, when you could ask and it would be given.
>
> It is within this kind of projection of a caring community that Jesus then says, "Do unto others as you would have them do unto you."

The "caring community" that Jesus projects is the "dream in the mind of the Creator." It is not yet fully realized, but in the church, this community of care, this "beloved community," sends up signs of life. Every now and then this community throws a party to recall that "God rejoices in our freedom to be who we are" and to "celebrate with all people the integrity of their being."

The church is the people who embody God's care for all of humanity. The sermon presses for the actual congregation to realize that the church is based on God's "*special caring* for those who have been despised and rejected and abused and oppressed." God shows such care through offering Jesus Christ to the world, the one who knows human suffering, who like us has "been there." In Christ, the church discovers its true identity as the community of the suffering redeemed.

In the final two paragraphs of the sermon, the two streams of theological anthropology and ecclesiology join to offer pastoral guidance to the congregation. In the one stream, we see humanity knee-deep in the creative waters of God. In the other, we see the Christ-formed church composed of those baptized in suffering love. Through sharing the suffering of Christ the church transcends but does not escape the sin of interpersonal violence and social suffering.

> The purpose of the church in this time is to create a group of people who understand that this God created us out of the same batch of divine creativity...My prayer is that we in this

congregation, slowly maybe, sometimes kicking and screaming and debating and shouting about it, will become a congregation where, when we look at one another and we see into the eyes of a brother or sister, we will understand their suffering and pain; we will be able to say, *I've been there*, so let me do unto this person even as I would have him or her do unto me.

God creates us all, the sermon reminds the hearers. And in this life, suffering comes to us all. So when we really see one another as suffering children of God united by Christ, mutual love and care will flow among our lives together.

One could argue that this sermon is too idealistic. Indeed, it would be an even stronger sermon if Forbes had offered more actual images of how the existing congregation is already functioning as a caring community in Christ (see chapter 5). The sermon does show the congregation laying wreaths of flowers on a grave, praying together in a vigil, and marching in an ecumenical parade. No doubt, other caring action occurs within the Riverside congregation. Greater emphasis here would have concretized the compelling pastoral picture of the church.

But all in all, starting with a very particular case of human suffering, the sermon moves outward to shape and define the pastoral nature of the church as a whole. Pastoral vision shines through the theology of the sermon, its analysis of the human situation, and its projection of the nature and mission of the church in the world. Forbes has a weekly opportunity to help bring this caring community a little closer to the pastoral ideals of mutuality, hospitality, and compassion. The sermon convinces us that when the church learns to take care, "not only are we taking care, we are creating a take-care system that will allow us once again to live, to walk freely in our streets, and to enjoy jogging in our parks." In this sermon's pastoral theology, care does move freely through the aisles of the sanctuary and hopefully out into the streets.

Talking Religion Defensively[2]

Fred B. Craddock

Dr. Craddock is the Bandy Distinguished Professor of Preaching and New Testament, Emeritus, of Candler School of Theology, Emory University, and is currently the pastor of Cherry Log Christian Church (Disciples of Christ) in

[2]The Cherry Log Christian congregation heard this sermon during Sunday worship. Dr. Craddock did not compose it in manuscript form. It has been transcribed and edited from a live audiocassette recording and is printed here with Dr. Craddock's permission.

Cherry Log, Georgia. He preached this sermon on John 4:5—5:42 on the Second Sunday of Lent, 1999.

Soon now, very soon, we are going to be able to do what we haven't been doing in two years. We haven't really been able to do it in two years. That is to get out and invite neighbors and friends and have them come and worship with us here at Cherry Log. We've tried such invitations a couple of times, but we've had about a hundred people, and they spilled out into the yard, and on benches, and onto the bumpers of trucks. It was like a gallon of milk spilled onto the floor; it just ran everywhere. It didn't work too well, but it was a nice occasion. But we're going to be able to do it now. We'll be on the hill, and there will be plenty of room. For many of you, this will simply be a matter of inviting people to come with you to worship. "Family, and friends, and neighbors, come and worship with us at Cherry Log." And that is good, very good. But some of you will have the opportunity to talk a little more deeply because somebody may engage you in conversation. And that's where some of us fall silent.

So it occurred to me a week or two ago that that some of you might like to know how it is that this particular tradition of the church, called Christian Church or Disciples, goes about talking to people about our faith and about Jesus Christ. You might wonder: Is there a special way that you talk about your faith? We don't know anything about this particular church. We show up, but we don't know much. We're learning how you observe communion, how you worship, what you sing, how you pray, and where you send your money to help other people. But how do you witness? How does the Christian Church witness?

Do you just kind of sit back and hope that people will come? Do you try to keep it a secret that people can apply if they want to? How do you witness? Do you make yourself obnoxious and take turns standing on the street corner and bothering people? Do you go into the ice cream parlors and ask people if they are saved when they're trying to decide between chocolate ripple and peanut butter crunch? What do you do? Do you stop at red lights, roll down the window, and say, "DO YOU KNOW JESUS?" Do you pass out tracts? How do you people do it? I mean, this is a new church. Although we're not all new to the faith, we're new here at Cherry Log. So I thought I should say something about how we witness.

May I say that in the history of this particular tradition the most instructive passage of scripture is the one that I've read to you. It is a conversation between Jesus and a woman at the well, Jacob's well, in Sychar in Samaria, which is in the mountains of central Israel. I want you to notice that it is a conversation. Jesus is not attacking her. He is not judging her. They are having a conversation.

Now, many of us think that we know what a conversation is. But let me remind you that a conversation can only take place if two people recognize at the outset that we have different backgrounds and traditions, different families, different values, and come from different parts of the world. Secondly, we have enough in common that we can talk. And thirdly, we will be open to each other in all honesty with the possibility of you changing me or me changing you. That is a conversation. A lot of times we say, "Oh, we had a great conversation." What we mean is, I sat there for thirty minutes listening to you talk. I said, "Uh-huh, un-uh, uh-huh." Or you sat there and listened to me for thirty minutes. Well, that was not a conversation. I'm talking about real conversation. It's difficult. We get ahead of the other people; we interrupt the other people; we do all kinds of things that are contrary to conversation.

Conversation at its best is difficult because we have gulfs to cross, such as gender gulfs between men and women. Sometimes you're hesitant to speak in public to this man or that woman. There are also race gulfs. We come from different cultures, different ethnic backgrounds, different economic status, different social standing, and different religious backgrounds. It's tough having a conversation. But what really makes having a conversation tough is that, when you get to religion, many people become defensive. By that I mean nothing ugly. Many people simply protect themselves. Now, the way you protect yourself, if you've never done this, is to change the subject. You know, tell a dirty joke. I get that sometimes. I talk about Jesus Christ, and this person who wants me to go away will become foul-mouthed. It works sometimes. Or you can ask an impossible question: "Well, what does your church teach about the age of the world? How old's the world?" That'll do it, you know. Sometimes you can just get angry. Let it be known you're angry! Claim that it's nobody else's business! Here's a good one. You'll run into this—the quick, easy answer. You say to someone, "We'd like for you to come and worship with us." And he says, "You know, I was just talking to my wife the other day and said that we ought to go down there. We'll be there Sunday." He's lying through his teeth, but it gets rid of you.

There are all kinds of ways to protect yourself from having a real conversation about faith. You've probably done some of them yourself. You could get a denominational squabble going like this woman in scripture. "You say you're supposed to worship in Jerusalem. That's what the Jews do. We say we worship here in Mount Gerezim in Samaria. Now, which is right?" That'll do it sometimes.

The difficulty with defensiveness is that it is hard to move past it in a gracious way in order to continue the conversation. The gender gulf is right there in the biblical story. "Well," the woman said, "a Jewish man talking to a Samaritan woman in public? Will miracles never cease? What is he really after? Who is he, anyway, this man talking to a woman?" Now, she's defensive; she's really defensive. I can understand it. I can appreciate the reason. It's because she has had five husbands, and she's living with a man now to whom she is not married. She has had it up to here with men! And here's a man who says, as he sits by the well, "Will you give me a drink?" So naturally she wonders, "What is his real subject?"

I want to pause here to say that this woman has been blamed for being a loose woman. She's had five husbands and now has a man who's not her husband. Let me remind you that in that culture it was not the woman's choice. The men passed the women around. One took her, then gave her a divorce; took her, gave her a divorce; took her, gave her a divorce. She didn't choose five husbands and another man—she was chosen! She has been passed around like a piece of meat. And a man says, "Will you give me a drink?" Do you understand her reaction?

I just asked a woman at Winn Dixie one day, "Uh, could you tell me where I can find the peanut butter?" I was looking for the peanut butter. And she turned around and looked at me, and said, "Are you trying to hit on me?" And I said, "Lady, I'm looking for the peanut butter." Later when I found it over in aisle five and had a jar of peanut butter, there she was. She said, "You were looking for the peanut butter." I said, "I told you I was looking for the peanut butter." She says, "Nowadays you can't be too careful." But I said to her, "Yes, you can." But I know. There is a reason for the protectiveness. It's because of the gender thing.

There's also the race thing. Now, I know I'm talking to people some of whom are not comfortable talking about the race thing. Get used to it! It's the Christian *way* to converse—across the racial gulf. Think about it. A Jewish man talks to a Samaritan woman. They didn't speak, Samaritans and Jews. They didn't have any discourse. People just avoided each other, crossed the street, did anything to keep from running into each other. It was the race thing. You see, when the Jews were taken into captivity, their captors took the professional people, the art people, and the skilled laborers into captivity to work for them. They left the poor, the "nobodies," and those with almost no education. These who were left intermarried with the local people, the Palestinians. The results were the Samaritans. So here we have a *Jewish* man talking to a *Samaritan*. It's the race thing.

In Atlanta there is a large, predominantly black Disciples of Christ church called the Ray of Hope. When the congregation was being formed, my wife, Nettie, was on the committee to get the church started. I was there at a service. We all ate together. There were several white people there, not many. After the service was over, the minister, Cynthia Hale, asked us to form a circle. So we formed a circle in the room. I was standing next to this young black boy who looked to be about six or seven. The minister said, "Take hands and we'll have prayers around the room." So I took the boy's hand. And when I held his hand, he looked up at me and said, "Are you a mean man?" I said, "No, I'm not a mean man." When it was over, his father on the other side of him said, "I'm sorry about what he said, but it's my fault." I said, "Well, I wasn't hurt by it. I'm sorry that he felt that I might be a mean man." He said, "It's because you're white. I have suffered so much that in the afternoon after work I take it home, and his young ears have picked up the things I've said. And so, he asked you because you're white, 'Are you a mean man?'" It was painful. He was probably six years old. Like your children at school. They can hear ethnic, ugly things, and you've got to spend half of your time clearing that out, clearing that out, and clearing that out, because it's wrong. It's hard to converse across the gulf of race.

And then there is the gulf of bad religious experiences. Some people have had such bad religious experiences. When I was a pastor up in Newport, Tennessee, I wondered a lot of times about one of the members of the church. So finally I asked her. I said, "Joanne, why is it as soon as the sermon is over, you just get up and head out?" She never said anything, but finally she told me. When she was just ten or eleven, she was in a service, and after the sermon they sang a hymn, and sang, and sang, and sang, and people started going through the congregation. She said, "The minister came down and took hold of my hand and said, 'Little girl, do you want to go to hell?' and it scared me to death. And so I leave before all of that starts." I said, "It's not going to start." But that is a bad religious experience.

I was asked to speak at a big church convention of a major denomination in Las Vegas. Why they had the church assembly in Las Vegas, I don't know. But it was in Las Vegas. I went out of the hotel and asked for a cab to go to the convention center where the gathering was held. I got in and I told the cab driver where I was going. He said, "Is that where all of those preachers and folks are gathering?" I said, "Yeah." He said, "Now, I want to tell you. Don't try to convert me. I'm Roman Catholic. I go to mass, my wife goes to mass, our kids go to mass, we're a Catholic family, and we're Christians. So if you want to convert, get yourself another cab!" I said, "I just want a ride out to the convention center." He said, "I've had four people try to convert me this morning, and I'm tired of it!"

Now, pretty soon when you start talking to people about Christ and the church and start inviting them to worship, to pray, to sing, and to listen to scripture with us, you'll find that some people have had some bad religious experiences. You want to be patient about it. But I think the deepest pain of all, the biggest thing to overcome, is the fear of not being accepted. There are people who attend churches for a pretty long time before they join because they want to know, "Will I really, really be accepted?" Now, to me, that seems a strange question to ask. But there are folk who have been hurt and embarrassed. And by the grace of God, and the will of God, and your good grace, that will never, ever be the case with us.

I wrote some time ago a little article for *Joe's News*, Joe Sisson's paper, in which I simply reminded the reader of a story Jesus told about a king who gave a banquet because his son was getting married. The folks who were invited didn't show up. And so the king said, "I want you to go out in the streets, and alleys, and out into the country and everywhere and bring the people in—the good and the bad—and have them come in to my banquet." So the servants went out and brought them in, the bad and the good, from everywhere, and they sat down at the table for the banquet. The king came in, and he saw a man there without a wedding garment, improperly dressed, and so the king made him leave. So the king said to the servants, "You go out and bring everybody." Now, if anybody has to leave, that's the king's business. That is not our business. Judging is God's business—not our business. Are we beginning to get that? All we do, our sole job is to say, "Everybody, everybody, everybody come!" And there'll never be a day when anybody, anybody, by that I mean anybody, is refused a place at the table.

And so the woman said, "Well, we think you ought to worship on this mountain, and you Jews think you ought to worship in Jerusalem." And Jesus said, "Woman, that's not the point. The point is—God is Spirit and Truth, and the time has come for everybody to worship God, not according to place—here or there—but according to God's own nature, which is Spirit and Truth." There is no such thing as my accepting you or your accepting me. It is God who has accepted all of us. When you bring the gospel of Christ to somebody, make sure you make it clear that what you're bringing was already theirs before you got there. There is no handing down or handing over. There is simply the sharing of the gospel.

I know defensiveness is tough. Protecting oneself is a difficult thing. I went by a person's home. There was no answer. I knew a family had moved in, but apparently there was nobody there. I went back the next day. A little girl came to the door. I said, "Hi," and she said, "Hi." Then her mother came to the door, and she said, "Come in," and I went in and sat down. And the little girl said, "I saw you here yesterday, but my mother hid in the closet." We got over that, but I knew exactly how the mother felt. Don't let religion be intrusive.

The woman at the well was so melted down by what Jesus said that finally she blurted it out. "Someday, someday, someday, a Christ will come and everything is going to be all right." And Jesus said, "He's here."

I don't know where the woman got that, but I have never met a person so secular, so disinterested, so apathetic, immoral, "I don't care," "get lost," angry; I have never met anyone so down, so out, so distant, but what if, given time, they will say something like this to you. "I know someday a Christ will come." And then you'll get to say, "He's here."

Commentary

We hear the unmistakable sounds of a pastor preaching among a congregation in this sermon. Though edited for written publication from a spoken event, the conversational tone of Craddock's sermon is audible as he engages scripture and the listeners. Craddock's characteristic emphasis on mutuality in preaching method fits this sermon's pastoral theological concern for mutuality within the ministry of the congregation.[3] In content and method, the preacher leans toward the hearers and invites their participation in the making of the sermon.

At first glance, the sermon's primary theological concern appears to be the witness of the church. How does the church talk about Jesus Christ? How do we witness to the love of God when we aren't even sure what we are doing? What about those persons who for good reason will be defensive when we witness? The sermon explores these questions in order to provide pastoral guidance (instruction) to the congregation about how to witness to the gospel.

The sermon, however, signals another pastoral intent besides guidance. The theological anthropology and ecclesiology of the sermon suggest a pastoral concern for reconciliation. The pastoral theology of the sermon seeks to construct a Christian community of mutuality and hospitality built on reconciliation of persons one to another. The sermon sets in motion pastoral care as reconciliation by proclaiming that Christian congregations care for others by the love of Christ, who through the congregation is doing the work of reconciliation in the world.

Theological Anthropology

Human Nature and Sin

Craddock grounds this sermon in the theological presupposition that God creates the human family as communal yet diverse. "We have different backgrounds and traditions, different families, different values, and we come from different parts of the world." We are distinctive by race, gender, and economics. Like Jews and Samaritans, we worship God differently. Such distinctions within the human family are not a threat to humankind. They do not indicate that anything is wrong within creation. Human difference is simply part of the diverse, created order.

Within this diversity, God creates us for mutuality with one another. The sermon develops this key theological claim, first by pointing out the importance but extreme difficulty of genuine conversation. Real conversation is mutual. Each partner is "open to each other in all honesty with the possibility of you changing me or me changing you." Humans, despite our diversity, do have enough in common to talk with one another.

---

[3]Craddock says, "At a time when pastoral care is being de-clericalized in the sense of equipping the whole church to be a community of caring and healing, preaching is giving a larger role to the congregation. This is not in the sense of proclaiming what the people want to hear but rather what they want to say. After all, it is the church's faith, the church's tradition, the church's message that is being spoken and not a private word that arrived with the preacher." "Preaching," *Dictionary of Pastoral Care and Counseling,* ed. Rodney Hunter et al. (Nashville: Abingdon Press, 1990), 944.

Authentic conversation is one way that we exercise our God-given humanity. This theological premise runs throughout the sermon. It is also one of the building blocks of Craddock's influential homiletic method.[4] God creates us for communion with one another. Those who can honestly talk with one another, from either side of the pulpit, within or outside the walls of the sanctuary, and who enjoy the give-and-take of free conversation, know what it means to be humans in communion.

The sermon's theological claim for human mutuality comes through in another way. Christians who witness to the gospel of Jesus Christ do so in such a way that it affirms human community. Christians do not harangue persons and put them on the defensive, asking crassly, "DO YOU KNOW JESUS?" We should not assume that every person we meet needs to adopt our approach to faith, as some assumed about the taxicab driver in the sermon. The cab driver's angry reaction to overly eager witnesses shows the rupture of human community: "If you want to convert, get yourself another cab!" Since God creates humanity for communion, we humans who become followers of Christ do everything we can to build up human community. This includes cultivating a modesty and profound respect for others in our witness. The sermon beckons the listeners to realize the God-given mutuality of human relationships. From the center of the sermon's theological anthropology arise the joyful sounds of God and humanity in communion.

Our enjoyment of human communion, however, is far from complete. Human mutuality is hard to come by. Interpersonal relationships are cracked. In image, story, and description, the sermon paints a recognizable picture of human fragmentation. While Craddock does not name the fissures among human beings as "sin," per se, he candidly points out the sinful human condition. For example, we often "attack" and "judge" one another instead of conversing. Or we interrupt and get ahead of one another. Such actions break genuine conversation (communion). This distortion of our true humanity is not an individual condition, inward and private. The ruptures of human nature occur between and among persons who, though born for togetherness, live in a state of broken communion.

Natural differences within the human community—gender, race, culture—cause flashpoints of defensiveness. Or worse still, persons use natural differences as reasons to dominate and oppress one another. The sermon's explanation of the oppressive divorce laws in the ancient Near East points out the unjust treatment of women in that day. At the same time, the story about shopping for peanut butter and the encounter with the woman in the Winn Dixie store suggests that ongoing gender

---

[4]See Fred Craddock, *Overhearing the Gospel: Preaching and Teaching the Faith to Persons Who Have Already Heard* (Nashville: Abingdon Press, 1978); and *As One Without Authority* (Nashville: Abingdon Press, 1979).

discrimination today creates suspicion and defensiveness between men and women. Then there is the painful incident that occurs when the white preacher attends worship in an African American congregation. There he encounters the suspicions of a young child. Why? Because of the "gulf of race," and because the child's father "has suffered so much" racial discrimination. "Like your children at school," Craddock reminds the congregation. "They can hear ethnic, ugly things, and you've got to spend half your time clearing that out." Craddock places all these experiences of human brokenness beside John's story of Jesus and the woman at the well. He claims that interpersonal sin is deep-seated within human nature and gives birth to assumptions of racial, cultural, and gender superiority that destroys human communion.

To top off all the brokenness within human society, the sermon shows that rejection, arrogance, cruelty, and discrimination plague the church. The church is not an island of purity afloat within a sinful culture. The church is all bound up with the same sin that is present within society. For example, some ministers frighten children with specters of hell. Some Christians berate fellow Christians. Some believers reject those who seek shelter within the church. Sometimes we use our faith as a battering ram rather than as a welcome table. This is no optimistic read on human nature. Craddock understands the severity of the human predicament, and he preaches that every human being, inside or outside the church, has some kind of "gulf" to cross to reach true communion. While Craddock has a keen eye for the ironic within human experience, and with it he provides some comic relief, he does not try to soften the problem. If God creates humanity for community, as the theological anthropology of this sermon suggests, the church and the wider human community has a long way to go to realize God's intentions.

Here we arrive at the pastoral perspective of the sermon. Humanity and the church need reconciliation. Seeing deeply into the breakdown of human communion, the sermon offers God's reconciliation in care-full response. "The biggest thing to overcome" is rejection, "the fear of not being accepted." This fear is not simply personal but interpersonal, not simply within the church but within the world at large. The greatest need among humanity is for the church to make good on the promise of reconciliation that Christ offers through the church to the world. This is how Christians care according to the pastoral theology of the sermon. Pastoral care is not solely defined by the preacher's relationships with the members of the church or personal interactions within the wider community. Neither is pastoral care built upon psychological exchanges and therapeutic interventions on the part of the pastor or specialized caregivers. Pastoral care, the theology of the sermon suggests, is the reconciling work of God and Jesus Christ through the members of the church, who embody in their witness and life together the ministry of reconciliation.

Human Responsibility and the Grace of God

Just who is responsible for the caring ministry of reconciliation that the sermon wants to bring about? The sermon beckons *the congregation* to take up the caring ministry of reconciliation within the church and the wider world. Craddock offers stories and discourse to help the congregation see how they can participate in the work of reconciliation. Here the sermon provides wise pastoral guidance. In Jesus' conversation with the woman at the well, the congregation sees the promise that they can overcome gender, cultural, and racial gulfs. In Ray of Hope Church, the people of Cherry Log Church see the faces of persons who seek racial reconciliation. At one point in the sermon, the preacher becomes quite direct regarding racial understanding. "Now, I know I'm talking to people some of whom are not comfortable talking about the race thing. Get used to it! It's the Christian *way* to converse–across the racial gulf." The negative examples of the cab driver and Joanne in the church at Newport, Tennessee, gently and with good humor suggest to the Cherry Log congregation how not to witness to the reconciling presence of Jesus Christ. Each of these elements of the sermon indicates the preacher's belief that the persons of the congregation do have the ability to be agents of reconciliation in the world. And the sermon offers to them pastoral guidance about how to carry out this responsibility.

Notice that the pastoral call to the congregation to take on the ministry of reconciliation emerges from God's grace. God acts through Jesus Christ to extend grace-full reconciliation to the human community. Our response(ability) takes wing from the ground of grace. It would be easy for another preacher working out of the same biblical text to allow the sermon to become moralistic. In such a sermon, Jesus' interaction with the Samaritan woman becomes the moral example for all the congregation to follow. "Now, go and do likewise," the sermon might admonish. But Craddock sets the caring ministry of the church upon the foundations of God's grace. This comes out most clearly at the end of the sermon. With respect to rejection of persons, he preaches, "There are folk who have been hurt and embarrassed. And by the grace of God, and the will of God, and your good grace, that will never, ever be the case with us." The ordering of grace in this sequence is telling. God comes first, then the congregation. Even more emphatic is Craddock's interpretation of the parable of the wedding banquet, which he borrows from Matthew 22:1–14 to underscore the priority of God's grace (and judgment). "Judging is God's business–not our business. Are we beginning to get that? All we do, our sole job is to say, 'Everybody, everybody, everybody come!' And there'll never be a day, never be a day when anybody, anybody, by that I mean anybody, is refused a place at the table." The church is responsible for offering reconciliation to others, but the gift and the outcome are in God's hands.

The theological point is crucial for the pastoral perspective of the sermon. Only when the church trusts in the priority of God's grace can it enter into mutual, caring relations with others. Forgetting grace, our efforts at reconciliation seem rude and silly at best ("Do you go into the ice cream parlors and ask people if they are saved when they're trying to decide between chocolate ripple and peanut butter crunch?") and downright destructive at worst ("Little girl, do you want to go to hell?"). God, through Christ and the Spirit, goes before the church. God is already present within the world. As Craddock says, "There is no such thing as my accepting you or your accepting me. It is God who has accepted all of us. When you bring the gospel of Christ to somebody, make sure you make it clear that what you're taking was already theirs before you got there. There is no handing down or handing over. There is simply the sharing of the gospel." While the good news of Jesus Christ comes to particular embodiment in the church, the gospel is not confined to the church. The responsibility of the caring church empowered by God's grace is to make sure that others have the opportunity to see what God has already given.

Freedom and Limits

The sermon is not sanguine about the prospects of human freedom. Left to our own devices, humanity turns natural differences such as gender and race into causes for discrimination. Persons often change God-given freedom into the freedom to oppress others. Some men dehumanize women as personal objects of desire and trade (the Samaritan woman). Some races systematically dominate others (the child and father at the Ray of Hope Church). Rather than enjoy one another in human freedom, we shout at one another, become defensive, or hide from one another across the gulfs of religion, culture, and economic status. Corrupted freedom causes people to avoid one another, cross the street, and do "anything to keep from running into each other."

Clearly, in the theological world of the sermon, there are limits to freedom that we transgress at great cost to human community. The negative examples in the sermon make this point. For example, the story about the cab driver illuminates what happens when Christians fail to respect the personal boundaries of others. A good conversation, like a genuine community, occurs within boundaries that give it shape. When we ignore these limits, conversation and community unravel.

The entire sermon, in one sense, is a pastoral endeavor to stake out the freedom and boundaries of Christian witness in the world. Craddock says that if we want to be a reconciling people in the world, we are free to say some things about Jesus Christ in certain ways and not free to say others. We are not free to accost people with Jesus while they are eating ice cream or driving taxicabs, at least if we want to make an effective witness to the grace-full care of God. We are not free to assume that our race, our culture, or our socioeconomic group is the only one that God loves. "Get used to it," Craddock says. The grace of God incarnated in Jesus Christ both limits the destructive potential of humanity and frees the Christian community to carry on the ministry of reconciliation in the world. As long as the church stays healthily aware of the wide yet sure boundaries of God's grace, it is free to act as a responsible witness in the world.

What has this got to do with the sermon as a pastoral endeavor? Quite a bit, because the theological anthropology of this sermon gives the congregation ample room and vivid images of how to care for others. The church cares for others by sharing the reconciling love of God. The sermon names the various necessary limits that can direct the congregation's caring ministry of reconciliation. In the sermon's theological anthropology, God is finally in charge. God offers judgment (limits) and grace (freedom) to the human community. With this assurance, the church is free to say to others, as the sermon does in the end, not by its own account but by the graciousness of God, "Christ is here."

Ecclesiology

Craddock preaches this pastoral sermon among a specific congregation. In the opening paragraph he calls the name of the congregation "Cherry Log." The whole sermon keeps in focus these particular hearers. Craddock is not preaching to an at-large body of people in the world or to some distant group of religious officials. The preacher has no bone to pick with outside parties (unless it is with certain segments of the church whose witness insults others), and he is not wrestling with his own internal, psychic struggles. The occasion of the sermon, a Sunday morning worship service of a particular congregation in a particular place, shapes the content, tone, and delivery of the sermon.

We learn along the way significant details about the congregation. They are completing the construction of a new building, "on the hill," that will provide them room to expand. Some of them drive trucks. They have "family, and friends, and neighbors," whom they can invite to worship. Some of the persons in attendance are new to the Disciples of Christ denomination and to this particular congregation at Cherry Log. A Winn Dixie store is in the community. The church is located somewhere outside Atlanta, Georgia. The congregation is probably white, and some people in the congregation are not comfortable conversing with persons of other races. All of this we learn about the actual church from the sermon. By sprinkling the sermon with these recognizable details, Craddock establishes communion (identification) with the congregation. The preacher pastor claims his place among the people. Craddock's skill at creating communion with the hearers will help bind them to the theological "world" of the sermon.

The sermon helps the congregation see themselves as an actual body of believers rather than as isolated individuals listening to the sermon. Craddock is not preaching from "heart to heart," as some pietistic interpretations of preaching would render. He is preaching as a representative member of the church who attempts to articulate the faith of the church. The concrete details of the sermon drawn from the life of the congregation and community, and the obvious connection of the pastor to the people, make it more possible for the preacher in this and similar sermons to help the congregation live into the theological fullness of being the church.

Theologically speaking, the church that the sermon imagines for the congregation is a reconciling community of believers who value mutuality and hospitality. In earlier chapters, we explored at length the importance of these values for a pastoral community. This church invites others "to worship, to pray, to sing, and to listen to scripture" with them in a spirit of grace-filled acceptance. "Everybody, everybody, everybody come." Notice the insistence of the rhetoric as Craddock through repetition establishes presence for the church's ministry of reconciliation. "There are folk who have been hurt and embarrassed. And by the grace of God, and the will of God, and your good grace, that will never, ever be the case with us." The sermon brings out a church where there will "never be a day when anybody, anybody, by that I mean anybody, is refused a place at the table." In short, the church of the sermon symbolizes and enacts the good news that through Christ, God accepts everyone.

We would be even more drawn into the sermon's theological view of the church if Craddock had been able to paint a picture of this reconciling community actually coming alive within the congregation. We catch a humorous glimpse of it in the opening paragraph when he compares the church's hospitality to "a gallon of milk spilled on the floor." One or two other pictures of the worshipers would bring the ecclesiology closer to the congregation's self-understanding. But the sermon clearly offers a vision of the church that invites the hearers to consider their identity and mission. For example, Ray of Hope Church provides an image of a congregation that is striving toward reconciliation. When the preacher reassures the former member of another church, Joanne, that he and this church will not manipulate her faith, he offers a positive image of reconciliation. And when Jesus, a Jew, accepts the woman at the well, a Samaritan, as a beloved child of God, the church sees the promise of racial, gender, and cultural reconciliation. All of these stories join together to invite the listening congregation to discover themselves as a care-full and reconciling people fashioned by God's grace. The communion that the preacher achieves with the hearers points the way to the much more important communion that occurs within the Christ-centered congregation and between the congregation and those beyond its walls.

The pastoral theology of this sermon imagines a church with open windows and doors. As the listening congregation inhabits a new building, the sermon makes a pastoral appeal to the people to become gracious hosts who offer living, reconciling water to all. Should the pastoral community actually form around the preacher's theological vision of the church, they should not be surprised when their care-full hospitality and compassion do indeed "spill out into the yard, and on benches, and onto the bumpers of trucks."

Just Say No[5]

Gina Stewart

Rev. Gina Stewart is Senior Minister of Christ Missionary Baptist Church in Memphis, Tennessee. She delivered this sermon on Exodus 1:15–22 in that congregation and at the chapel service of Memphis Theological Seminary on February 3, 1999, during the celebration of Black History Month.

It is an old, old story that is rich with contemporary application. It is a story about genocide, labor relations, economic oppression, political domination, control issues, fear, abuse of power and privilege, policy coercion, monopolies, and the extent that one will go to preserve their own interest. It is a text about the power of evil and the corruption associated with absolute power. Against the backdrop of evil and corruption, it is also a story about a God who is our ultimate authority and what happens when we submit to God's authority over human authority.

Shiphrah and Puah were not exactly household names. In scripture, they lived in relative obscurity. They were not considered to be persons of influence or affluence. They had no impressive pedigree. They had no political power. They were two ordinary women who did extraordinary things. By some estimations they were considered weak. But these two women demonstrated enormous courage because they were used by God to shape the redemptive history of the nation of Israel.

As the story unfolds, we find that it is a defining moment in history. A change in the political structure has taken place, and a new administration is in charge. The new king of Egypt has no commitment or loyalty to prior agreements made by his predecessor. Privileges granted by the previous administration have been withdrawn and forfeited.

Nevertheless, this small but favored nation is poised for liberation. They have preferred status because they are a nation chosen by God to receive

---

[5]Used by permission of the author.

the promises of God. They are powerful and fruitful. But this favored status makes them a *threat* to the empire. Although these people of Israel had done nothing wrong to the Egyptians, and there were no indications of conspiracy, the king, suffering from fear and worry about the loss of control, permits his imagination and insecurity to get the best of him by engaging in a game of "what if":

- What if these Hebrews continue their trend of birthing babies like rabbits?
- What if the Hebrews join our enemies and start a war against us?
- What if these Hebrews escape our country and our control over them?

In reality, the king anticipates a potential exodus and departure of cheap labor that imperial government will no longer be able to control. Out of his anxiety, the king generates a fresh policy of forced labor. Whips were cracked, commands were barked, with the Hebrews bending over bricks for building and bending over fields for planting. Bent backs were intended to decrease the expanding number of Hebrews. But in spite of the forced labor, the Hebrews continued to multiply.

With the failure of plan A, Pharaoh instituted plan B. Pharaoh enlisted the aid of two Hebrew midwives: Shiphrah and Puah. On call day and night. Always ready at a moment's notice. Dependable, experienced, reliable, women with years of experience with childbirth. No doubt they had seen it all: long labors, stillbirths, the death of mothers in childbirth, and the physical handicaps. Surely Pharaoh could depend upon them to cooperate with his plan. They were weak and powerless and they had to obey him. After all, he was their boss, and he was responsible for their paycheck. Most importantly, he was the king. Pharaoh explains to them that for the good of the nation they were asked to kill every Hebrew male at birth.

But Pharaoh had no idea what he was asking. Pharaoh was operating out of an imagined threat to Egyptian national security and self-preservation. But the midwives were operating out of a moral commitment. They remained true to their vocation. How does a midwife, whose primary vocation is grounded on the hope of assisting in bringing life, make a career change from a midwife to a pallbearer?

But these two ordinary women were not as weak as Pharaoh thought they would be. No doubt Pharaoh probably saw two powerless women in bondage to a system. In bondage to a job. In bondage to a paycheck. But Shiphrah and Puah knew who they were and whose they were. They understood that their vocation meant assisting with life, not death. They deliberately chose to let the Hebrew boys live. When Pharaoh learned of their civil disobedience and insubordination, the midwives were called in for a reprimand. But the midwives told him that the Hebrew midwives delivered with more vigor than the Egyptians did. In essence, these two Hebrew midwives said no to Pharaoh.

What would make these women say no to Pharaoh? What would make them risk reprimand, maybe even punishment, for what they did? Surely they had to know that Pharaoh could fire them or subject them to stiff punishment. Surely they had to know the consequences of insubordination. The king was accustomed to obedience. Despite the instruction given to kill, the midwives disobeyed the king because they feared/reverenced God more than they feared or reverenced the king (Ex. 1:17). And to reverence God is to reverence God's value system. A value system that is countercultural to the world's system. A value system that values human life over a paycheck or a position. A value system which sees and appreciates the spark of God in every individual but particularly in the life of an unborn child. A value system which understands that to abort a child is to, in essence, abort future possibilities. A value system that caused them to dare to practice insubordination.

What does it mean to say no to Pharaoh from a contemporary perspective? To say no to Pharaoh means to ask value questions. To say no to Pharaoh means to ask caring questions. To say no to Pharaoh means to ask authority questions. To say no to Pharaoh means, as much as lies within the scope of our abilities and scope of influence, to do the will of God. To say no to Pharaoh means that in the midst of a technologically astute culture, there must also be a presence of a vital witness to our faith through our actions. To say no to Pharaoh means to partner knowledge, technological capabilities, and political privilege with a moral commitment to humanity. To say no to Pharaoh means to become advocates who work to change the attitudes and mores of our communities for the better. To say no to Pharaoh means to be advocates and activists for peace and well-being. To say no to Pharaoh means to work for the balance of justice. To say no to Pharaoh means to seize the opportunity to apply our faith and to boldly and defiantly resist injustice when necessary. To say no to Pharaoh means that we must continually ask the question: How does biblical faith inform or shape my decisions and my ability to relate to all people as children of God? To say no to Pharaoh is to say no to evil.

To say no to Pharaoh is to personally adopt the spirit of Shiphrah and Puah. To say no to Pharaoh means that we, as insignificant as we may be, have the power just like these two midwives to make a difference in the world. To say no to Pharaoh means to offer ourselves to be used of God as instruments in God's hand to accomplish God's awesome purposes. To say no is to join in with that great cloud of witnesses who feared God as the ultimate authority: people like Harriet Tubman, who led slaves to freedom on the underground railway; people like the abolitionists, who fought and spoke out against slavery; Ida B. Wells, who dared to speak out against lynching when no one else would; Dietrich Bonhoeffer, a theologian who dared to speak out against the Holocaust; Medgar Evers, who lost his life in Mississippi fighting for the right to vote; Rosa Parks, who refused to move to the back of the bus or Dr. Martin Luther King, Jr., who believed that a person should not be judged by the color of his or her skin but by the content of his or her character; Rev. Robert Graetz, a caucasian Lutheran pastor, who shattered racial boundaries and gained a unique eyewitness perspective on the role of ministry in crisis during his active participation in the Montgomery bus boycott; Nelson Mandela, who spent twenty-seven years in prison in opposition to apartheid. All these persons were just ordinary people, but when they said yes to God and no to Pharaoh, God used them to do extraordinary things. To say no to Pharaoh is what Jesus did, when he deliberately chose to take the more direct route through Samaria to confront prejudice and discrimination rather than avoid it. To say no to Pharaoh is to reject the practice of racism, sexism, and classism. To say no to Pharaoh is to say no to whoever our slavemaster is: Greed, Self-indulgence, Power, Pride, Need for Control, Jealousy, and Materialism.

And it is very important that we say no to Pharaoh because Pharaoh is not dead. Pharaoh is not dead because Pharaoh is an institution. Pharaoh is any institution or person who controls our lives. Pharaoh is anyone or anything that stands in our way of claiming our high calling from God.

And because Pharaoh is not dead, we need more people like Shiphrah and Puah who have the courage to obey God rather than humanity. This may seem to contradict biblical teaching that believers should obey the law and respect the governing authorities. And scripture does teach that we are to obey those who are in authority over us. But we must also recognize that there are limits to human authority. Sometimes God's people have to resist human authority in order to obey God. Pharaoh was in charge, but Pharaoh was commanding nothing less than infanticide. Whenever there is a conflict between human command and God's command, it is always better to obey God than to obey humanity. Respect and preservation of life are top priorities in the kingdom of God.

The blood of hundreds of slaves who lost their lives in the middle passage demands that we recognize the limits of human authority. The blood of millions of Jews killed during the Holocaust demands that we recognize the limits of human authority. The blood of Emmett Till demands that we recognize the limits of human authority. The blood of those little girls bombed in a church one Sunday morning in Alabama demands that we recognize the limits of human authority. The blood of Martin Luther King, Jr., and Malcolm X demands that we recognize the limits of human authority. And, as if that is not enough, the blood of Jesus, the crimson tide that flows from Calvary, the scarlet thread that unites all of us—male and female, Jew and Greek, bond and free—demands that we recognize the limits of human authority. When human authority rejects the *imago dei* of other human beings; when human authority fails to see the value in other human lives; when human authority values property over person; when human authority violates God's moral authority, the law has already been broken. Jesus explained it this way in response to the question: "Master what is the greatest commandment in the law?" Jesus said unto him, "Thou shalt love the Lord thy God with all thy heart, and with all thy soul, and with all thy mind. This is the first and great commandment. And the second is like unto it, Thou shalt love thy neighbor as thyself. On these two hang all the law and the prophets."

Commentary

At first glance this sermon seems short on identifiable pastoral material. Many preachers would designate this a "prophetic" sermon. Indeed, in the opening lines the preacher's interpretation of the biblical text moves the hearers toward the social concerns of "genocide, labor relations, economic oppression, political domination." Stewart understands Pharaoh's oppression and the subversive, resistant action of the midwives, Shiphrah and Puah, through the interpretive lens of social liberation. In content, tone, and delivery, the sermon prophetically challenges the hearers to say "no" to Pharaoh, which means "to boldly and defiantly resist injustice when necessary." The sermon is unapologetically prophetic. The preacher wants to rouse the congregation to claim the power of God, like Shiphrah and Puah, and place the weight of their lives into the balance for justice.

But I have claimed throughout this book that such separation between the prophetic and pastoral is an unhelpful distinction in preaching. In the sermon, Stewart does not rail like a lone voice in the wilderness against the forces of injustice. She preaches the sermon pastorally among her own people, an African American Baptist congregation in the southern part of the United States, many of whose members know firsthand "bondage to a system...bondage to a job...bondage to a paycheck." The hearers can readily identify with the struggles of the Hebrews and the courageous actions of Shiphrah and Puah.

Stewart offers to the congregation, as Walter Brueggemann suggests, an "alternative world" in which to dwell. It is a world whose inhabitants recognize God's countercultural value system. It is a world whose people rely on God's strength to live triumphantly in the face of the contemporary forces of Pharaoh. The sermon enacts among the people that God's ways will ultimately prevail. At this theological and contextual level, the sermon is pastoral through and through.

Theological Anthropology

Human Nature and Sin

The sermon clearly understands the power of sin and evil within creation. Pharaoh personifies the "corruption associated with absolute power" and the extent that humanity will go to preserve self-interest. If self-interest is served by destroying the lives of entire communities, then humans are ready and capable of killing a community's firstborn children. If we need cheap labor to fund our own political, economic, and social advancement, we are ready to "crack the whip," "bark the commands," and put the poor to work in the brickyards of contemporary society. Like it or not, Stewart preaches that we live against "a backdrop of evil and corruption." Sin runs deep within the veins of the human community.

Nevertheless, the preacher resists the temptation to allow the sermon to slide into moral dualisms. Just when the hearers might think that the sermon views Pharaoh as outside of the church, the preacher reminds the congregation of its own sinfulness. "To say no to Pharaoh is to say no to whoever *our* [emphasis mine] slavemaster is: Greed, Self-Indulgence, Power, Pride, Need for Control, Jealousy, and Materialism." The listeners may want to think that sin is socially external to the church, but with this turn in the sermon, the preacher recalls for the congregation its own complicity with the forces of destruction, its own temptation to align with Pharaoh. Christians struggle against all manner of false "authority," against "anyone or anything that stands in our way of claiming our high calling from God." The church engages in a protracted conflict against powers that dominate and destroy human community. These forces are not simply outside us (social sin) or inside us (individual sin), but all mixed up among "ordinary people."

Admittedly, the sermon tips toward a social interpretation of sin. Thus, the pastoral concern of the sermon emphasizes social liberation. But the preacher does not let the congregation off the hook by placing sin outside the walls of the church. Out of pastoral concern for the congregation, she urges the hearers to overcome all manner of sin–social, individual, and interpersonal. She wants us to say no to all the forces that corrupt our human relationships and to "relate to all people as children of God." No rose-colored glasses for this preacher and this sermon when assessing the human situation. When the preacher looks toward humanity, she gauges just how destructive we often are. We can say "no" to Pharaoh, she preaches, but she knows the task will not be easy.

Human Responsibility and the Grace of God

Here the clearest pastoral care elements of the sermon come into focus. First, the sermon offers moral guidance for the congregation. Second, by offering such guidance, the sermon sustains the congregation as it does the work of changing "our communities for the better." The pastoral theology of the sermon stresses that human beings exist for a purpose. Namely, we are "instruments in God's hand to accomplish God's awesome purposes." And what are God's purposes? God's purposes are freedom for all of humanity, peaceable relations among races and nations, dignity for every single child of God.

The image of God is stamped on every person, the sermon proclaims ("image of God" appears three times in the sermon), though we often fail as a society to see it. The hearers have the responsibility to help God restore persons in God's image. Ida B. Wells, Dietrich Bonhoeffer, Rosa Parks, Robert Graetz, and Nelson Mandela all witness to God's purposes for humanity. Like them, and like Shiphrah and Puah, the sermon urges the hearers to shoulder a "moral commitment to humanity." At times, this will mean resisting all kinds of human authority, because God's authority supersedes that of the human community.

The pastoral intent of the sermon comes through clearly in this call to human responsibility in a world where "God's value system…is counter-cultural to the world's system." People who care about one another and the world will often find that their compassion runs up hard against moral opposition. But a caring, compassionate people know that love of God and neighbor requires moral strength to preserve the purposes of God.

It's important to notice that the sermon grounds the moral responsibility of the congregation in the power of God. This sermon is not an optimistic or liberal call to more human courage, more personal sacrifice, more protest in the name of protest. It would have been easy enough for Stewart to lift up Shiphrah and Puah as moral exemplars for the community without spotlighting their theological motivations. But Stewart grounds the anthropology of the sermon in theology. Moral responsibility arises from the "promises of God" given to the Hebrews of scripture and passed on to succeeding generations. Shiphrah and Puah do not act of their own volition. They act out of reverence for God, who has chosen them. God gives them their vocation to preserve life. Everything they do is in response to the theological reality that God, the ultimate authority, gives them the power to act.

The congregation is probably not surprised when at the end of the sermon the preacher points toward Jesus upon Calvary as the one who empowers them to resist sin and destruction. While the sermon does not directly explore the gift of grace through Christ, it doesn't need to. The final sequence gives such strong presence to the redemptive work of Jesus Christ–tracing redemptive suffering through the blood of slaves to that of Martin Luther King, Jr.–that we can hardly miss the divine source of human moral responsibility. The pastoral community knows that it has loving work to do in the world. But our pastoral action flows from God's compassion for all creation that comes to focus in the sacrificial love of Jesus Christ.

Some listeners might object to the people in the sermon's roll call of saints. The heroic accomplishments of Ida B. Wells, Martin Luther King, Jr., Medgar Evers, and Nelson Mandela might seem unattainable to many in the pew. But the preacher balances these "famous" members of the communion of the saints with "ordinary," even nameless people like "the hundreds of slaves who died in the middle passage," "the millions of Jews killed during the Holocaust," and "those little girls bombed in a church one Sunday morning in Alabama." The unknown and the well known actually compose the roll call of faith. They are all heroes and heroines of the faith whose witness rings true within the African American community. They are the ones who have carried forward the moral struggle for liberation and have paid the dear price of life itself.

Further still, the preacher narrates the biblical story of Shiphrah and Puah so that these two women represent the little-known, "ordinary" people in the pew. The sermon skillfully presences Shiphrah and Puah. "They had no impressive pedigree. They had no political power. They were two ordinary women who did extraordinary things…They had seen it all: long labors, stillbirths, the death of mothers in childbirth, and the physical handicaps." Shiphrah and Puah do not rescue the Hebrew babies from the jaws of death by their own courage. They deliver liberation by the awesome power of God. If these two women answering the call of God can resist Pharaoh, so can the people who hear the sermon. Others have done it. And the congregation stands in that same line of the communion of the faithful.

This is where the sermon makes its pastoral theological claim on the congregation. The sermon's pastoral intent is to stir up a congregation of Shiphrahs and Puahs who know "who they are" and "whose they are." We do not need personal pep talks; we cannot rely on ourselves. God is the "ultimate authority" who leads the Shiphrahs and Puahs of this world and who enables us to say "yes to God." Our human responsibility is to offer prophetic pastoral care for others in the world. The power of God enables us to do so.

Freedom and Limits

Stewart grounds the sermon in the anthropological assumption that human freedom is only possible for those who trust and obey God. "There are limits to human authority," she reiterates. In a restatement of the classic theological conflict between divine and human authority, she states that finally the authority of God and the sacrifice of Christ supersede human authority. "When human authority rejects the *imago dei* of other human beings; when human authority fails to see the value in other human lives; when human authority values property over person; when human authority violates God's moral authority, the law has already been broken." In moral dilemmas within society, Christians can choose to exercise their God-given freedom to obey the laws of faith and conscience rather than those of the state or nation. Christians are people who care for others in the name of God, not in the name of nation or prosperity or even human decency. Shiphrah and Puah are conscientious objectors to the corrupted human authority of Pharaoh. Likewise, Christians from time to time must profess allegiance to God's higher authority.

But notice the preacher's honesty even as she seeks to pastorally guide the congregation toward responsible exercise of Christian freedom. She knows such moral commitment isn't facile. "To say no to Pharaoh means, as much as lies within the scope of our abilities and scope of influence, to do the will of God." Knowing the will of God and doing it are two different matters. The scope of our abilities varies, as does the range of our influence. Limits remain. We may be on the way to liberation and have the freedom to choose to do the right thing when confronted with injustice, but we haven't arrived yet. Even more, often the cost of human freedom is suffering and sacrifice. The sermon most fully presences faithful suffering in Christ. In short, caring for others and for the world is costly business. If we want to be free, as God intends for us to be, sometimes suffering will follow. In the interest of genuine, liberating care, the preacher refuses to paint a comforting picture of the birth of freedom.

Ecclesiology

The preacher speaks directly to the congregation as a people. She intends for the corporate body, the church, to hear this sermon. She signals this in the very first paragraph by her choice of pronouns, using "our" and "we" consistently throughout the sermon. This cannot be overstressed, because time and again contemporary pastoral preaching focuses either on individuals in distress or on the ills of society (see chapter 4). Stewart knows that the people before her are the ones who care. She isn't trying to shape public policy, though the congregation may choose to take up such a ministry. The care of the sermon doesn't linger long on personal needs, for it wants to midwife a caring community within a culture that is often care-less.

Several images of the church interact in the sermon: covenant people (people of God), "a nation chosen by God to receive the promises of God"; exodus community, "a nation poised for liberation"; and a countercultural moral community, "countercultural to the world's system...with a moral commitment to humanity." These scriptural images of the church reinforce one another and give the sermon a clear ecclesiological focus. They are the constitutive images of the sermon. A righteous and loving God calls together a people who become agents of God's righteous love in the world. At the heart of the sermon we find a church "with a moral commitment to humanity...to become advocates who work to change the attitudes and mores of our communities for the better." Importantly, this clear statement of ecclesiological purpose falls structurally at the center of the sermon. From that point forward, the sermon reinforces this central claim by spotlighting the commitments of those who have gone before the congregation to "make a difference in the world." A skillful use of repetition ("To say no to Pharaoh means..."), the juxtaposition of phrases ("no to Pharaoh," "yes to God"), and the rapid recitation of the roll call of the communion of the saints binds the congregation together as God's people who have a clear identity and purpose within creation.

We can reasonably hope that this congregation, if reinforced by such preaching over time, will embody the core virtues of a pastoral community–mutuality, hospitality, and compassion. There is a basic leveling of status and authority throughout the sermon. The church relates to "all people as children of God" who "reject the practice of racism, sexism, and classism." If the church is anything, it should be a people united in Christ: "male and female, Jew and Greek, bond and free," who "insignificant [the irony is clear] as we may be have the power just like these two midwives to make a difference in the world." This very pastoral, prophetic sermon rests upon the creative labor of Shiphrah and Puah, and like them, it seeks to give birth to a God-centered community whose members care passionately for the world.

The Silence of God[6]

Barbara Brown Taylor

Rev. Barbara Brown Taylor holds the Harry R. Butman chair of religion and philosophy at Piedmont College in Demorest, Georgia. She was the rector of Grace-Calvary Episcopal Church in Clarkesville, Georgia, when this sermon was preached. This sermon was delivered at Calvary Episcopal Church in Memphis, Tennessee, during Lent, 1993.

> Is not this the fast that I choose: to loose the bonds of injustice, to undo the thongs of the yoke, to let the oppressed go free, and to break every yoke? Is it not to share your bread with the hungry, and bring the homeless poor into your house; when you see the naked, to cover them, and not to hide yourself from your own kin? (Isa. 58:6–7)

Almost everyone has a story to tell about the first time God let you down. Maybe you were eight, or ten, or twenty. You did everything right, just the way you had been taught. You knelt by your bed, you clasped your hands in front of you, and you prayed for all you were worth. You gave yourself away; you held nothing back. You asked God for a sign, a hand, a map, a cure, and you waited, confidently, for God's answer to your prayer. Only it never came. Your need was not addressed, not directly, and you either learned to pray another way or else you gave it up altogether, because God turned out to be more stubborn than you had thought—more stubborn or more distant, but in either case, not who you had thought.

"Why do we fast, but you do not see?" God's people ask in the fifty-eighth chapter of Isaiah. "Why humble ourselves, but you do not notice?" It is not just an individual complaint; it is a human complaint that affects our lives in

---

community as well as our lives at home. "Why do we worship, but you do not reveal yourself to us? Why do we pray, Sunday after Sunday, for peace, for health, for safety, but you do not give us those things? Why is the world so far from our desires for it, and why don't you speak—loudly and clearly— so the whole world can hear?"

God's silence is stunning, especially for those of us who talk a lot. We think, perhaps, that we can solve the problem by making more noise ourselves, but it is only when we stop, and hush, that the silence can teach us anything: namely, that our disillusionment is not a bad thing. Take the word apart and you can begin to hear what it really means. Dis-illusion-ment. The loss of illusion. The end of make-believe. Is that a bad thing? Or a good thing? To learn that God's presence is not something we can demand, that God's job is not to reward our devotion, that God's agenda may in fact be quite different from our own. Is that a bad thing or a good thing to know?

"Announce to my people their rebellion," God says to the prophet Isaiah, "to the house of Jacob their sins. Yet day after day they seek me and delight to know my ways, as if they were a nation that practiced righteousness and did not forsake the ordinance of their God" (Isa. 58:1–2). That is how God answered the chosen people when they wanted to know where he had gone, and it is one of those answers that makes you wish for the silence again. "It is not I who have forsaken you," God says to the people, "but you who have forsaken me. If you cannot hear me, it is because you have strayed far from my voice. It is not I who am ignoring you, but you who are ignoring me."

The big disillusionment for the chosen people was that God was not where they thought. They thought God was supposed to be with them when they prayed and fasted and studied their scriptures. They thought nothing pleased God more than to find them on their knees, dressed in sackcloth, and covered with ashes—but they were wrong.

God was not at their prayer desks with them. God was out in the streets, warming his hands over a can of burning garbage with a bunch of drifters, delivering sacks of groceries down at the housing project, handing out blankets to those who slept shivering in the bushes. God was not parked in their sanctuaries, waiting for one of them to stop by for a talk. God was in the emergency room at the city hospital, in the waiting room at the labor pool, in the lobby at the police station, not only to comfort those who were stuck there but also to stir them up—reminding them of their birthright, their inherent nobility, reminding them that they were the long-lost sons and daughters of heavenly royalty, who were meant for more excellent lives.

"Is not this the fast that I choose," God said to the sackcloth-and-ashes crowd, "to loose the bonds of injustice, to undo the thongs of the yoke, to let the oppressed go free, and to break every yoke?" The big disillusionment for the chosen people was that they could not serve God without serving their neighbors. Their relationship to God was not separable from their relationship to other people, especially the least of them. They had hoped they could keep their faith a private matter between them and their God, but it turned out to be an illusion.

"It is a great mistake to suppose that God is chiefly interested in religion," wrote an archbishop of the last century, and Isaiah seems to agree. God is not interested in religion; God is interested in human beings, and particularly in the demolition of our illusions: that we can hold ourselves apart from one another, that we are not related to one another, that some people are simply destined to be winners and others to be losers and that there is nothing to be done about it, except perhaps to build some walls and install some security systems and relocate some neighborhoods in order to keep the one from spilling over into the other.

"Will you call this a fast, a day acceptable to the Lord?"

I am guilty. Ten months ago, I relocated my neighborhood, leaving the big city of Atlanta for a little town in North Georgia. I left because it was time for a change, but I also left because I was tired of being afraid all the time, and locking my doors all the time, and defending myself against people I was called to serve. Not the ones inside the church. I did all right with them. It was the ones outside the church who spooked me: the men who congregated in the parking lot late at night with bottles in paper bags; the women who hurled abuse at the receptionist for giving them one more telephone number to call instead of the help they needed; the children who clung to their mothers' legs with eyes one hundred years old. They were only the tip of the iceberg, and I knew it. I knew the city was full of catacombs where people existed on very little light and air, where bullets flew and babies' stomachs growled and old people froze to death in their beds because they could not pay their utility bills.

So I left. I had an illusion that the country would be different, and for the first few weeks it was. All I saw were the cows, and the clouds, and the fields full of wildflowers. But once I had gotten used to those, I started seeing other things: the Mexican children playing in the drainage ditch at the trailer park, the Laotian women coming out of the chicken-processing plant with their hair in white nets, the old folks at the grocery store with almost nothing in their carts, trying to decide between beans and cereal for supper. I had an illusion that the country would be different, but God disillusioned me.

Hiding ourselves from our kin is not a city issue or a rural issue but a human issue, and living with the fact of it is like living with a sore that will not heal. Everywhere you turn, it hurts. In order to hide from your brothers and sisters, you have to avert your gaze a lot. You have to learn when to look and when not to look. You have to plan your routes through town very carefully. Tinting your windows helps, or wearing dark glasses. Better yet, stay home altogether, or live somewhere with a guard at the gate. We can do that. That is one of our choices, but if we do, then we should not be surprised when we ring God and get no answer, or leave a message that is never returned, because we cannot hide ourselves from our kin without hiding ourselves from God. Isn't that a kick in the pants? We cannot defend ourselves against each other without defending ourselves against God.

A couple of years ago I decided to use public transportation whenever I could. It was an environmental commitment at that point; I had not really thought about the social consequences, most of which became clear to me the first time I boarded a Greyhound bus for Augusta. I was the only middle-class white lady aboard that day, and while I settled myself in my seat with my Walkman and my theological journals, my fellow passengers greeted each other loudly and started spreading their belongings around.

Once we got underway, it was like a block party on wheels. People asked each other their names and tried to figure out if they knew any of the same people in Augusta. They passed fried chicken around and fell asleep on each other's shoulders. They held each other's screaming babies and traded stories that made them howl with laughter, while the middle-class white lady, sitting up front all by herself, turned up the volume on her Walkman and read about the kingdom of God.

God has given us another way, a way as old as Isaiah and as up-to-date as the evening news. We can surrender our illusions of separateness, of safety and superiority. We can leave our various sanctuaries and seek God where God may be found, gathering in the streets—or in the Greyhound bus station—to figure out how to untie the fancy knots of injustice and how to take the yokes of oppression apart. We can pool our resources so that the hungry have bread and the homeless have houses and the naked have something to cover their shame. Above all, we can learn to claim our own kin, asking them what their names are, telling them our own, and refusing to hide from them anymore. "Then your light shall break forth like the dawn," says the Lord, "and your healing shall spring up quickly…Then you shall call, and the Lord will answer; you shall cry for help, and he will say, Here I am" (Isa. 58:8–9).

If God is silent, it may be because we are not speaking God's language yet, but there is still time. God has taught us how to break the silence and has even given us the words. "Here I am." They are the words we long to hear, but they are also the words God longs for us to speak—to stand before a sister, a brother, and say, "Here I am."

Those of us who decide to try it should listen real hard when we are through, because there is likely to be an echo in the air—not silence anymore, but the very voice of God, saying, "Yes. Hello. Welcome home. Here I am. Here I am."

Commentary

This sermon promises in the opening paragraph to deal with a specific pastoral theological concern: Where in the world is God? Why does God seem so silent whenever we come to God directly with our human needs? The problem is not limited to angst-ridden individuals. Had Taylor focused the sermon on the God-abandoned individual, we might have heard a therapeutically oriented sermon akin to those critiqued in earlier chapters. But she is casting a wider net. The silence of God is "a human complaint," she says, "that affects our lives in community as well as our lives at home." And the community that she has in mind is the pastoral community, the Christian congregation who prays "Sunday after Sunday, for peace, for health, for safety," but does not hear an answer from God.

The questions and answers, the silence and shouting, that Isaiah mediates between God and Israel are the questions and answers that Taylor explores between God and the contemporary church. The sermon gathers in the congregation as a people and asks them to consider again the relationship between God, humanity, and the church. How does the church come to hear God, anyway? What is the relationship between our worship of God and our care for those beyond the walls of the sanctuary? These are probing questions that drive the sermon. The underlying pastoral theology upon which Taylor bases her answers reveals a pastoral care that offers reconciliation between God, the hearers, and the neighbor. And it suggests a gentle yet sure moral guidance of the church toward its caring ministry in the world.

Theological Anthropology

Human Nature and Sin

The sermon stakes its theological claim for human nature on the *imago dei,* similar to the sermons of Forbes and Stewart. God creates human beings as brothers and sisters of one another in God's own image. All persons are "sons and daughters of heavenly royalty." By our birthright we are kin to one another, and we "cannot hide ourselves from our kin without hiding ourselves from God." Those who worship God inside the sanctuary are related by creation to those "in the waiting room at the labor pool, and in the lobby at the police station." The illusion that we can separate ourselves from one another, that "some people are simply destined to be winners and others to be losers," is just that—an illusion. The sermon rests upon this foundational anthropological premise. God creates human beings to enjoy redemptive relationships with one another. We can ignore this essential interpersonal nature of humanity, but we do so at the cost of losing our relatedness to God.

The sermon presences the communion that God desires for humanity in various ways, but it is especially effective in the Greyhound bus scene. While there may be some idealization of the riders on the bus, Taylor paints an earthy picture of the reign of God, complete with laughter and babies and fried chicken. This is the humanity that God had in mind at the first creation and that God seeks in the new creation. Here men and women, boys and girls share the joyful presence of one another and the rich satisfaction of human communion. The sermon shines a spotlight on this human "block party on wheels" and says to the congregation, This is a moving picture of God's care-full community. This is how God intends for all members of the human community to care for one another.

This lively, interactive human fellowship, however, is incomplete. There are cracks within the communion. The preacher has distanced herself from the wider human community, especially those on the margins of society. "I had an illusion that the country would be different," she says, explaining her move from the city. She watches the activity of the wider human community from a distance, separated by her Walkman and her theological journals. She reads about the kingdom of God when all around her people are experiencing it. The church as a whole, figured in the sermon as Israel, retreats into the secure walls of the sanctuary, where it can avoid the ones in the street. "The big disillusionment for the chosen people was that God was not where they thought...God was not parked in their sanctuaries, waiting for one of them to stop by for a talk." Commenting on Israel's (the church's) retreat from others, the sermon says, "They had hoped they could keep their faith a private matter between them and their God, but it turned out to be an illusion." Although God creates humanity for community, the church and its members repeatedly deny the ties that bind person to person. We withdraw from those persons who are different socially, economically, and racially, until, like Israel, we forget the nature of righteousness.

Pastorally speaking, the sermon wrestles with sin as separation from God and one another. But this is not the estrangement of the Christian existentialist alone in the world. Separation is the condition and sin of corporate humanity. The reason we cannot hear God is because we have hidden from one another. "Hiding ourselves from our kin is not a city issue or a rural issue but a human issue, and living with the fact of it is like living with a sore that will not heal." This human tendency to separate ourselves from others is particularly problematic for the church, because the church must live with Isaiah's prophetic reminder that it cannot serve God without serving the neighbor. Taylor's irony is pointed: The silence of God shouts of the church's sin.

The main pastoral intention of the sermon, therefore, is to offer reconciliation between the church and those whom the church disregards, on the one hand, and between the church and God, on the other. The pastoral theology of the sermon invites the listening congregation "to claim our own kin, asking them what their names are, telling them our own, and refusing to hide from them anymore." Reconciliation on the human level will be matched by divine/human reconciliation. The church's "Here I am," spoken to those outside of the sanctuary, will be echoed by God's

"Here I am" to the church. The movement of the sermon itself is toward reconciliation as it progresses from silence to the renewal of conversation between God, church, and the other.

Such reconciliation may seem like a grand pastoral order, but the preacher understands that godly care overcomes impediments to human community. The first step toward genuine reconciliation is for the church to break the silence that separates those inside the church from those outside the church. The church will effect such reconciliation not by assuming that it holds the keys to salvation. Rather, the church will act on the theological conviction that God is "out in the streets, warming his hands over a can of burning garbage" and "in the emergency room at the city hospital." Persons outside the church, sometimes more powerfully than those inside the church, witness to the love of God. Reconciliation will come, and the silence of God will be broken, whenever the church begins to listen more intently to the voice of the other, the stranger who is a caring child of God.

Human Responsibility and the Grace of God

Another pastoral intent of this sermon emerges through the preacher's convictions about human responsibility. If God is silent within the church and in the lives of its members, it is not because God refuses to speak but because *we* have strayed from the voice of God. "It is not I who am ignoring you, but you who are ignoring me." Humanity must take responsibility for ignoring God by heeding God's call in Isaiah. Taylor does not have to push the point very hard, because the scripture passage that governs the sermon does the pushing. "Is not this the fast that I choose: to loose the bonds of injustice...Is it not to share your bread with the hungry, and bring the homeless poor into your house." The sermon challenges the hearers, just as the preacher challenges herself, to admit that by fencing ourselves off from others, we close ourselves off to God. Without haranguing the congregation about its shortcomings or raising the flag of moral crusade, the sermon offers gentle moral guidance to the hearers about how they should live in the world. "We can pool our resources so that the hungry have bread and the homeless have houses and the naked have something to cover their shame. Above all, we can learn to claim our own kin." Notice the inclusive nature of the rhetoric through its use of the pronouns *we* and *our,* as Taylor maintains identification with the listeners. She is not preaching at the people, but among them. She assumes that humans are responsible moral agents in God's world, and she offers the same thoughtful pastoral direction to her hearers that she prescribes for herself.

The question might arise as to *how* the church is supposed to act on its moral responsibility with respect to others. Clearly the sermon assumes an incarnational understanding of God. God is much more immanent than transcendent. When God is so closely aligned with the human poor and suffering, is there any divinity and grace left to empower the Christian community to act responsibly? Or does the sermon, in liberal fashion, finally cast us back on our own will, which by the preacher's own theological convictions is deeply flawed? These questions bear weighty pastoral significance. Because if the sermon offers moral, pastoral guidance to the community, there must be some theological support for our action. Otherwise, the church will despair over its own inability to respond in faith or ignore the pastoral guidance altogether.

The point is subtle in the sermon, but Taylor maintains the priority of grace. Admirably, she does not attempt to wrest Jesus Christ as God's offer of grace into a sermon that is governed by Hebrew Scripture. No, we hear the divine initiative in the silence of God. By refusing to speak on our command, God beckons us back to right relations with God and one another. God is prior and present to humanity, even if we have forgotten God. "If you cannot hear me, it is because you have strayed far from my voice. It is not I who am ignoring you, but you who are ignoring me." God is the silent Presence whose very silence convicts the believing community of its faithlessness and empowers the believing community to act with righteousness. Because God, the great "I Am," is already at home, already present to those who act and believe in God's name, the church learns to say to the neighbor, "Here I am," that is, to act responsibly in the world. "God has given us another way, a way as old as Isaiah and as up-to-date as the evening news," the preacher reminds the congregation. When the church recalls that God has already given us to one another through creation—a gift of God, not of our own doing—we can fulfill the prophetic call to righteousness. This pastoral sermon does not urge the hearers to fulfill an impossible moral demand. It calls us to be who we already are regardless of creed, or race, or socioeconomic status—sisters and brothers of the same God.

Freedom and Limits

One final aspect of the sermon's theological anthropology deserves comment before we explore its ecclesiology. Much of this sermon's pastoral impact stems from the preacher's awareness that humanity walks a tightrope between freedom and limits. We can in freedom exert moral influence in our world. Empowered by God's presence, we can offer care to others that matters. Indeed, the sermon is quite hopeful on this point. Responsible use of our God-given freedom can lead us to dismantle our "security systems" and "take the yokes of oppression apart." This is how caring Christians act, the sermon proclaims. We do taste the bread of Christian care, and we are free to share it liberally within church and community.

But Taylor stops far short of claiming unlimited freedom for the human being. Left to unfettered freedom, humanity bumps smack against the imposing barrier of the silence of God. Imagining that we can conjure up a

God of our own making, we come to a moment of profound disillusionment. "To learn that God's presence is not something we can demand, that God's job is not to reward our devotion, that God's agenda may in fact be quite different from our own." God is the only One in all creation who is fully free, this theology suggests. When the human community realizes this, we can begin to hear the voice of God that guides humanity in our use of freedom.

We should not overlook the pastoral significance of these theological claims. They assert that God directs Christian care because God is the one who sets the terms of human life in the first place. We are free to do otherwise than listen to the voice of God, but we should not be surprised when we wake up in a desolate country far from the sounds of God. Those who seek to live compassionately, carefully, will honor the limits of human freedom, knowing that our best hope is to listen attentively for God, who not only announces our "rebellion," but who says "your healing shall spring up quickly." Such pastoral theological convictions help the congregation avoid placing too much confidence in their own well-laid plans while it anchors them in the promises of God.

Ecclesiology

Taking a cue from Isaiah 58, the sermon constructs the church as Israel, the people of God. "'Why do we fast, but you do not see?' God's people ask." The address of the sermon is communal. Taylor does not preach to individuals or to some abstraction of society. She preaches to those "in community," the ones in the sanctuary. The sermon speaks to the contemporary Israel who gathers together in the sanctuary to worship and pray "Sunday after Sunday, for peace, for health, for safety." At first, the silence of God puzzles the people, but they soon discover that God's refusal to speak is because they have forsaken God, not the other way around. The church has made the age-old mistake of separating sacred ritual from lives of mercy and compassion. The church retains its identity as God's people throughout the sermon, but the church must rediscover its purpose.

The pastoral nature of the sermon comes into clear focus as Taylor invites the hearers to consider the true mission of the church. God leads the church away from rituals of "sackcloth and ashes" into the city of human need, "full of catacombs where people exist on very little light and air, where bullets fly and babies' stomachs growl and old people freeze to death in their beds because they cannot pay their utility bills." Beyond the walls of the sanctuary, despite our best efforts to evade them, is a whole world of people whom God loves: "Mexican children playing in the drainage ditch at the trailer park…Laotian women coming out of the chicken processing plant…and old folks at the grocery store…trying to decide between beans and cereal for supper."

The vivid but terse imagery of these and similar passages magnifies rhetorical presence in the sermon. It is one of the powerful components of Taylor's preaching. Hearing and seeing such vivid pictures of life outside the sanctuary, the persons in the pew (the church) cannot easily shut them out. The walls begin to crack between the church and world as the pastoral preacher guides the congregation to embrace its true calling. The sermon slowly and gently guides the church to remember that "their relationship to God was not separable from their relationship to other people, especially the least of them." The church will not hear the voice of God when it learns to pray better but when it learns that prayer cannot be cut off from caring concern for others. God goes before the church into the world. Indeed, God resides among the lives of those from whom the church often hides.

The sermon wants to mold the hearers into a pastoral community. The preacher does not chastise individuals for their selfishness or elevate human concern for others to heroic status. The sermon wants to shape a people into the caring folk whom God intends them to be. Though the words do not appear in the sermon, hospitality and compassion are the communal virtues that the preacher seeks to form within the people. At the end of the sermon, Taylor holds before the hearers a picture of the church as a compassionate and hospitable community, "leaving our various sanctuaries and seeking God where God may be found, gathering in the streets," or pooling "our resources so that the hungry have bread and the homeless have houses and the naked have something to cover their shame." The pastoral community will "learn to claim our own kin, asking them what their names are, telling them our own, and refusing to hide from them anymore." The church comes out of the stained-glass shadows and breaks the silence by entering into caring relationships with others. The echo here of Matthew 25 is unmistakable. The church lives by giving itself away for others (compassion). The church hears the voice of God in the voice of the poor, the hungry, and the prisoner (hospitality, mutuality). At bottom, this pastoral sermon builds the church on the caring love of God so that the church's life will be care-full. Who cares in this sermon? The church cares, *and* those beyond the church care. Above all, God cares.

Personal Stories

One additional comment might be helpful about the preacher's use of personal stories in the sermon. The preacher relates two personal experiences: a move from Atlanta to a town in North Georgia and a ride on a Greyhound bus. Intentional self-disclosure occurs in these stories. A confessional tone governs them both. Indeed, Taylor introduces the first story by saying, "I am guilty."

Some hearers could take issue with this use of personal experience in the sermon, and some of my earlier comments in the book might suggest the same. But notice, Taylor presents these stories with utmost homiletical restraint. Committed to the church's need to hear God, she does not allow her personal stories to take over the sermon. There is, as she says elsewhere, "no hogging of the hermeneutic."[7] Following her own cautions about the use of personal experience in preaching, Taylor doesn't use the stories to focus the spotlight on herself.[8] In the first instance, the spotlight shines on the many people whom Taylor sees outside the church who pose a challenge to the church's illusion of security. In the second instance, the camera focuses on the rollicking and fleshly incarnation of the kingdom of God among the riders of the Greyhound bus.

The preacher is clearly in these stories and learns something from her own experience. This may distract some hearers. But as I see it, in both instances, Taylor presents herself as a *representative* of the church. She is not so much singling herself out as establishing rhetorical communion (identification) with the listening congregation. She says to the gathered congregation, "These are *our* illusions of safety and security. This is what the upside-down world of the kingdom of God really looks and sounds like if *we* can open our eyes and ears." Her immediate shift of pronouns following each story, from *I* to *We*, indicates this intention. Presented by a less skillful preacher, the stories might detract from the pastoral intent of the sermon. But the preacher respects her hearers. She understands the power of language. These, combined with her overall homiletical skills, keep the sermon focused on its primary pastoral theological concerns of reconciling and guiding the people of God in the world.

God Hears

G. Lee Ramsey, Jr.

Rev. G. Lee Ramsey, Jr., preached a version of this sermon on Genesis 21:8–21 in July 1996 at Bethlehem United Methodist Church in Clarksville, Tennessee, where he was serving as pastor.

This is the story we forget—the one about Hagar and Ishmael. We often remember the story before this one. You know, old Sarah and Abraham after so many years of waiting finally have a son, Isaac, just as God promises. We cackle along with Abraham and Sarah. We toast the baby's birth. Finally, God fulfills the promise. But amid all the celebration, we forget about the slave woman Hagar and her son Ishmael. How quickly we overlook Abraham's firstborn—Ishmael. How easily the church pushes into the shadows the

[7]Barbara Brown Taylor, *When God is Silent* (Cambridge, Mass.: Cowley Publications, 1998), 114.

[8]Commenting on Jesus' use of stories in the gospels, Taylor says, "He also did not star in his own stories," ibid., 76.

woman who in obedience to Abraham and Sarah gives birth on their behalf. We want to be rid of these two. The woman does not really belong. Now that Isaac is born, this other child must go. Maybe Ishmael and Hagar remind us too much of our own desperation. So off we shove them into oblivion with a bag of bread and a jug of water. They stumble farther away from us. In time, they become no more than phantoms flickering across the screens of our awareness. It's easy, really, to forget about Hagar and Ishmael.

Can we focus again upon them? Can we bring the mother and child back into view? See Hagar and Ishmael—the abandoned and abused, AIDS babies, starving parents and children from Rwanda to Clarksville. Can we see them out there wandering through the empty places? Do we spot them in the wastelands of our cities? The mother holds the child upon her hip. Exhausted, she shuffles silently along our streets. Now she stops to peer into a can. She turns over some trash; then she's off again. Ishmael's hunger gnaws at Hagar. His thirsty need tortures her. After weeks of trying, Hagar cannot find a way to feed Ishmael. So there in an overgrown vacant lot, the mother thrusts the infant underneath some bushes and runs away, now fast, now falling. She lunges away groping for distance. Hagar scrambles far enough away not to have to face the death of her own child. She collapses. She wails. Her moans rise and drown out the whimpering of her own dying baby. Ishmael cries like an orphaned lamb, and homeless Hagar wails.

Now listen. A remarkable thing happens. God hears. As Hagar and Ishmael scream in the wilderness, God hears. Then God speaks. "Take the boy, Hagar. Hold him fast with your hand. And I will give you both a future." God hears the wails of Hagar and Ishmael and promises a full life right smack in the middle of the desert of death. Others have silenced Hagar, shut her up and shut her out, but not God. God's ears work quite well. God hears the shouts and the whispers. You can count on that. As a matter of fact, this is not the only time God hears the sounds of those who cry out. Baby Moses cries in the bulrush—God hears. The voice of a broken man says, "Jesus, Son of God, save me"—God hears. A bleeding woman from the crowd reaches out, pleads for the healing touch of Christ—God hears. God hears because that's the way God is. Not despite abandonment but because of abandonment, our God hears. No voice shall remain mute to God, certainly not the cries of God's children, whom the world often tunes out. God is like a mother to whom you are talking in our fellowship hall. You know how loud and lively things can get in there during a fellowship lunch. You think the conversation is on track when you notice that she isn't fully present. She says, "Excuse me a minute. Hear that?" You say, "Hear what?" She says, "That cry. That's my child." Lost to the crowd but not unto God. God anticipates the cries of Hagar and Ishmael. Our God hears.

What about the hearing of the church? We listen with God's ears, you know. The church is the community who listens with the ears of God. We are the people who for the love of God cannot plug up our ears to the cries of Hagar and Ishmael. In Nashville there is a small congregation, Edgehill United Methodist Church, that gathers to worship in a converted garage-sanctuary on the edge of a low-income community. Recently, right in the middle of the sermon, a distressed man entered the worship service and began calling for the preacher's attention. The preacher stopped the sermon and walked directly to the man. He calmed the man down. Then the preacher told him that he wanted to hear all about what was happening. He invited the man to let a couple of the "sisters and brothers" help him until the sermon was over. By that time, two members of the congregation had literally embraced this crying man and were offering consolation. Later, the preacher left the sanctuary with the man to hear his story. It turned out that the man's wife was dying. Somebody's got to listen. Even in our worship right here at Bethlehem, you see, the church can hear the cries of Hagar and Ishmael. On Sunday mornings when one of you stands to make announcements about the needs of the homeless in our city, and you tell us how we can support the work of Clarksville Urban Ministries, we are listening for Hagar and Ishmael. For what would our worship be without the honest intent to serve God and our neighbor in need? Surely we cannot call our worship "the liturgy," the "service" of God, unless we are able to hear and respond to the cries of Hagar and Ishmael. Church folk hear. We gather every Sunday in auditoriums, hearing places. Because we are the people who listen to God and all of God's children.

Do you remember what God does? God offers to Hagar and Ishmael water without price. God gives to thirsting humanity a well in the desert, water from a rock. Not just to a few, but God gives this water to all God's people. No one shall be cast out. "Ho, everyone who thirsts, come to the waters [and drink]," says the prophet Isaiah (55:1). Run, Hagar, get your dehydrated son and bring him to the stream of living water. There's plenty of room in the cool shallows for all of God's people to drink and play. There's water enough for Isaac *and* Ishmael, water for the firstborn and the last. We need not worry that God's water will run dry.

Like last week at the cancer walk, Relay For Life. Have you ever seen so many people having so much fun? Here we are, Bethlehem Church, in our booth selling ice cream right between the Baptists with barbecue and the Harley Riders for Health. Everybody is talking, laughing, raising money for the same purpose—to remember those who have died from cancer and raise funds for research to prevent cancer in the future. Well, in case you've forgotten, it's about a hundred and twenty degrees out there at ten o'clock in the morning. So what's the most popular booth at the entire event? It's the water station. The kids and adults are going in and out of that misting tent like it's a backyard sprinkler. And those ice-cold bottles of crystal clear water, they taste as cool and fresh as a Smoky Mountain spring in April. People stand there in line to get a bottle of that water and then just circle back around and get in line again for another one. And the best part about the water is that it's free. FREE. Free water for all who pass by—the sick, the healthy, cancer survivors, supporters of those with cancer, the bereaved, Baptists, Methodists, motorcycle riders, old, young—it doesn't matter; the water is free. That's what God provides for all of God's children—free, living water. God offers water without price.

You see, the church who hears with the ears of God is in the caring business. Our call as God's people comes from those who plead for water and bread. Sometimes the church is guilty of ignoring the thirst of our own sisters and brothers. We forget that the same God who gives us life gives life to Hagar and Ishmael. Hagar and Ishmael are part of us, all members of God's family. Finally, there is enough water and food for all God's children. The work of the church is to open up the watering stations and let the healing gifts of God flow. It doesn't have to be all that complicated. Our youth have shown us through their work with the Appalachia Service Project how simple yet meaningful it is to share a cup of cold water with someone else. They'll tell you that the Hagars and Ishmaels who live in the hills of Appalachia know God quite well, and that deep streams of care flow within those hills. Or take a look at a few church women over near Raleigh, North Carolina. They began thinking and praying about all the women in prison who are mothers. With some Spirit-fired imagination, hard work, and cooperation from prison officials, they fixed up a couple of rooms, a den and a kitchen, right there on the prison grounds. There the mothers not only can see their children but rock them in rocking chairs, play games with them on the floor, and cook good meals, like macaroni and cheese, for their own children. They call it the MATCH house, which stands for Mothers And Their Children. It's an oasis in the middle of the prison. Why does the church do such crazy things? Because the church hears with the ears of God. We are in the caring business.

Look, we believe in a God who hears. We belong to a people who listen to the thirsty cries of Hagar and Ishmael with the ears of God. When the parched voices of God's children pierce the world, God answers with free-flowing waters. The church, as God's people, cannot help but offer the water that revives, the water that sustains to the lonely, afraid, illegitimate, homeless, or abandoned. After all, the name Ishmael means "God hears." The name Ishmael means "God hears." Can we who call ourselves God's people remember that? God hears. God hears.

Commentary

I attempt to allow one central symbol from Genesis 21, the hearing of God, to guide the form and content of this sermon. This is what I refer to in chapter 3 as the hub symbol, or constitutive image of the sermon. Just as God hears the cries of Hagar and Ishmael, I hope to quicken the hearing of the congregation to those whom we often tune out. Hagar and Ishmael function symbolically to represent various kinds of people–homeless women and children, persons with AIDS, prisoners, the abused—whom the church too easily ignores. Signaled in its anthropology and ecclesiology, the pastoral intent of the sermon is to offer healing to the congregation and to amplify the congregation's sustaining care of others, especially for those whom church and society cast out.

Theological Anthropology

Human Nature and Sin

This sermon, like all the previous ones in this book to one degree or another, assumes a theological anthropology of communion. God creates all humanity as brothers and sisters of one another. Ishmael, like Isaac, is the legitimate son of Abraham. He and Hagar belong just as much to the human family as anybody else. "Hagar and Ishmael are part of us, all members of God's family." God does not reject Ishmael and Hagar in the scripture even though Israel does; rather, God makes Ishmael, like Isaac, the leader of a nation. Each has his place on the earth, and all human beings trace their lineage back to God.

Furthermore, God creates humanity with the capacity to "hear" one another. In this case, hearing implies compassionate concern for one another, like a mother hearing the cries of her child above the noise of a fellowship dinner. Joy reverberates through human community when we truly hear one another. "Everybody is talking, laughing…right between the Baptists with barbecue and the Harley Riders for Health." Comfort flows through community when sisters and brothers hear the cry of a bereaved man in worship and convert their hymns of praise into embracing arms. This is how God intends for the human community to live. We listen to one another because in genuine speaking and hearing between persons we enact our God-given communion.

The problem is, we forget. The first line of the sermon names our forgetfulness. "This is the story we forget." Later on, I say, "We forget that the same God who gives us life gives life to Hagar and Ishmael." And in response to our forgetfulness of others, the sermon asks, "Do you *remember* what God does?" The entire sermon attempts to recall for the listeners, to bring to hearing again, who we are in relation to God and one another, especially who we are in relationship to those outside the walls of church and social "respectability." While I do not directly name this forgetfulness as sin, the theological assumption underlies the sermon. At one point I say that the church "is guilty of ignoring the thirst of our brothers and sisters." Our inability to remember the Hagars and Ishmaels of the world causes the unchecked suffering of men, women, and children from "Rwanda to Clarksville…in the wastelands of our cities."

It may be a subtle point, but sin in the sermon isn't so much a malignant desire to harm others as it is a desperate move to put distance between us and the other. "Maybe Ishmael and Hagar remind us too much of our own desperation." We'd rather toast the abundant promise of Isaac's birth than own up to the prior responsibility to Ishmael. So out of our own anxiety we conveniently push Hagar and Ishmael away; then, we forget.

The pastoral perspective of the sermon now comes into view. Our own forgetfulness, our poor hearing, needs to be healed. "What about the hearing of the church?" the sermon asks. "Surely we cannot call our worship 'the liturgy,' the 'service' of God, unless we are able to hear and respond to the cries of Hagar and Ishmael." This is an indirect though nonetheless intentional call to confession (accountability), a necessary first step in the healing process.

Healing of the church, however, and this is crucial, is not for our own sake but in order for the church to be able to heal and sustain others. I attempt to give concrete examples of the healing and sustaining care of the hearing church: the man in worship at Edgehill United Methodist Church, Clarksville Urban Ministries, the youth group and the Appalachia Service Project, Relay for Life, the mothers and children in prison. So the care of the sermon has a dual intent: to heal the congregation of its forgetfulness and to guide the congregation toward compassionate concern for others. The church may temporarily need hearing aids until we are able to perceive the sound of the cries of others. But once we remember (hear again) who we are, the care of the church will flow toward others like springs in the desert.

In addition to healing and guiding, a third pastoral intent runs through the sermon—reconciliation. To remember is to be reconnected to someone or something that has been lost or forgotten. The eucharistic prayers include prayers of *anamnesis*, or remembering, in which the church is "re-membered," "re-united," "re-connected" to one another and God through Jesus Christ. The sermon's appeal to the congregation to remember (hear again) the voices of the forgotten ones outside the sanctuary suggests the reconciling dimension of pastoral care. Pastorally speaking, the sermon wants to bring together those who are separated by physical condition, creed, or class and join them together around the healing fountain of God. The story from the cancer walk points toward this pastoral theme. "Free water for all who pass by—the sick, the healthy, cancer survivors, supporters of those with cancer, the bereaved, Baptists, Methodists, motorcycle riders, old, young—it doesn't matter, the water is free." Similarly, the reference to the youth group's work among the people of Appalachia represents an overcoming of barriers, as does the story about the prison mothers. The sermon attempts to paint pictures of reconciling events within the community and invites the listening congregation to take on this pastoral ministry of reconciliation.

Human Responsibility and the Grace of God

The sermon appeals to the congregation to quicken its sensitivity to the Hagars and Ishmaels of society. The final lines of the sermon are a direct entreaty to congregational moral responsibility. "Can we who call ourselves God's people remember that? God hears." The sermon hopes to encourage within the congregation the pastoral virtues of mutuality, hospitality, and compassion. Our human tendency is to forget about the homeless and women in prison, but our Christian moral responsibility is to listen and respond to their calls as children of God. The sermon allows, and here my own Wesleyan roots show through, no shirking of ethical response to the needs of others regardless of how well we worship. For what would our worship be without the honest intent to serve God and our neighbor in need? Holiness of heart and life go hand in hand.

I think, however, that the sermon avoids becoming moralistic and falling into a theology of works righteousness. A liberation motif does run throughout the sermon that in the tension between works and grace potentially tips the scales toward human action. But God offers the first and last response to human need in the sermon. Unlike the fallen and forgetful human community, "God hears." When the focus switches from God's response to that of the church, the mood is indicative rather than imperative. "We listen with God's ears, you know. The church is the community who listens with the ears of God." Thus, I attempt to remind the church of who we already are (indicative) rather than, in activist fashion, demand of the listening congregation a radical response (imperative). The fact is that the actual congregation of Bethlehem United Methodist Church is already a congregation that hears the voices of others in the community. So the sermon invites them to become *better* listeners, more attuned to others with the ears of God.

Yes, the sermon challenges the congregation to hear more clearly, but it is because God already hears. "God hears because that's the way God is." The church cannot by its own efforts fine-tune its hearing. God will heal the church's hearing. "Baby Moses cries in the bulrush—God hears. The voice of a broken man says, 'Jesus, Son of God save me'—God hears." Each of these biblical allusions reinforces that God is the first one to hear and heal.

God is the One in scripture and sermon who offers water without price. The church can establish an "oasis in prison" for mothers and children, because God has already provided for the church an oasis in the desert. Youth can extend a "cup of cold water" to families in Appalachia, because God has already placed "deep streams of care within those hills." Baptismal allusions that unconsciously reinforce the priority of grace lie beneath the surface of these water images. Through the hearing church, God will offer the healing "water that revives, the water that sustains."

Very few christological elements appear in the sermon because I am preaching from the Hebrew Scriptures. I mention this because earlier in the book (chapters 4 and 5) I stress the importance of christology for pastoral preaching. Too many pastoral sermons in the liberal tradition seem to leave Jesus Christ out, reducing christology to noble human action. This is a problem that Christian preachers need to address. Nevertheless, trusting in the providence and grace of God revealed in both Hebrew and Christian scripture, I do not see any need to shoehorn Jesus into this particular sermon. I do not suggest that caring for the hungry, the abandoned, the abused, and the imprisoned is an easy or even noble thing for the church to do. The church cares because God cares, and God through Jesus Christ and the Holy Spirit is the theological basis for the church. God is the One who provides healing and wholeness (salvation) in the scripture passage, and God is the main character of this sermon. The sermon wants to bring out the church's care for others, but this care is rooted in God. The God of the sermon hears the cry of Hagar and Ishmael (God not only speaks but listens), has compassion for them (suffers with them), and provides them the means of salvation (healing). It is this very same God who becomes incarnate in Jesus Christ and whom, in another sermon based in Christian scripture, I would bring out through christology. The main point here is that in pastoral sermons, God in any or all of the trinitarian manifestations (Creator, Redeemer, Sustainer) is the primary actor. This theological focus allows the pastoral preacher to derive congregational care (responsibility) from God, not the other way around.

Freedom and Limits

I attempt to strike a balance between the anthropological poles of freedom and limits as I characterize humanity in the sermon. The sermon may appear too optimistic to some readers, suggesting that human beings and the church are more capable of exercising freedom responsibly than we actually are. Admittedly, the sermon provides various hopeful images of the church without exploring many constraints. But in the beginning and end (the literal limits) of the sermon, I recognize the boundaries to human freedom. At the start of the sermon, whether we like it or not, something limits our capacity to remember Hagar and Ishmael. We have selective memories. Something causes us to cope with our own desperation (anxiety) by shoving away those who are destitute. This is not so much a transgression of boundaries as it is a corruption of human freedom.

The sermon asks: Can we hear Hagar and Ishmael? And while it attempts to persuade the congregation to say yes, the answer is not fully assumed even at the end of the sermon. Can we as God's people remember that? God hears. In other words, while the sermon wants to construct a people who freely care for others, it recognizes that we may abuse our God-given freedom. It's possible for us to turn a deaf ear to the cries of others. Or we may overlook the fact that God is the one who provides the oasis in the desert. We may attempt to take control of care by our own hands, or we may assume that the hungry of the world are somebody else's problem. Either way, the wellspring of compassion will run dry, and we will become deaf to the cries of others. Only when the church discovers its own freedom within the wide boundaries of God's grace, a grace bountiful enough for Hagar and Sarah, Ishmael and Isaac, will we be able to carefully embrace others.

Ecclesiology

As you might expect from my comments in chapter 5, the church of the sermon is based on two biblical models: the people of God and the church for others (servant community). I state this ecclesiology in various ways throughout the sermon. "We belong to a people who listen to the thirsty cries of Hagar and Ishmael with the ears of God." Or again, "We are the people who for the love of God cannot plug up our ears to the cries of Hagar and Ishmael." Compassion and hospitality characterize this church as a pastoral community. "You see, the church who hears with the ears of God is in the caring business." I try to name as directly as possible the healing care of the church. "The work of the church is to open up the watering stations and let the healing gifts of God flow." Since God hears Hagar and offers healing (saving) water to her, the ones who call themselves God's people will do the same. The church discovers its identity and mission in the God who hears. "We listen with God's ears, you know."

I attempt to present recognizable and seriously imaginable images of the church for the listening congregation. Several images of the actual congregation appear in the sermon (announcing needs of the homeless in Clarksville, participating in the Relay for Life, and the youth ministry's working with the Appalachia Service Project). I hope that these positive images of the congregation's hearing and responding to others will affirm the existing pastoral work of the body by reminding them of who they already are. This is the important work of identification within the sermon. Remember who you are, the sermon says–a people who hear with the ears of God.

At the same time, I present two other images of the church beyond the existing congregation (Edgehill Church, the prison ministry in North Carolina). Each of these images is not too far removed from the Bethlehem congregation. The first is close by geographically, in Nashville. The other, the ministry with women in prison, is carried out by several church women, presumably a lot like some of the women who hear the sermon. I attempt to closely align this final story of the church with the scripture passage itself, since both stories concern rejected mothers and their children. Hopefully, these images stretch the actual imagination of the congregation. They attempt to paint fresh pictures of the church as a caring community that will beckon the listening congregation forward.

I hope that these corporate images of the caring church as a healing, sustaining, and reconciling people of God will achieve presence for the hearers. If not, and they may not, it is helpful for the pastoral preacher to remember that each sermon, like the worship of the entire congregation, is an offering to God. But if the church of this sermon does become embedded within the self-understanding of the congregation, we might reasonably hope to discover a pastoral community with "ears to hear" and the compassion to respond to the needs of others.

Conclusion

Every Sunday pastoral preachers stand in the pulpit to offer God's healing and reconciling, guiding and sustaining care to congregations. When life is broken open in Memphis or Oklahoma City, Iraq or Israel, Serbia or Rwanda, as it is every day in the lives of those who people the congregation, the preacher's job is to name the caring presence of God among the Christian community in the world.

This crucial task of pastoral preaching is primarily a theological endeavor. Pastoral preaching is theological despite the fact that the language of other disciplines, such as psychology and sociology, tends to drown out the voice of pastoral theology in contemporary preaching. Admittedly, some gains occur through preachers' application of modern psychological insight to the sermon. For example, the most astute preacher pastors gain clarity about the depths of the human personality that the preached gospel seeks to encounter. This, in turn, leads some preachers to offer more sensitively attuned sermons that can bear the weight of human need. Nevertheless, many contemporary preachers eagerly stumble around within the relatively new house of psychotherapeutically informed pastoral care, grasping first one theory of human behavior and then another, to haul up into the pulpit and apply to this week's scripture text and sermon, all in the name of pastoral care and all with mixed results. Meanwhile, we leave theology, homiletic and pastoral, in the study. But preaching is pastoral–care-full– because of the way that the preacher handles the theology of the sermon, especially its understanding of the human being and the church.

Preaching is indeed pastoral, whether the preacher is aware of it or not. At bottom, the pastoral perspective of preaching is rooted in the theological anthropology and ecclesiology of the sermon. We can understand the pastoral nature of our sermons by paying close attention to the pastoral theology within the sermon itself: Who cares in the sermon? What kind of church does the sermon seek to build? I hope that the examples of chapter 6 will help the readers with the task of pastoral theological assessment of their own sermons.

To be sure, the pastoral care of sermons will vary from preacher to preacher and Sunday to Sunday. Sometimes the care of the sermon will offer reconciliation or moral guidance to the congregation; at other times, healing or sustaining. But over time, if we look closely at the theology of our sermons, we will probably discover pastoral theological patterns that we will want to either reinforce or correct. The first step is to become aware that pastoral care is occurring through the theology and language of the sermon. The next is to decide what to do about it. Hopefully, some of the pointers in these pages will help.

Pastoral preaching forms communities who care for the world with the love of God. This is a significant challenge, for it is the dearth of authentic community in the Western world that calls for our most creative ministry at the beginning of the twenty-first century. These Christian pastoral communities, formed through our preaching and pastoral care, are signs of God's care-full presence among all of creation. They resemble, ever so faintly, the fullness of God's care among humanity. Within the pastoral community, we see the dim outlines of the suffering and resurrected Christ whom God offers as care for the world. We witness these pastoral communities, in part, wherever in Christian congregations pastoral preaching binds folks together in mutuality, hospitality, and compassion as they share God's caring love for creation.

Yet preacher pastors will not place their ultimate trust in themselves or the pastoral community. Such trust we reserve for the One who cares enough to create a world in love and redeem it in grace. For all our preaching and caring, the best we can muster in faith among a people of faith are but offerings of gratitude that we entrust back into the arms of God, the One who cares.

Select Bibliography

Aden, Leroy, and J. Harold Ellens, eds. *Turning Points in Pastoral Care: The Legacy of Anton Boisen and Seward Hiltner.* Grand Rapids, Mich.: Baker, 1990.

Allen, Ronald J. "The Relationship Between the Pastoral and the Prophetic in Preaching." *Encounter* 49 (Summer 1988): 173–89.

——, Barbara S. Blaisdell, and Scott B. Johnston. *Theology for Preaching: Authority, Truth, and Knowledge of God in a Postmodern Ethos.* Nashville: Abingdon Press, 1997.

Ammerman, Nancy Tatom, et al. *Congregation & Community.* New Brunswick, N. J.: Rutgers University Press, 1997.

Augustine, Bishop of Hippo. *Writings of Saint Augustine, On Christian Doctrine* The Fathers of the Church Series. Translated by John J. Gavigan. New York: CIMA, 1947.

Barth, Karl. *The Word of God and the Word of Man.* Translated by Douglas Horton. New York: Harper & Brothers, 1928.

Baxter, Richard. *The Reformed Pastor.* London: Nisbet & Co., 1860.

Bellah, Robert, et al. *Habits of the Heart: Individualism and Commitment in American Life.* Berkeley, Calif.: University of California Press, 1985.

Berger, Peter, and Thomas Luckmann. *The Social Construction of Reality.* New York: Doubleday & Co., 1965.

Berry, Wendell. *What Are People For?* San Francisco: North Point Press, 1990.

Billman, Kathleen D. "Pastoral Care as an Art of Community." In *The Arts of Ministry: Feminist-Womanist Approaches,* edited by Christie Cozad Neuger, 10–38. Louisville: Westminster John Knox Press, 1996.

Bond, L. Susan. *Trouble With Jesus: Women, Christology, and Preaching.* St. Louis: Chalice Press, 1999.

Bondi, Roberta C. *Memories of God: Theological Reflections on a Life.* Nashville: Abingdon Press, 1995.

Bonhoeffer, Dietrich. *Life Together.* New York: Harper & Row, 1954.

——. *Worldly Preaching: Lectures on Homiletics.* Edited by Clyde E. Fant. New York: Crossroad, 1991.

Brooks, Phillips. *Lectures on Preaching.* New York: E. P. Dutton, 1877.

Brown, Paul B. *In and For the World: Bringing the Contemporary into Christian Worship.* Minneapolis: Fortress Press, 1992.

Browning, Don S. *The Moral Context of Pastoral Care.* Philadelphia: Westminster Press, 1976.

——. *Religious Thought and the Modern Psychologies.* Philadelphia: Fortress Press, 1987.

Brueggemann, Walter. *Cadences of Home: Preaching Among Exiles.* Louisville: Westminster John Knox Press, 1997.

Buttrick, David. *A Captive Voice: The Liberation of Preaching.* Louisville: Westminster/John Knox Press, 1994.

——. *Homiletic: Moves and Structures.* Philadelphia: Fortress Press, 1987.

Campbell, Alastair. *Rediscovering Pastoral Care.* Philadelphia: Westminster Press, 1981.

Campbell, Charles L. *Preaching Jesus: New Directions for Homiletics in Hans Frei's Postliberal Theology.* Grand Rapids, Mich.: Eerdmans, 1997.

Capps, Donald. *Pastoral Counseling and Preaching: A Quest for an Integrated Ministry.* Philadelphia: Westminster Press, 1980.

Childs, Brian H., and David W. Waanders, eds. *The Treasure of Earthen Vessels: Explorations in Theological Anthropology: In honor of James Lapsley.* Louisville: Westminster/John Knox Press, 1994.

Chopp, Rebecca S. *The Power to Speak: Feminism, Language, God.* New York: Crossroad, 1992.

Clapp, Rodney. *A Peculiar People: The Church As Culture in a Post-Christian Society.* Downers Grove, Ill.: Intervarsity Press, 1996.

Clarke, Erskine, ed. *Exilic Preaching: Testimony for Christian Exiles in an Increasingly Hostile Culture.* Harrisburg, Pa.: Trinity Press International, 1998.

Clebsch, William A., and Charles R. Jaekle. *Pastoral Care in Historical Perspective.* Englewood Cliffs, N. J.: Prentice Hall, 1964.

Cooke, Bernard. *Ministry to Word and Sacraments: History and Theology.* Philadelphia: Fortress Press, 1976.

Couture, Pamela D., and Rodney J. Hunter, eds. *As One Without Authority.* Nashville: Abingdon Press, 1979.

——. *Pastoral Care and Social Conflict: In honor of Charles Gerkin.* Nashville: Abingdon Press, 1995.

Craddock, Fred B. *Overhearing the Gospel: Preaching and Teaching the Faith to Persons Who Have Already Heard.* Nashville: Abingdon Press, 1978.

Crawford, Evans C., and Thomas H. Troeger. *The Hum: Call and Response in African American Preaching.* Nashville: Abingdon Press, 1996.

Dawn, Marva J. *Reaching Out Without Dumbing Down: A Theology of Worship for the Turn-of-the-Century Culture.* Grand Rapids, Mich.: Eerdmans, 1995.

Douglas, Jane Dempsey, and James F. Kay, eds. *Women, Gender, and Christian Community.* Louisville: Westminster John Knox Press, 1997.

Dudley, Carl S., ed. *Building Effective Ministry: Theory and Practice in the Local Church.* San Francisco: Harper & Row, 1983.

——, and Sally A. Johnson. *Energizing the Congregation: Images that Shape Your Church's Ministry.* Louisville: Westminster/John Knox Press, 1993.

Dulles, Avery. *Models of the Church.* New York: Doubleday, 1974.

Edwards, O. C. "Preaching and Pastoral Care." In *Anglican Theology and Pastoral Care,* edited by James E. Grifiss, 154. Wilton, Conn.: Morehouse-Barlow, 1985.

Eslinger, Richard. *A New Hearing.* Nashville: Abingdon Press, 1987.

Farley, Edward. *Good and Evil: Interpreting a Human Condition.* Minneapolis: Fortress Press, 1990.

———. "Preaching the Bible and Preaching the Gospel." *Theology Today* 51, no.1 (April 1994): 90–104.

Forbes, James. *The Holy Spirit and Preaching.* Nashville: Abingdon Press, 1989.

Fosdick, Harry Emerson. *The Living of These Days.* New York: Harper, 1956.

———. "Personal Counseling and Preaching." *Pastoral Psychology* 3, no. 22 (March 1952): 11–15.

———. "What Is the Matter With Preaching?" *Harpers Monthly Magazine* 157 (July 1928): 133–42.

Foss, Sonja K., Karen A. Foss, and Robert Trapp, *Contemporary Perspectives on Rhetoric.* Prospect Heights, Ill.: Waveland, 1991.

Frei, Hans W. *The Eclipse of Biblical Narrative: A Study in Eighteenth and Nineteenth Century Hermeneutics.* New Haven, Conn.:Yale University Press, 1974.

Gerkin, Charles V. *Crisis Experience in Modern Life: Theory and Theology in Pastoral Care.* Nashville: Abingdon Press, 1979.

———. *Prophetic Pastoral Practice: A Christian Vision of Life Together.* Nashville: Abingdon Press, 1991.

Glaz, Maxine, and Jeanne Stevenson Moessner, eds. *Women in Travail and Transition: A New Pastoral Care.* Minneapolis: Fortress Press, 1991.

Gonzalez, Catherine, and Justo Gonzalez. *The Liberating Pulpit.* Nashville: Abingdon Press, 1994.

Graff, Ann O'Hara. *In the Embrace of God: Feminist Approaches to Theological Anthropology.* Maryknoll, N.Y.: Orbis, 1995.

Graham, Larry Kent. *Care of Persons, Care of Worlds: A Psychosystems Approach to Pastoral Care and Counseling.* Nashville: Abingdon Press, 1992.

Gregory the Great. *Pastoral Care.* Ancient Christian Writers series. Translated by Henry Davis. Westminster, Md.: Newman Press, 1950.

Grierson, Denham. *Transforming a People of God.* Melbourne, Australia: The Joint Board of Christian Education, 1984.

Gustafson, James. *Treasure in Earthen Vessels: The Church as a Human Community.* New York: Harper, 1961.

Hall, Douglas John. *The Future of the Church: Where Are We Headed?* Etobicoke, Ont.: The United Church Publishing House, 1989.

———. *Professing the Faith: Christian Theology in a North American Context.* Minneapolis: Fortress Press, 1993.

Hall, Thor. *The Future Shape of Preaching.* Philadelphia: Fortress Press, 1971.

Hanson, Paul D. *The People Called: The Growth of Community in the Bible.* San Francisco: Harper & Row, 1986.

Harris, Maria. *Fashion Me a People.* Louisville: Westminster/John Knox Press, 1989.

Hauerwas, Stanley. *Christian Existence Today: Essays on Church, World, and Living in Between.* Durham, N.C.: Labyrinth, 1988.

——, and William H. Willimon. *Resident Aliens: Life in the Christian Colony.* Nashville: Abingdon Press, 1989.

Hilkert, Mary Catherine. *Naming Grace: Preaching and the Sacramental Imagination.* New York: Continuum, 1996.

Hiltner, Seward. *Preface to Pastoral Theology.* Nashville: Abingdon Press, 1958.

Hodgson, Peter. *Winds of the Spirit: A Constructive Christian Theology.* Louisville: Westminster/John Knox Press, 1994.

Holifield, E. Brooks. *A History of Pastoral Care in America: From Salvation to Self-Realization.* Nashville: Abingdon Press, 1983.

Hopewell, James F. *Congregation: Stories and Structures.* Philadelphia: Fortress Press, 1987.

Howard, Robert R. "Gender and Point of View in the Imagery of Preaching." *Papers Of the Annual Meeting of the Academy of Homiletics* (1992): 35–45.

Hudson, Mary Lin, and Mary Donovan Turner. *Saved From Silence: Finding Women's Voice in Preaching.* St. Louis: Chalice Press, 1999.

Hunter, Rodney, et al., eds. *Dictionary of Pastoral Care and Counseling,* Nashville: Abingdon Press, 1990.

Jackson, Edgar N. *How To Preach to People's Needs.* New York: Abingdon Press, 1956.

Jay, Eric G. *The Church: Its Changing Image Through Twenty Centuries.* 2 vols. London: SPCK, 1977–78.

Johnson, Elizabeth A. *Consider Jesus: Waves of Renewal in Christology.* New York: Crossroad, 1990.

Keller, Catherine. *From A Broken Web: Separation, Sexism, and Self.* Boston: Beacon, 1986.

Kiefert, Patrick. *Welcoming the Stranger: A Public Theology of Worship and Evangelism.* Minneapolis: Fortress Press, 1992.

Kirkpatrick, Frank G. *Community: A Trinity of Models.* Washington, D.C.: Georgetown University Press, 1986.

Lakoff, George, and Mark Johnson. *Metaphors We Live By.* Chicago: University of Chicago Press, 1980.

Lasch, Christopher. *The Culture of Narcissism: American Life in an Age of Diminishing Expectations.* New York: W. W. Norton, 1978.

Lindbeck, George. *The Nature of Doctrine: Religion and Theology in a Postliberal Age.* Philadelphia: Westminster Press, 1984.

Lischer, Richard. *A Theology of Preaching: The Dynamics of the Gospel.* Abingdon Preacher's Library. Nashville: Abingdon Press, 1981. Repr. Durham, N.C.: Labyrinth, 1992.

——. "The Limits of Story." *Interpretation* 38 (January 1984): 26–38.

——, and William H. Willimon, eds. *Concise Encyclopedia of Preaching.* Louisville: Westminster Press, 1985.

Long, Thomas G. *The Witness of Preaching.* Louisville: Westminster Press, 1989.

——, and Edward Farley, eds. *Preaching As a Theological Task: World, Gospel, Scripture: In honor of David Buttrick.* Louisville: Westminster John Knox Press, 1996.

Lose, David J. "Narrative and Proclamation." *Papers of the Annual Meeting of the Academy of Homiletics* (Oakland, Dec. 4–6, 1997): 22–45.

McClure, John S. *The Four Codes of Preaching: Rhetorical Strategies.* Minneapolis: Fortress Press, 1991.

——. *The Roundtable Pulpit.* Nashville: Abingdon Press, 1995.

McElvaney, William K. *Preaching from Camelot to Covenant.* Nashville: Abingdon Press, 1989.

McGee, Lee. *Wrestling With the Patriarchs: Retrieving Women's Voices in Preaching.* Nashville: Abingdon Press, 1996.

McIntyre, John. *The Shape of Christology.* Philadelphia: Westminster Press, 1966.

McKnight, John. *The Careless Society: Community and Its Counterfeits.* New York: Basic Books, 1995.

McLuhan, Marshall. *The Medium is the Message.* New York: Random House, 1967.

McNeill, John T. *A History of the Cure of Souls.* New York: Harper, 1951.

Miller-McLemore, Bonnie J. *Also a Mother: Work and Family as Theological Dilemma.* Nashville: Abingdon Press, 1994.

——, and Brita L. Gill-Austern, eds. *Feminist and Womanist Pastoral Theology.* Nashville: Abingdon Press, 1999.

Mills, Liston O. "Seward Hiltner's Contributions to Pastoral Care and Counseling." *Pastoral Psychology* 29, no.1 (Fall 1980): 10.

Minear, Paul S. *Images of the Church in the New Testament.* Philadelphia: Westminster Press, 1960; repr. 1975.

Mitchell, Henry H. *Celebration and Experience in Preaching.* Nashville: Abingdon Press, 1990.

Moyd, Olin P. *The Sacred Art: Preaching and Theology in the African American Tradition.* Valley Forge, Pa.: Judson Press, 1995.

Mudge, Lewis S. *The Sense of a People: Toward a Church for the Human Future.* Philadelphia: Trinity Press, 1992.

Nelson, C. Ellis, ed. *Congregations: Their Power to Form and Transform.* Atlanta: John Knox Press, 1988.

Neuger, Christie Cozad, ed. *The Arts of Ministry: Feminist-Womanist Approaches.* Louisville: Westminster John Knox Press, 1996.

Nichols, J. Randall. *The Restoring Word: Preaching as Pastoral Communication.* San Francisco: Harper, 1987.

Niebuhr, H. Richard. *The Purpose of the Church and Its Ministry.* New York: Harper & Row, 1956.

——, and Daniel D. Williams, eds. *The Ministry in Historical Perspectives.* New York: Harper & Row, 1956.

Noren, Carol M. *The Woman in the Pulpit.* Nashville: Abingdon Press, 1991.

O'Day, Gail R., and Thomas G. Long, eds. *Listening to the Word: Studies in Honor of Fred B. Craddock*. Nashville: Abingdon Press, 1993.

Oden, Thomas C. *Care of Souls in the Classic Tradition*. Theology and Pastoral Care Series. Edited by Don S. Browning. Philadelphia: Fortress Press, 1984.

——. *Pastoral Theology: Essentials of Ministry*. San Francisco: Harper, 1983.

Ong, Walter J. *The Presence of the Word: Some Prolegomena for Cultural and Religious History*. Minneapolis: University of Minnesota Press, 1967, 1981.

Palmer, Parker J. *The Company of Strangers: Christians and the Renewal of America's Public Life*. New York: Crossroad, 1988.

Pannenberg, Wolfhart. *Anthropology in Theological Perspective*. Translated by Matthew J. O'Connell. Philadelphia: Westminster Press, 1985.

——. *The Church*. Philadelphia: Westminster Press, 1983.

Patton, John. *Pastoral Care in Context: An Introduction to Pastoral Care*. Louisville: Westminster/John Knox Press, 1993.

Perelman, Chaim. *The Realm of Rhetoric*. Translated by William Kluback. Notre Dame, Ind.: University of Notre Dame Press, 1982.

——, and L. Olbrechts-Tyteca. *The New Rhetoric: A Treatise on Argumentation*. Translated by John Wilkinson and Purcell Weaver. Notre Dame: University of Notre Dame Press, 1969.

Pruyser, Paul W. *The Minister as Diagnostician*. Philadelphia: Westminster Press, 1976.

Ramsey, G. Lee, Jr. "Preaching and the Rhetoric of Care: Forming A Pastoral Community for Care in the World." Ph.D. dissertation, Vanderbilt University, 1998.

Ramshaw, Elaine. *Ritual and Pastoral Care*. Philadelphia: Fortress Press, 1987.

Ramshaw, Gail. *Worship: Searching for Language*. Washington, D.C.: Pastoral Press, 1988.

Randolph, David J. *The Renewal of Preaching*. Philadelphia: Fortress Press, 1969.

Reid, Clyde. *The Empty Pulpit: A Study in Preaching as Communication*. New York: Harper & Row, 1967.

Ricoeur, Paul. *The Rule of Metaphor*. Toronto: University of Toronto Press, 1977.

Rieff, Phillip. *The Triumph of the Therapeutic: Uses of Faith After Freud*. Chicago: University of Chicago Press, 1966.

Rose, Lucy Atkinson. *Sharing the Word: Preaching in the Roundtable Church*. Louisville: Westminster John Knox Press, 1997.

Russell, Letty M. *Becoming Human*. Philadelphia: Westminster Press, 1982.

——. *Church in the Round: Feminist Interpretation of the Church*. Louisville: Westminster/John Knox Press, 1993.

Schüssler Fiorenza, Elisabeth. *In Memory of Her: A Feminist Reconstruction of Christian Origins*. New York: Crossroad, 1983.

——. *Jesus, Miriam's Child, Sophia's Prophet: Critical Issues in Feminist Christology.* New York: Continuum, 1995.

Simmons, Martha J., ed. *Preaching on the Brink: The Future of Homiletics: In honor of Henry H. Mitchell.* Foreword by Gardner Taylor. Nashville: Abingdon Press, 1996.

Smith, Archie, Jr. *The Relational Self: Ethics and Therapy from a Black Church Perspective.* Nashville: Abingdon Press, 1982.

Smith, Christine M. *Preaching as Weeping, Confession, and Resistance: Radical Responses to Radical Evil.* Louisville: Westminster/John Knox Press, 1992.

SteinhoffSmith, Roy Herndon. *The Mutuality of Care.* St. Louis: Chalice Press, 1999.

Stokes, Allison. *Ministry After Freud.* New York: Pilgrim Press, 1985.

Stratman, Gary D. *Pastoral Preaching: Timeless Truths for Changing Needs.* Nashville: Abingdon Press, 1983.

Switzer, David K. *Pastor, Preacher, Person: Developing a Pastoral Ministry in Depth.* Nashville: Abingdon Press, 1979.

Taylor, Barbara Brown. *When God Is Silent.* Cambridge, Mass.: Cowley Publications, 1998.

Thistlethwaite, Susan B. *Metaphors for the Contemporary Church.* New York: Pilgrim Press, 1983.

Tisdale, Leonora Tubbs. *Preaching as Local Theology and Folk Art.* Minneapolis: Fortress Press, 1997.

Townes, Emilie M., ed. *A Troubling in My Soul: Womanist Perspectives on Evil and Suffering.* New York: Orbis, 1993.

Tracy, David. *The Analogical Imagination: Christian Theology and the Culture of Pluralism.* New York: Crossroad, 1981.

Van der Geest, Hans. *Presence in the Pulpit.* Atlanta: John Knox Press, 1981.

Van Seters, Arthur, ed. *Preaching as a Social Act: Theology and Practice.* Nashville: Abingdon Press, 1988.

Wardlaw, Don M., ed. *Preaching Biblically: Creating Sermons in the Shape of Scripture.* Philadelphia: Westminster Press, 1983.

Weaver, Richard M. *Language Is Sermonic: Richard M. Weaver on the Nature of Rhetoric.* Edited by Richard L. Johannesen, Rennard Strickland, and Ralph T. Eubanks. Baton Rouge, La.: Louisiana State University Press, 1970.

Webb, Joseph M. *Preaching and the Challenge of Pluralism.* St. Louis: Chalice Press, 1998.

Webber, Robert E., and Rodney Clapp. *People of the Truth: The Power of the Worshiping Community in the Modern World.* San Francisco: Harper & Row, 1988.

Wilder, Amos N. *Early Christian Rhetoric: The Language of the Gospel.* New York: Harper & Row, 1964.

Williams, Daniel Day. *The Minister and the Care of Souls.* New York: Harper & Row, 1961.

Willimon, William H. *Worship as Pastoral Care*. Nashville: Abingdon Press, 1979.

Wilson, Paul Scott. *A Concise History of Preaching*. Nashville: Abingdon Press, 1992.

Wimberly, Edward P. *African American Pastoral Care*. Nashville: Abingdon Press, 1991.

Witten, Marsha Grace. *All Is Forgiven: The Secular Message in American Protestantism*. Princeton, N.J.: Princeton University Press, 1993.

Index